197

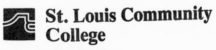

D1071443

WANG YANG-MING
AND
KARL BARTH

A Confucian-Christian Dialogue

Heup Young Kim

University Press of America, Inc.
Lanham • New York • London

Copyright © 1996 by
University Press of America,® Inc.
4720 Boston Way
Lanham, Maryland 20706

3 Henrietta Street
London, WC2E 8LU England

Library of Congress Cataloging-in-Publication Data

Kim, Heup Young
Wang Yang-ming and Karl Barth : a Confucian-Christian dialogue /
Heup Young Kim.
p.   cm.
Includes bibliographical references.
1. Confucianism--Relations--Christianity. 2. Christianity and other
religions--Confucianism. 3. Wang, Yang-ming, 1472-1529. 4. Neo-
Confucianism. 5. Barth, Karl, 1886-1968. 6. Philosophy,
Comparative. 7. Christianity and culture--Korea.   I. Title.
BR128.C43K56 1996   299'.512'72--dc20   95-46069 CIP

ISBN 0-7618-0226-6 (cloth: alk: ppr.)

In Memory of Mother

Nam Joung-Sook (1924-83)

CONTENTS

vi

•

Abbreviations

CSL
: Wang Yang-ming, *Ch'uan-hsi lu:* Trans. Chan Wing-tsit. *Instructions for Practical Living and other Neo-Confucian Writings by Wang Yang-ming.* New York: Columbia University Press, 1963.

Instructions
: Other Confucian Writings by Wang Yang-ming. Trans. Chan Wing-tsit. *Instructions for Practical Living and other Neo-Confucian Writings by Wang Yang-ming.* New York: Columbia University Press, 1963.

I/1
: Karl Barth. *Church Dogmatics: The Doctrine of the Word of God.* Vol. 1, Part 1. 2nd ed. Trans. G. W. Bromiley. Edinburgh: T. & T. Clark, 1975.

I/2
: Karl Barth. *Church Dogmatics: The Doctrine of the Word of God.* Vol. I, Part 2. Trans. G. T. Thomson & Harold Knight. Edinburgh: T. & T. Clark, 1956.

II/2
: Karl Barth. *Church Dogmatics: The Doctrine of God.* Vol. II, Part 2. Trans. G. W. Bromiley et. al. Edinburgh: T. & T. Clark, 1957.

III/2
: Karl Barth. *Church Dogmatics.* Vol. III, Part 2, *The Creature.* Trans. Harold Knight et.al. Edinburgh: T.& T. Clark, 1960.

IV/1
: Karl Barth. *Church Dogmatics: The Doctrine of Reconciliation.* Vol. IV, Part 1. Trans. G. W. Bromiley. Edinburgh: T. & T. Clark, 1956.

IV/2
: Karl Barth. *Church Dogmatics: The Doctrine of Reconciliation.* Vol. IV, Part 2. Trans. G. W. Bromiley. Edinburgh: T. & T. Clark, 1958.

IV/3
: Karl Barth. *Church Dogmatics: The Doctrine of Reconciliation.* Vol. IV, Part 3. Trans. G. W. Bromiley. First Half. Edinburgh: T. & T. Clark, 1961; Second Half. Edinburgh: T. & T. Clark, 1962.

•

Acknowledgment

The completion of this book would not have been possible without the encouragement, guidance, support, and caring of numerous people. This work has begun as a dissertation presented for the degree of Doctor of Philosophy in the Graduate Theological Union, Berkeley, 1992; it has since been revised. I am deeply grateful to the members of my doctoral committee in the Graduate Theological Union and the University of California at Berkeley: Professors Claude Welch, Judith Berling, Benjamin Reist, Edmond Yee, and John Jamieson. The manuscripts in various stages have been read by Professors Stuart McLean of the Phillips Graduate Seminary, Ted Peters of the Pacific Lutheran Theological Seminary, Jae Hyun Chung of the Sungkonghoe University, Seoul, James Emerson and David Ng of the San Francisco Theological Seminary, and Rev. Heng Sure of the Berkeley Buddhist Monastery. I am deeply indebted to these people for their thoughtful comments and valuable suggestions. Special thanks are due to John Dillenberger, Professor Emeritus of the Graduate Theological Union, and Professor Philip Ivanhoe of the Stanford University for their careful reading and editorial suggestions of the final manuscript.

Most of all, my appreciation goes to my family without whose fidelity, love, and support this work would never been written. Even sacrificing her youth and dreams, Joung Hee has undertaken the hardship of financial burdens throughout my graduate studies. Kwang Suk and Sonia have been patient and filial in enduring the pain and suffering as the children of a seminarian father. The memory of my mother, Joung-Sook Nahm, to whom this book is dedicated, has been a profound source of theological inspiration. Finally, I submit this work as the beginning of my way of uttering an East Asian doxology in Jesus Christ.

I am grateful to the following publishers for their permission to quote their materials.

The T. & T. Clark Ltd. has given permission to quote materials from Karl Barth, *Church Dogmatics*, Copyright © 1932-81 by T & T Clark Ltd. Reprinted by permission of T. & T. Clark Ltd.

The Columbia University Press has given permission to quote material from *Instructions for Practical Living and Other Neo-Confucian Writings*, Chan Wing-tsit, 1963, © Columbia University Press, New York. Reprinted with permission of the publisher.

The Princeton University Press has given permission to quote material from Chan Wing-tsit; *A Source Book in Chinese Philosophy*. Copyright © 1963 by Princeton University Press. Reprinted by permission of Princeton University Press.

The University of California Press has given permission to quote material from Wei-ming Tu, *Neo-Confucian Thought in Action: Wang Yang-ming's Youth (1472-1509)*, Copyright © 1976 by the Regents of the University of California. Reprinted by permission of the University of California Press.

Professor Tu Wei-ming has given permission to quote material from Tu Wei-ming, *Humanity and Self-Cultivation: Essays in Confucian Thought*, 1978, Copyright © by Lancaster-Miller Publisher. Reprinted by permission of Tu Wei-ming.

•

Introduction

The Confucian-Christian Context

This study is grounded in my existential struggle as a Christian who has been raised in a Korean family steeped in a thousand-year history in Confucianism.[1] The more I study Christian theology, the more I become convinced how deeply Confucianism is embedded in my soul and body, my spirituality. Subtly but powerfully, Confucianism still works inside me, as my native religious language. If theology involves the response of one's total being to God, it also entails a critical wrestling with this embedded Confucian tradition. Doing East Asian theology necessarily involves the study of Confucianism as a theological task.

I would not be the only person who sees this theological dimension of Confucianism. East Asian Christians often experience this aspect in one way or the other, because Confucianism is still deeply present in the heart of the people of East Asia. Religiously, as Tu Wei-ming said, "East Asians may profess themselves to be Shintoists, Taoists, Buddhists, Muslims, or Christians, but by announcing their religious affiliations seldom do they cease to be Confucians."[2] Socially, East Asian countries in general may still be defined as Confucian societies, even though this stage of the East Asian civilization is called a "post-Confucian era."[3]

The remarkable economic successes of the so called "four tigers" or "four little dragons" of Asia—Singapore, Hong Kong, Taiwan, and South Korea—and Japan have drawn attention to Neo-Confucianism.[4] Wm. Theodre de Bary states it well:

Nevertheless, the dramatic successes of these countries in rapid modernization, by contrast to the slow pace of development elsewhere in Asia, Africa, and South Africa, and all the more notably in the absence of great natural resources other than their human endowment, has drawn new attention to a factor long overlooked in the common background of the peoples of East Asia: a long-shared process of intellectual and moral preparation through Neo-Confucianism. Whereas previously the Neo-Confucian influence had been seen as inimical to modernization (and it was unquestionably averse to certain aspects of westernization), the idea that the peoples of China, Japan, Korea, Taiwan, Hong Kong, and Singapore have benefited from the love of learning, commitment to education, social discipline, and personal cultivation fostered by Neo-Confucianism can now be entertained.[5]

De Bary also finds that Neo-Confucianism, "the common background of the peoples of East Asia," is "the most plausible rationale" and "the key" to understanding the attitude of "the inward-looking civilizations of East Asia" in their modern encounter with "the expansionist West:"

Neo-Confucianism furnished the most plausible rationale for East Asian civilizations preoccupied with their own inner development—self-centered in the positive sense of being inner-directed, conservative of their energies, and concentrated in their efforts. To my mind, Neo-Confucianism is also the key to understanding how later on, in the eighteenth and nineteenth centuries, the inward-looking civilizations of East Asia would appear to the expansionist West to be ingrown, self-contented, smug, and isolationist, while the West would seem to East Asians the very embodiment of uncontrolled aggressiveness—power on the loose, bound to no moral and spiritual center.[6]

Neo-Confucianism is a distinctive feature of the East Asian religio-cultural complex. In this regard, Hans Küng also made a helpful correction in his book with Julia Ching, *Christianity and Chinese Religions*.[7] Against the dipolar view generally accepted in the World Council of Churches circle (namely, Middle Eastern and Indian religions), Küng argued for a tripolar view of World Religions. He said that East Asian Religions such as Confucianism should be regarded as "a third independent religious river system" of sapiential character, "equal in value," in contrast to "the first great river system, of Semitic origin and prophetic character," and "the second great river system, of Indian origin and mystical character." And he advocated Confucian-

Christian dialogue in which Christianity and Confucianism are to be "equal partners . . . in terms of both value and status."[8]

Since Confucianism is a distinctive feature of its religio-cultural complex, Christians in East Asia live in the Confucian-Christian context. Everyday, East Asian Christians experience the collision and the fusion of the two religious traditions in one way or the other. Doing theology in this context compels a genuine intrareligious dialogue between Confucianism and Christianity. No matter what kind of experiences they may have had with Confucianism, hence, Confucian-Christian dialogue is constitutive of doing East Asian theology.

The need for the Confucian-Christian dialogue is particularly imperative in Korea. Here, I argue that Korea displays the most strong Confucian-Christian context and, thus, that the Korean Church is the ideal locus for the Confucian-Christian dialogue of a global significance. There are at least three reasons. First of all, Korea is the only county in East Asia where Christianity is no longer a small minority religion but takes a leading role in society. Membership in Christian churches in Korea has reached a quarter of the population.[9]

Secondly, in the history of East Asia, Korea was most strongly influenced by Confucianism, and it still is. Tu Wei-ming said, "Among all the dynasties, Chinese and foreign, the long-lived Choson (Yi) in Korea (1392-1910) was undoubtedly the most thoroughly Confucianized."[10] J. H. Grayson also claimed, "It is only in Korea that we find a society in which the predominant political, cultural, and social influences were and are Confucian."[11] He also said:

> It is an interesting fact that Confucianism in no other society in East Asia took as strong a hold on the culture as it did in Korea during the Chosun dynasty (1392-1910). China as a continental nation with a cosmopolitan society always had many cultural factors present which would mitigate against the development of a monolithic society. Consequently, although Confucianism originated in China, it never had the overall impact on Chinese society that Neo-Confucianism had on Korea over the five hundred years of the last dynasty. In Japan, Confucianism was primarily a concern of the ruling elite and the associated scholarly class.

Grayson argued that since "Confucianism still influences Korean society in the social sphere on both the structural and cognitive levels," "Korea may still be called a Confucian society."[12]

Thirdly, Korean Christianity is basically a Confucian Christianity. Both Roman Catholicism and Protestantism in Korea originated from Confucian social concern and has developed on Confucian conceptual foundations.[13] Korean Christianity has distinctively Confucian roots. Both Roman Catholic and Protestant missions in Korea were initiated not by outsiders, but insiders, primarily Confucian activists who envisioned Christianity as the new vehicle to bring renewal to their Confucian country in decay.

As Buddhism was introduced to China through Taoist categories, Christianity was naturally introduced to Korea through Confucian conceptual vocabularies. The Confucian-Christian dialogue, in fact, has been operative since the beginning of Korean Christianity. The Korean Roman Catholic Church is unique in this regard. Even before the first official priest landed in the country, a brilliant Confucian scholar Yi Pyok (1754-1786), self-taught in Christianity, wrote *Sung-gyo Yo-ji* (Essentials of the Holy Teaching), perhaps the first theological treatise written by Korean.[14] Another Confucian Chóng Yak-jong (1760-1801), also wrote *Chu-gyo Yo-ji* (Essentials of the Lord's Teaching), perhaps the first theological writing in Korean.[15] In the Korean Protestant Church, the Bible was translated mostly by Confucian scholars. The Korean Protestant Bible, which is still most favored by conservative churches, is full of Confucian concepts. Korean Protestant Christianity also has been introduced and developed through Confucian conceptual categories. Unfortunately, their anti-indigenous bias obstructed the natural development of Confucian-Christian dialogue. However, there were some exceptions, such as Ch'oe Pyong-hon (1885-1927) and Yun Sung-bum (1916-1979) who continued the dialogue explicitly.[16]

More than ever before, Vatican II has led the Korean Roman Catholic Church to establish a more open attitude toward issues of inculturation.[17] However, deeply influenced by exclusive forms of Neo-Calvinism, Korean Protestant Churches with the attitude, more or less, of "Christ against Culture"[18] have suppressed the possibility of a dialogue with Confucianism. Yet, the practical situation of Korea Protestant Churches seems to be the opposite of these Churches' theoretical position. Yoon Yee-heum reported an astonishing survey result that more than ninety percent of so called "self-identified" church-going Korean Protestant Christians are virtually "practical members" of the Confucian "soft" community who still hold Confucian moral norms and practice traditional Confucian social customs.[19] This is provocative. For this implies that, even though most Korean

Protestant Christians identify themselves as Christians, they are still Confucians in a practical sense. This may be clear evidence for the existence of the Confucian-Christian context and even reveal a case of a *de facto* dual religious identity.

A Concrete-Universal Approach
Toward a Christian Theology of Religions

My concern begins especially with the situation of Korean Presbyterian Churches which hold an exclusivist attitude to indigenous culture and religions.[20] Within a century, the Korean Presbyterian Church has become the largest Christian denomination not only in Korea, but also among the allied Reformed Churches in the world. It is a Presbyterian success story in mission history. In this regard, my hypothesis is that this success was possible because there are striking similarities between Neo-Confucianism and Reformed Christianity. While some would claim the success was due to the superior doctrines of the Calvinist or Reformed theology, a more important reason could be the similarities between Korean Confucianism and Neo-Calvinism (i.e., the Old Princeton theology) which American Protestant missionaries brought to Korea.

In fact, Neo-Calvinist Orthodoxy was an excellent counterpart of the Koreanized Ch'eng-Chu (Neo-Confucian) Orthodoxy. These two traditions have a remarkable "religious affinity."[21] For example, they share a strong stress on loyalty toward Orthodoxy, stubborn literalism toward canonical texts, rigorous zeal toward personal piety, emphasis on the family and stern propriety in human relationships. The Presbyterian success story can be viewed as a marriage between Puritanical Neo-Calvinism and the Koreanized Neo-Confucianism. Koreans who were historically embedded in Ch'eng-Chu [Neo-Confucian] "moral rigorism" need not go far to understand Calvinist "worldly asceticism."[22]

In appearance, Korean Presbyterian churches have tried to eliminate radically their non-Christian indigenous elements. At a deeper level, however, this uncritical attitude seems to produce rather the opposite result. Some forms of Korean Presbyterianism would be a *de facto* reconstitution of the deteriorated Neo-Confucianism of the late Chosun Dynasty in Christian guise.[23] Korean Presbyterianism tends to be fundamentalistic, conservative, highly individualistic, overzealous in the pursuit of external reputation, culturally exclusive, socially stubborn, politically insensitive, highly bureaucratic, and structurally vulnerable to corruption. Since these malevolent traits are covered up with a new garb of the Christian faith in another petrified form of fundamentalism, the situation is very deceptive and even dangerous.

Confucianism, as the cultural-linguistic matrix for Korean theology, naturally calls for serious theological clarification and scrutiny. In such a deceptive situation, the need for such a theological examination is even more critical. Confucianism in this context is no longer merely a matter of an academic and cross-cultural discussion, but it entails a serious theological task related to the practice of faith in a concrete community. This involves a task beyond dialogue, that is more than an a priori speculative comparison of Confucianism and Christianity for intellectual edification, but a theological imperative for an *a posteriori* thematization of the content of the faith for a specific community, i.e., the Korean Churches. However, this enterprise will not limit the scope to Korean theology, but to use this concrete point of departure for both the more general study of the Confucian-Christian encounter and for a constructive East Asian theology of religions; that is, an approach which is concrete and thus universal.

The unusual strength of the Korean Presbyterian Christianity in comparison with those in the other East Asian countries is not *a creatio ex nihilo*.[24] But there must be a theological reason for the strength. In a distinctively "plurireligious" context,[25] the reason is inevitably in a form of "theology of religions." That is to say, a viable theology of religions is already operative in the Korean Church, which can promote a crucial paradigm for the global theology of the third millennium.[26] Its thematization is a concrete-universal approach toward that constructive East Asian Christian theology of religions.

Wang Yang-ming and Karl Barth

This book is a beginning of that theological enterprise. As partners in the dialogue, I choose two major figures, one from each tradition; Wang Yang-ming (1472-1529) and Karl Barth (1886-1968). The reasons for the selection of these two figures are twofold.[27] First, both Wang and Barth are historically relevant to and constructively import-ant for the Confucian-Christian encounter in the Korean Church. Second, Wang and Barth are major figures, so well representing their respective traditions to be proper partners for the Confucian-Christian dialogue. Wang Yang-ming, a sixteenth-century Chinese Confucian scholar-general, was a seminal thinker and a great reformer in the history of Confucianism.[28]   Karl Barth, a twentieth- century Swiss professor of theology, was one of the most significant Church theologians in the history of Western Christianity since the Reformation.[29]   Especially, I will focus on their doctrines related to their common issue of humanization; i.e., the Neo-Confucian teaching of self-cultivation and the Christian doctrine of sanctification (for the reason for this selection, see the next section).   Likewise, the first and main task of this book involves an interpretation of the writings of Wang Yang-ming and Karl Barth on these doctrines.

The primary text for Wang Yang-ming's teaching on self-cultivation is *Ch'uan-hsi lu* (The Instructions of Practical Living),[30] in which "all of Wang's fundamental doctrines are contained."[31]   However, it is a difficult task to talk about East Asian thought in western languages and conceptual categories.   As Mou Tsung-san said, there was no linguistic category equivalent to the western notion of "philosophy" in Classical Chinese.[32]   While Western philosophy stresses "objectivity" and "knowledge," Chinese philosophy focuses on "subjectivity" and "inner morality."[33]   East Asian thinkers in general do not believe that the Tao can be neatly packaged into a conceptual system.   Rather, they fear losing profound and ineffable meanings of the Tao in the process of conceptualization and its inevitable decontextualization.   Wang Yang-ming was particularly suspicious of "intellectual argumentation as an adequate means of communicating this type of knowledge."[34]   He had a "suspicion of language," and refused to put his learning in written form.[35]   The main text of the Confucian part, *Ch'uan-hsi lu*, also was not a systematic treatise written by himself, but a collection of his conversations and communications compiled by his students. To make Confucianism more communicable in the contemporary discourse, however, it is necessary to construct an integrated set of understandings, which I call confuciology.   Analogously as theology is a type of discourse that articulates a coherent reflection on faith in a theistic paradigm (*fides quaerens intellectum*), confuciology designates a type of discourse that coherently articulates a faith in the Confucian paradigm.[36]   Tu Wei-ming and Julia Ching, contemporary Wang Yang-ming scholars, have made excellent contributions to the interpretation of Neo-Confucian thought in western, philosophical, and theological languages.[37]   I will rely on their interpretations to formulate a confuciology of Wang Yang-ming. For the romanization of Chinese words, I will use the Wade-Giles system.

The primary text for Karl Barth's doctrine of sanctification is the second part of Karl *Barth's Church Dogmatics, Vol. IV, The Doctrine of Reconciliation*.[38] Basically, I will give my own interpretation of this main text of the Christian part, but will also use contributions of contemporary Barth studies, particularly those of Eberhard Jüngel.[39]

This book centers on three tasks: an interpretation of Confucian and Christian doctrines, an interfaith dialogue, and a constructive East Asian Christian theology of religions. The first task is to construct a confuciology of self-cultivation and a theology of sanctification. When interpreting each text, I will attempt to maintain its organic coherence in its own context (to tell the story in its own terms).[40] The second task is to develop a Confucian-Christian dialogue based on these more communicable discourses, i.e., Wang's confuciology of self-cultivation and Barth's theology of sanctification. In the dialogue, I will compare homologous concepts and explore functionally equivalent terms and points of contact between the two different religious paradigms. I will see commonalities in the two traditions,[41] and take note of their differences. Their points of convergence will illuminate eventually their essential distinctiveness. Finally, the third task is to propose some insights for a constructive Christian theology of religions based on the Confucian-Christian dialogue.

How to Be Fully Human?

Without doubt, Confucianism and Christianity are quite different religions. But there are similarities in these two traditions, which is perhaps a most intriguing theoretical reason for the so-called "miracle" of the Korean Christian mission. Confucianism and Christianity share a common interest in the issue of humanity.[42] Furthermore, the special interest in both traditions lies in a practical, pedagogical question of "how to be fully human" rather than the theoretical, philosophical apprehension of "what is a human being." This central problematic for both traditions has produced distinctive, but comparable doctrines in each tradition; namely, self-cultivation and sanctification. Hence, I will use this common issue of "how to be fully human" as the starting question for the dialogue, or the *koan* for this book. In fact, as Tu Wei-ming demonstrated, "learning to be human," is the central issue of the whole Confucian enterprise.[43] Furthermore, humanization is a globally important issue. The contemporary situation of the wider ecumenism demands a "dialogical participation" in "the common quest for a new humanism" ("Is not ultimate salvation an 'eschatological humanization?'").[44] This post-modern world seriously seeks for what I call "the new Tao of radical humanization."

As a Confucian-Christian dialogue in search of the Tao for humanization, this book will establish the main thesis: In the light of two paradigmatic teachings of Wang Yang-ming and Karl Barth, self-cultivation and sanctification are thickly resemblant views of a common issue, i.e., how to be fully human, or the Tao of radical humanization. The dialogue may furnish some crucial insights for new humanism necessary to the contemporary world and provide a viable point of departure for doing a constructive East Asian Christian theology of religions. Since Jesus Christ is the prototype of humanity for Christians, the search for the Tao of humanization is inevitably connected to the quest for the Tao of Jesus Christ. In transcending the differences between the two traditional visions, i.e., the anthropo-cosmic mode of Confucianism and the theo-historical mode of Christianity, the Tao of Jesus Christ would envision for us the new the-anthropo-cosmic mode of humanism. This Tao of Jesus Christ, as a more proper phrase than the traditional term Christology, would bring us a more appropriate post-modern paradigm of Christology. For example, Jesus Christ as the Tao of new cosmic humanity is very much relevant to the burning issues of today: liberation, dialogue, and ecology.

Confuciology and theology are of radically different religious paradigms; briefly, anthropocosmic versus theo-historical paradigms. Each paradigm has its own world of categories in different styles. Hence, it is hard to find a categorization equally adequate to both traditions. Nevertheless, I will employ four basic categories in the exposition of their discourses: (1) the prolegomena, (2) the humanity paradigm, (3) the humanization method, and (4) the root-metaphor. However, it should be noted that each paradigm is organically construed. One category in a paradigm cannot be separated from another, all are closely interrelated.

The first category, prolegomena, means a preliminary remark for the exposition. It gives an introduction, explains the point of departure and the context from which the two thinkers begin their confuciology and theology. Both Wang and Barth start their own formulation with a paradigm shift from the orthodox tradition. In this paradigm change, the two thinkers emphasize congruently that epistemic understanding of the ontological humanity without its actual practice is not only insufficient but also wrong. Hence, the prolegomena includes both the nature of their paradigm shifts and their arguments on the issue of theory and praxis.

The second category, the humanity paradigm, denotes an exposition of humanity in three themes of the root-paradigm of humanization, the paradigm of humanity, and the problem of evil. The root-paradigm signifies the primordial or ontological content of humanity that constitutes the exemplary pattern of radical humanization. Note that paradigm here does not mean a tradition, but is more broadly defined; i.e., the basic model of humanity that "sets the limits on the range of acceptable models."[45] The root-paradigm denotes the ultimate root of humanity which explicitly refers to its relationships with the transcendent and other beings (the vertical and the horizontal). The paradigm of humanity focuses more on the horizontal side (with others). For Wang and Barth, the root-paradigms are the innate knowledge of the good (*liang-chih*) and the humanity of Christ (*humanitas Christi*), whereas the paradigms are *jen* and *imago Dei*. Furthermore, both of them speak to the problems of evil after the humanity paradigm.

The third category, the humanization method, refers to the way to achieve radical humanization; in other words, the Tao of radical humanization points to the specific answer to the question of how to be fully human. The final category, the root-metaphor, denotes the key concept that demonstrates the Tao of humanization; i.e., sincerity (*ch'eng*) and love (*agape*).[46] These themes can be put in the following table.

Starting Question : "How to be Fully Human?"

	Confucianism **Wang Yang-ming** **Self-Cultivation**	**Christianity** **Karl Barth** **Sanctification**
prolegomena		
paradigm shift	identity of mind and principle	Gospel and law
theory and praxis	unity of knowing and acting	unity of theology and ethics
humanity-paradigm		
root-paradigm	*liang-chih*	*humanitas Christi*

paradigm	*jen*	*imago Dei*
evil	selfish desires	sloth
humanization-method	extension of *liang-chih*	direction of the Holy Spirit
root-metaphor	*ch'eng*	*agape*

The Plan of the Book

Hence, this book will consist of three main parts and a conclusion. Each part will have four chapters, and each chapter will deal with a category. In some cases the order of the chapters does not follow that presented above. For example, although Barth's doctrine of *agape* is transparent as the root-metaphor of sanctification, Wang's notion of *ch'eng* is more subtle. Wang's metaphor must be treated in connection with the doctrine of the unity of knowing and acting. Thus, the chapter on *ch'eng* will be in the second place, instead of the last, while the chapter on *agape* will be in the last

In the first two expository parts, I will concentrate on interpreting each discourse in its own context. I will seek to be faithful to its own intratextuality and avoid the error of a categorical imposition and decontextualization.

In the third part, I will attempt a Confucian-Christian dialogue based on the two expositions. At the same time, I will compare correlative and homologous themes.

Finally, in the conclusion, I will review the thesis and propose some Confucian modes of Christology as examples. The following is a brief description of the materials I will cover in each chapter in this book.

Part I: the Confucian Paradigm, Wang-Yang-ming's confuciology of self-cultivation. In Chapter 1, by introducing Confucianism as a living faith, I will examine Wang's doctrine of the identification of mind-and-heart and principle (*hsin chi li*), his paradigm shift from Chu Hsi's doctrine of the investigation of things (*ko-wu*). This shift leads to his formulation of the unity of knowing and acting (*chih-hsing ho-i*), a topic in Chapter 2. This doctrine entails a concrete-universal approach of co-humanization, summarized in a Confucian root-metaphor of sincerity (*ch'eng*). In Chapter 3, I will delineate Wang's doctrine of the innate knowledge of the good (*liang-chih*), the root-paradigm of self-cultivation and his understanding of evil (selfish desires). In Chapter 4, I will examine the doctrine of *chih liang-chih* (the extension of *liang-*

chih), his cardinal doctrine in which, he claimed, all Confucian insights of self-cultivation are summarized.

Part II: the Christian Paradigm, Karl Barth's theology of sanctification. In Chapter 5, introducing a relationship of Karl Barth's theology and world religions, I will investigate Barth's structural scheme of Gospel and law, a paradigm shift from the traditional doctrine of law and Gospel, and his assertion of the unity of theology and ethics. In Chapter 6, I will explicate Barth's doctrines of *humanitas Christi*, royal humanity, real human nature, and sin and the human condition. In Chapter 7, I will look into Barth's doctrine of sanctification which involves his Spirit Christology, pneumatology, the call to discipleship, the awakening to conversion, the praise of works, and the dignity of the cross. In Chapter 8, I will examine Barth's understanding of Christian love (*agape*), the root-metaphor of sanctification.

Part III: an attempt at a Confucian-Christian dialogue. In Chapter 9, I will develop a methodology for the dialogue between Wang's confuciology of self-cultivation and Barth's theology of sanctification. Then, I will attempt a Confucian-Christian dialogue on the themes of the prolegomena--paradigm shift (*hsin chi li* vs. Gospel and Law), the point of departure (*li-chih* vs. faith), and the unity of ontological knowledge and ethical practice--in Chapter 10; on those of the humanity paradigm--the root-paradigm (*liang-chih* vs. *humanitas Christi*), the paradigm of humanity (*jen* vs. *imago Dei*), and the problem of evil (selfish desires and evil)--in Chapter 11; and on those of the humanization method--self-cultivation and sanctification--and the root-metaphors--sincerity (*ch'eng*) vs. *agape*--in Chapter 12.

In the conclusion, I will review the main thesis that self-cultivation and sanctification are thickly resemblant views of the common issue, "how to be fully human." Regarding the Confucian-Christian dialogue as a dialogical participation in the common quest for the *Tao* of humanity, I will suggest three modes of humanism: *jen*, *ch'eng*, and *Tao*. Attempting a constructive Christian theology, I propose five models of Christology based on the dialogue: *Tao*, *Sage*, *Ch'eng*, *Jen*, and *Liang-chih*. Finally, in the postscript, I will propose those models for a new post-modern paradigm of Christology in the the-anthropo-cosmic vision, that is to say, Jesus as the *Tao* for a new cosmic humanity.

PART I

THE CONFUCIAN PARADIGM

WANG YANG-MING'S CONFUCIOLOGY OF SELF-CULTIVATION

Chapter 1

•

Prolegomena

Ever since the West began to have an impact on East Asian civilization, Confucianism[1] has tended to be despised, forgotten, and neglected. However, the dramatic successes of the modernization of Japan and the so-called "four tigers" call for a renewed appreciation of its role in East Asia. Confucianism is still powerfully operative as a living tradition for the East Asian people.[2] However, religiously, Confucianism calls for great subtlety on the part of religious scholars, because it "does not fit with the conventional definition of a 'higher world religion.'"[3] Unlike other religions, Confucianism is not an expansionist, missionary religion by nature. It has no church ("organizational vehicle") and clergy ("leadership elite"), and it is difficult to identify the institutional voice which represents the tradition. It appears in the "homeless category." Thus, many scholars who are accustomed to seeing religion in terms of its parochial nature and proselytizing function have underestimated the religious dimensions of Confucianism. And Confucianism is often regarded merely as a "finite, historical, secular, and culturally specific" social ethic.[4]

However, the contemporary East Asian scene cannot accept this reductionistic view.[5] Confucianism not only has survived under one of the fiercest and longest debates in the history of human thought,[6] but also it still remains a living tradition for contemporary East Asian people. Küng argued for Confucianism as "a third great religious river system" comparable with two other great river systems (Semitic and Indian). Recently, scholars of religion began not only to affirm the religious dimensions of Confucianism, but also to regard Confucianism as a faith.[7]

Confucianism as a Living Faith

Tu Wei-ming argued that a plausible reason for "the Confucian tradition to undergo profound transformations without losing its spiritual identity" is because it has a capacity for religious transcendence.[8] W. C. Smith made a distinction between "religion" and "being religious."[9] While "religion" signifies an institution distinguished by a set of dogma, "being religious" means a "spiritual self-identification of the living members of a faith community."[10] Arguing that Confucianism fits the second definition, Tu defined the Confucian meaning of "being religious" as *"ultimate self-transformation as a communal act and as a faithful dialogical response to the transcendent."* The ultimate self-transformation implies the never-ending, ever-broadening, and ever-deepening process of learning to be fully human, a process of establishing and enlarging within a community. Although it is not as explicit as the idea of the "wholly other" in Christianity, the Confucian commitment to become fully human necessarily involves a transcendent dimension, establishing "a constant dialogical relationship with Heaven."[11]

Furthermore, Tu defined Confucianism as a faith in the intrinsic possibility of human self-transcendence, or "the perfectibility of human nature through self-effort," or simply, "a faith in self-transcendence."[12] Tu said:

> The Confucian "faith" in the intrinsic meaningfulness of humanity is a faith in the living person's authentic possibility for self-transcendence. The body, the mind, the soul, and the spirit of the living person are all laden with profound ethicoreligious significance. To be religious, in the Confucian sense, is to be engaged in ultimate self-transformation as a communal act. Salvation means the full realization of the anthropocosmic reality inherent in our human nature.[13]

Self-Cultivation, the Central Confucian Project

The center of the Confucian faith lies in the project of self-cultivation, more precisely, "learning to become more authentically or more fully human." It begins from the concrete life situation, 'the living person here and now,' focusing on the self. Because of this focus, Confucianism is also characterized as the 'learning for the sake of the self.' However, self here does not mean an autonomous, self-fulfilled ego in the modern, Western sense, but "a center of relationships" with an emphasis of "a communal quality."[14] Harmonizing human relations is the cardinal Confucian virtue. Confucians know that this harmony cannot be achieved without the transformation of selfhood ("Selfhood as Creative Transformation").[15] Self-cultivation is "a precondition" for harmonizing human relations, and the priority of self-cultivation in Confucianism is "irreversible."[16] Hence, Wang Yang-ming said, "To study is nothing but self-cultivation."[17]

Self-cultivation (*hsiu-shen*) is thus at the center of Confucian project. It is regarded even as "an end rather than a means" of Confucian learning. Unless learning is for the sake of learning, it cannot be a true learning, but for the sake of other reasons such as fame, position, and wealth. However, self-cultivation as the end does not mean the "private possession of a single individual but a sharable experience that underlies common humanity." It is properly understood as the process of "the broadening of the self to embody an ever-expanding circle of human relatedness."[18]

These points are well founded in *The Great Learning*, one of the Four Books, the most authoritative Neo-Confucian texts.[19] *The Great Learning* "gives the Confucian educational, moral, and political programs in a nutshell."[20] It is an indispensable guideline to Confucian adult education. Chu Hsi underscored the book as "the gate through which the beginning student enters into virtue."[21] *The Great Learning* states:

> The Way [*Tao*] of learning to be great (or adult education) consists in manifesting the clear character, loving the people, and abiding (*chih*) in the highest good.
> The ancients who wished to manifest their clear character to the world would first bring order to their states. Those who wished to bring order to their states would first regulate their families. Those who wished to regulate their families would first cultivate their own personal lives [*hsiu-shen*]. . . . when the personal life is cultivated, the family will be regulated; when the family is regulated, the state will be in order; and when the state is in order, there will be peace throughout the world. From the Son of Heaven down to the common people, all must regard cultivation of the personal life as the root or foundation. There is never a case when the root is in disorder and yet the branches are in order.[22]

This passage announces three important points. First, it introduces three root-metaphors of *the Great Learning*; (1) "manifesting the clear character," (2) "loving the people," and (3) "abiding in the highest good." Yi T'oegye (1501-1570), a great Korean Neo-Confucian scholar, explained their relationship; the first one as "substance" (*t'i*), the second as "function" (*yung*), and the third as "the goal of substance and function."[23]   Second, it includes the famous phrase with respect to the outer application of learning in four stages: self-cultivation (*hsiu-shen*), regulating the family (*ch'i-chia*), ordering the state (*chih-kuo*), and bringing peace throughout the world (*ping t'ien-hsia*).   It delineates that the Confucian way to realize the meanings of those root-metaphors is to begin to practice them from the most concrete locus, self, and to expand through the concrete stages of human relatedness; e.g., family, state, and the world. This implies a "concrete-universal approach," a spiral movement of creative transformation from the particular to the universal, from the inner to the outer, and from selfhood to the cosmos (a theme of the next chapter). Third, this passage explicitly defines self-cultivation as "the root and foundation" of the Confucian project, because self-cultivation is the concrete point of departure for the universal harmonization.

Paradigm Shift:
Hsin chi li (The Mind-and-Heart Is the Principle)

Li

Neo-Confucianism is also known as *li hsüeh*, literally, the school of the principle. This highlights that the concept of *li* (principle) is a cardinal Neo-Confucian concept. *Li* signifies a built-in structure, pattern, or standard which sustains the order of universe as a whole. As Ch'en Ch'un explained, *li* and *Tao* (the Way) are generally the same except the former is more concrete while the latter is broader. [24]   *Li* is also associated with (*i*) righteousness: *li* refers to 'substance' (the ontological reality), while *i* refers to 'function' (its existential norm). *Li* signifies the transcendent principle of truth and goodness that is both formative and normative.   Although *li* is generally translated as principle, it does not have the connotation of an abstract universality as the English word principle has.[25]

Originally, *li* was not a Confucian notion, but a Neo-Confucian construction in response to Chinese Buddhist philosophy. *Li* acquired an important status in the thought of the Five Masters of Northern Sung—the founding fathers of Neo-Confucianism—Chou Tun-i (1017-

1073), Shao Yung (1011-1077), Chang Tsai (1020-1077), Ch'eng Hao (1032-1085), and Ch'eng I (1033-1107). When the Ch'eng brothers (Ch'eng Hao and Ch'eng I) first argued "being presupposes principle" (*li* as the ground of being), *li* became a basic Neo-Confucian term. The Neo-Confucian fathers faced a dilemma in the contradiction between the ultimately one *Li* and ubiquitously many *li*[s] (a Neo-Confucian version of the problematic of one versus many or transcendence versus immanence). Ch'eng I tried to resolve it with his famous doctrine of *li-i fen-shu*, meaning principle is one but its manifestations are many.[26]

To solve the existential problem of evil, Ch'eng-Chu scholars established a distinction between nature (*hsing*) and mind-and-heart (*hsin*). Although original human nature is always good and identical with principle, evil can occur because the mind-and-heart is contingent and vulnerable. They also postulated the reason in a relationship between *li* and *ch'i* (material force); for example, principle is good, but the vulnerability happens owing to a disturbance of *ch'i*. *Ch'i*, literally signifying breath, vapor, ether, vital force, or energy, is "the stuff out of which beings are formed." It is the agent that both concretizes (differentiates and individuates) and energizes all beings to realize the harmony.[27] However, the Ch'eng brothers were divided on the relationship between *li* and *ch'i*. Ch'eng Hao espoused a monistic view (*li* and *ch'i* are same), whereas Ch'eng I a dualistic understanding. Chu Hsi achieved a synthesis which harmonized these two views, providing a systematic explanation of their relationship.[28] In this synthesis, Chu Hsi postulated further that principle is prior to material force, which Wang Yang-ming rejected.[29]

Ko-wu *(the Investigation of Things)*

In addition to the four stages of the outer dimension, *the Great Learning* delineates another four steps pertaining to the inner dimension; namely, the investigation of things (*ko-wu*), the extension of knowledge (*chih-chih*), the sincerity of the will (*ch'eng-i*), and the rectification of the mind-and-heart (*ch'eng-hsin*). *The Great Learning* states:

> Those who wished to cultivate their personal lives would first rectify their minds. Those who wished to rectify their minds would first make their wills sincere. Those who wished to make their wills sincere would first extend their knowledge. The extension of knowledge consists in the investigation of things. When things are investigated, knowledge is

extended; when knowledge is extended, the will becomes sincere; when the will is sincere, the mind is rectified; when the mind is rectified, the personal life is cultivated; when the personal life is cultivated, the family will be regulated; when the family is regulated, the state will be in order; when the state is in order, there will be peace throughout the world.[30]

Editing *The Great Learning* as one of the *Four Books* in 1190, Chu Hsi underscored *ko-wu* as the essential stage for the four inner dimensions of self-cultivation. Since then, this notion has been the chief controversial problem within Neo-Confucianism[31] And Chu Hsi taught that *ko-wu* is "to grasp the *li* inherent in things by a systematic and gradual investigation."[32]

Wang Yang-ming had been fascinated by this idea of Chu Hsi's since childhood and continuously struggled with it before his own enlightenment. His chronological biography (*Nien-p'u*)[33] contained an interesting anecdote. Wang resolutely attempted to comprehend the idea that universal principle (*li*) is everywhere, embodied even in a tree and a blade of grass.[34] He and a friend undertook the project to grasp the meaning of *ko-wu* through the task of investigating a bamboo grove. His friend tried first, but gave up after three days of intensive study. Wang continued for seven days, but he also became completely exhausted and physically ill.[35] Wang was caught in a dilemma, "the tension between self-knowledge and external learning," or in Confucian terms, "the conflict between the 'inner' (*nei*) or 'outer' (*wai*)." Persuaded by Chu Hsi, Wang endeavored to arrive at self-realization through an external understanding of the *li* inherent in the bamboo, but he failed. Wang made other attempts later, but he failed again. He could not resolve "the root issue—how to arrive at internal self-realization through external investigation." The central question of "bridging the gap between *hsin* (heart-mind) and *li*" was yet unanswered. These frustrating experiences prompted him to leave Confucianism for a while, and he looked to Taoism and Ch'an Buddhism.[36]

Wang could not settle this issue until he achieved an enlightenment in 1508 during his political exile at Lung-ch'ang, a primitive region of mountains and forest. There, he built a sarcophagus, sat in front of it, and meditated. One night, he achieved sudden enlightenment, "a monumental event not only in the personality development of Wang Yang-ming but also in the history of Chinese thought."[37] Tu described it dramatically:

One night, in the "outpost of advancing day," it suddenly occurred to him that the true meaning of *ko-wu*, a concept that he had encountered almost twenty years previously, was to be found internally rather than externally. According to the commonly accepted account, what happened was quite dramatic: In the midnight watches, when he was sleeplessly tossing and turning, suddenly he felt as if he had heard a voice talking to him about the issue of *ko-wu*. Unconsciously he called out and jumped out of bed. His servants were startled. For the first time Yang-ming came to the realization that "My own nature is, of course, sufficient for me to attain sagehood. And I have been mistaken searching for the *li* in external things and affairs (shih-wu)." He then reflected upon the words of *the Five Classics*, that he had learned by heart as "witness" (*cheng*) to his new realization. He found that they were completely in harmony with it.[38]

Hsin chi li *(The Mind-and-Heart Is the Principle!)*

Through the enlightenment Wang realized that the *li* is not an external thing, but already *sufficient* in his own *hsin* (mind-and-heart). Later, he said about his struggle with Chu Hsi's interpretation of *ko-wu*:

People merely say that in the investigation of things [*ko-wu*] we must follow Chu Hsi, but when have they carried it out in practice? I have carried it out earnestly and definitely. In my earlier years my friend Ch'ien and I discussed the idea that to become a sage or a worthy one must investigate all the things in the world. But how can a person have such tremendous energy? I therefore pointed to the bamboos in front of the pavilion and told him to investigate them and see. Day and night Mr. Ch'ien went ahead trying to investigate to the utmost the principles in the bamboos. He exhausted his mind and thoughts and on the third day he was tired out and took sick. At first I said that it was because his energy and strength were insufficient. Therefore I myself went to try to investigate to the utmost. From morning till night, I was unable to find the principles of the bamboos. On the seventh day I also became sick because I thought too hard. In consequence we sighed to each other and said that it was impossible to be a sage or a worthy, for we do not have the tremendous energy to investigate things that they have. After I had lived among the barbarians for [almost] three years, I understood what all this meant and realized that there is really nothing in the things in the world to investigate, that the effort to investigate things is only to be carried out in and with reference to one's body and mind, and that if one firmly believes that everyone can become a sage, one will naturally be able to take up the task of investigating things.   This idea, gentlemen, I must convey to you. (CSL: 249)

Wang claimed that *hsin* has the intrinsic possibility of self-transcendence in the process of attaining sagehood. *Hsin* has been a principal concept of East Asian thought since Mencius, but its meaning is difficult to grasp within the Greek philosophical framework that distinguishes body and soul, as well as emotion and reason. Whereas mind signifies only the faculty of reasoning in much of Western thought, *hsin* has "conative as well as cognitive and affective meanings" in East Asian thought.[39] Since mind does not convey its full meaning, "mind-and-heart" is a better translation.[40] Furthermore, for Mencius, *hsin* is not merely a physiological or psychological idea, but also has "an ontological basis for moral self-cultivation."[41] Wang had realized the truth of this Mencian claim again. He proclaimed, as Lu Hsiang-shan once did against Chu Hsi, "THE MIND-AND-HEART IS THE PRINCIPLE" (*hsin chi li*). He discussed this with one of his disciples, Hsü Ai:

> I [Hsü Ai] said, "With reference to the sentence, 'Only after knowing what to abide in can one be calm' in *the Great Learning*, Chu Hsi considered that 'all events and things possess in them a definite principle.' This seems to contradict your theory."
> The Teacher said, "To seek the highest good [the abiding point] in individual events and things is to regard righteousness as external. The highest good is the original substance of the mind [*hsin chih pen-t'i*]. It is no other than manifesting one's clear character to the point of refinement and singleness of mind. And yet it is not separated from events and things. When Chu Hsi said in his commentary that [manifesting the clear character is] 'the realization of the Principle of Nature to the fullest extent without an iota of selfish human desire,' he got the point."
> I said, "If the highest good is to be sought only in the mind, I am afraid not all principles of things in the world will be covered."
> The Teacher said, "The mind [*hsin*] *is* principle [*li*]. Is there any affair in the world outside of the mind? Is there any principle outside of the mind?" (CSL: 6-7)

In the discussion, Wang identified "the highest good," the last root-metaphor of *The Great Learning,* with the original substance of the mind-and-heart, or *hsin*-in-itself (*hsin chih pen-t'i*). He also affirmed that the first root-metaphor, "manifesting the clear character," denotes the full realization of the highest good immanent in the mind-and-heart. In the primordial and ontological sense, hence, the mind-and-heart is "the embodiment of the Principle of Nature [*T'ien-li*], which requires not an iota added from the outside" (CSL: 7).[42] Although *li* is transcendent, it does not necessarily mean it is only external. For Wang, *li* is not such a conceptual, static notion as in Chu Hsi interpretation, but a dynamic concept in close association with the "existing self."[43] Chu Hsi tends to objectify *li* and sharply distinguishes it from *hsin*. However, this is wrong. *Li* must be construed in a non-dualistic relation to *hsin*. Wang developed the doctrine of *hsin chi li* precisely in order to correct Chu Hsi's excessive objectification of *li* apart from *hsin*.

Wang made a philological argument to support the doctrine through a proper interpretation of *ko-wu*. The first character of the word, *ko*, historically, has three major interpretations: "to oppose" (*han*), "to arrive at" (*chih*), and "to correct" (*cheng*).[44] Ssu-ma Kuang (1019-1086), the eminent statesman-historian of the Sung dynasty, understood *ko-wu* in the first sense, "to guard against" selfish desires stimulated by external things. Chu Hsi, following Ch'eng I, used the second meaning, "to grasp the *li* inherent in things by a systematic and gradual process of investigation." However, Wang contended for the third interpretation, "to rectify" one's thought. Hence, *ko-wu* is not to investigate the external phenomena, but to rectify one's own affairs. He said, "To investigate is to rectify. It is to rectify that which is incorrect so it can return to its original correctness. To rectify that which is not correct is to get rid of evil, and to return to correctness is to do good. This is what is meant by investigation."[45] And Wang argued that this interpretation is in accordance with Mencius' original intention:

> The word *ko* in *ko-wu* is the same as the *ko* in Mencius' saying that "A great man rectified (*ko*) the ruler's mind." It means to eliminate what is incorrect in the mind so as to preserve the correctness of its original substance. Wherever the will is, the incorrectness must be eliminated so correctness may be preserved. (CSL: 15)

He argued that Chu Hsi's division of *hsin* and *li* repeats the same mistake Kao Tzu made in the fourth Century B.C.E. For the fundamental error in Kao Tzu's heresy was that righteousness is conceived as an exterior virtue. This presupposes a separation between righteousness and *hsin*. Wang argued that this fallacious presupposition was precisely the point Mencius endeavored to clear off:

What Chu Hsi meant by the investigation of things is "to investigate the principle in things to the utmost as we come in contact with them." To investigate the principles in things to the utmost as we come in contact with them means to look in each individual thing for its so-called definite principles. This means to apply one's mind to each individual thing and look for principle in it. This is to divide the mind and principle into two. To seek for the principle in each individual thing is like looking for the principle of filial piety in parents. If the principle of filial piety is to be sought in parents, then is it actually in my own mind or is it in the person of my parents? If it is actually in the person of my parents, is it true that as soon as the parents pass away the mind will lack the principle of filial piety. . . From this we know the mistake of dividing the mind and principle into two.

Such division is the doctrine of Kao Tzu who taught that righteousness is external to the mind, a fallacy which Mencius strongly attacked. You know the defect of devoting oneself to external things and neglecting the internal, and becoming broad but lacking essentials. (CSL: 98-99)

Philosophically, Cheng Chung-ying argued that an essential differences between Chu Hsi and Wang Yang-ming is the "onto-epistemic difference between the *hsin* (heart-mind) and the *hsing* (nature)."[46] In Chu Hsi's doctrine of *ko-wu, hsin* is more epistemolog-ized (*hsing* is ontologically given): in Wang's doctrine of *hsin chi li* it is more ontologized (*hsin* is also ontologically given). Wang had the tendency to absorb nature into mind-and-heart, while Chu Hsi had that to absorb mind-and-heart in nature. However, Wang would be more concerned with the epistemological fallacy due to the dualism between *hsin* and *hsing*, a Chinese version of the subject-object distinction. Wang said, "The mind is the nature of man[47] and things, and nature is the principle. I am afraid the use of the word 'and' makes inevitable the interpretation of mind and principle as two different things" (CSL: 33).

A Neo-Confucian Paradigm Shift

In Mencius, *hsin* already has all-embracing dimensions, affective, epistemological, and ontological. Wang's doctrine of *hsin chi li* enhances this inclusiveness even further and opens a new dimension of Neo-Confucianism. It is not only a philosophical swing of the onto-epistemic pendulum of Neo-Confucianism, but also it has a profound theological implication. It constitutes a paradigm shift that enables Neo-Confucianism to enter into Soteriology. His proclamation that "the

mind-and-heart is the principle" would be a soteriological leap expressed in Neo-Confucian language. It provides an ontological basis for the
Confucian way of salvation, an expression even more immediate and
dynamic than Tu's, "the full realization of the anthropocosmic reality
inherent in our human nature."[48]

In his spiritual journey, associated with the characteristics of *k'uang*
(mad ardor), Wang expressed an immediate, passionate, existential, and
intense spiritual longing. His enthusiastic quest for self-realization
resonates with Luther's intense yearning for salvation. What Luther did
with corrupt Roman Catholicism, Wang did with Ch'eng-Chu Neo-
Confucianism which became like "dry wood and dead ashes." Perhaps,
his crisis was intensified both by his natural propensity of "mad ardor"
and by the soteriological aspiration of Ch'an Buddhism. Finally, he
exploded in a childlike, but creative spirit of Tseng Tien, and produced
the proclamation "the mind-and-heart is the principle!" The claim
would be saying in Neo-Confucian language, "Self-realization comes
from nowhere else, but only from within our mind-and-heart!" It
resonates with Luther's battle cry for Reformation, saying in Christian
language that justification comes from nowhere else, but only from
within our faith. For both of them, the matter is not related to
something outside such as formal proprieties in the Society or that of
visible sacraments in the Church, but ultimately pertains to one's own
subjectivity. Just as Luther's doctrine of *sola fide* (justification by faith
alone) radically changed the course of Christian theology, Wang's
doctrine of *hsin chi li* (self-realization in the mind-and-heart alone)
reshaped the path of East Asian thinking. Both of them marked a major
paradigm shift for each tradition.

Basing himself on Thomas Kuhn, Hans Küng argued that Christian
theology developed through continuous paradigm shifts. Küng said,
"New discoveries arise through a highly complex and usually long,
drawn-out process of *replacement of a previously valid model of
explanation or 'paradigm' by a new one.* They arise through something that is neither fully rational nor fully irrational--and in any case
more revolutionary than evolutionary--a *"paradigm change."* [49]
Analogously, Confucianism also seems to have developed through the
process of paradigm shifts. Paradigm shift would be a more appropriate
term than evolution, the term Chan Wing-tsit used.[50]

In Wang's confuciology, I see a salient example of Neo-Confucian
paradigm shift. Chu Hsi's paradigm has dominated East Asian
Confucian thought as a whole, being regarded as the orthodox

Confucian teaching. However, Wang constituted a crucial paradigm shift, radically departing from this orthodox interpretation of Chu Hsi. For many years, Wang was occupied with Chu Hsi's ruling paradigm, the normative interpretive tradition of his community for his time. However, Wang discovered anomalies in Chu Hsi's paradigm and experienced a spiritual crisis, particularly in the issue of *ko-wu*. Through his sudden enlightenment, he finally realized that the root cause for the anomalies is in looking at self-realization in the wrong place and based on the false dualism of *hsin* and *li*, inner and the outer, self and non-self, and subject and object. Wang's paradigm shift of *hsin chi li* is an "urgent remedial measure" to correct this defect which betrayed the Confucian faith in primordial human goodness (CSL: 94).

Christian Reformers such as Martin Luther and John Calvin (1509-1564) used the authority of St. Augustine of Hippo (354-430) in their paradigm changes (Reformation) against the then dominant scholastic theology. Similarly, Wang relied on the authority of Mencius in his revolt against Chu Hsi's ruling tradition. Like these Christian Reformers, Wang did not simply reiterate Mencius' sayings, but rearticulated them through the new hermeneutical filters of his time, including the Taoist-Buddhist filter, though Mencius could not have known these new conceptual materials.[51] Although a paradigm change produces many differences, literally speaking, it does not necessarily mean an exit or a discontinuity from a tradition. On the contrary, it warrants a continuity of the tradition as an authentic living faith that can respond dynamically to the context, even through revolutionary changes.

Chapter 2

•

Root Metaphor: *Ch'eng* (Sincerity)

Li-chih (the establishment of the will)

The goal of self-cultivation, the primary Confucian project, is to establish the ultimate humanity that dwells naturally in the highest good. Since ultimate humanity denotes sagehood in Confucianism, self-cultivation is to attain sagehood. For Wang, this project does not begin "with an external method but with an inner decision." The main concern is not with metaphysical questions such as the "delicate issue of why," but "the concrete and urgent problem of *how* to become a sage." However, Chu Hsi's doctrine of *ko-wu* is in the final analysis an external method. Chu Hsi actually "subsumed" self-cultivation "under a whole complex of metaphysical presuppositions such as the dichotomy between *hsin* and *li*."[1] Wang said:

> In his doctrine of *ko-wu*, Wen Kung [Chu Hsi] lacked a basis [*t'ou-nao*]. For instance, he said [that among the methods of investigating things] is 'the examination of one's subtle thoughts and deliberations.' [Being the most fundamental,] this should not be grouped together with 'searching for the principles of things in books,' 'testing them in one's conspicuous activities,' and 'finding them out in discussion.' He lacked a sense of relative importance." (CSL: 204)

In this passage, Wang said that metaphysical elements which appeared in Chu Hsi's doctrine of *ko-wu* are neither foundational, of the first priority, or primary. Wang argued that the true point of departure of the Confucian project is not so much in such speculative postulation as in one's inner decision making and genuine commitment to become a sage, namely *li-chih* (the establishment of will). As faith is the starting point for the Christian discipleship, *li-chih* is that for the Confucian discipleship.

When banished to Lung-ch'ang, Wang taught his students four principles of self-cultivation:[2] (1) Students must establish their wills on learning (*li-chih*), study diligently (*ch'in hsüeh*) learning how to become a sage, (3) continuously reform their errors according to the learning (*kai-kuo*),[3] (4) and motivate and invoke other Confucianists to the good by means of reproof and criticism (*tse-shan*). *Li-chih* is the first principle in the first priority, the first requirement to become his personal disciple. *Li-chih* involves not only one's complete and total commitment. but also "continuous assurance."[4] Comparing *li-chih* to the Kierkegaardian notion of "qualitative change," Tu said:

> The structure of *li-chih* is analogous to that of existential decision in the Kierkegaardian sense; it is a fundamental choice that requires an ultimate commitment; it is a qualitative change that affects the entire dimension of one's being; and it is an unceasing process that demands constant reaffirmation.[5]

However, *li-chi* as a qualitative change is different from the Christian notion of faith in some respects. Whereas *li-chih* denotes one's will to attain sagehood through self-transformation, faith is related to one's trust in salvation by the "wholly other." As Tu clarified, "The qualitative change in Confucianism, unlike its counterpart in Christianity, is not an either-or leap of faith, but a both-and return to the self." *Li-chih* is not so much related to a "mystic experience of the transcendent Absolute" or the revelation of God as "an enlightening experience of the immanent Self."[6]

Confucius' famous autobiographical statement in the *Analects*, "At fifteen, I set my heart on learning"[7] presents a classic example of *li-chih*, a life-long commitment to self-transformation at an early age. Hsün Tzu (313-238 B.C.?) also said, "the art of learning occupies the whole of life; to arrive at its purpose, you cannot stop for an instant. To do this is to be a man; to stop is to be a beast." [8] Mencius divided human beings into two groups, the great body (*ta-t'i*) and the small body (*hsiao-t'i*): "*Ta-t'i* refers to the intrinsic moral feelings that make man uniquely human; *hsiao-t'i* refers to the basic instinctual demands that make man a part of the animal kingdom." This distinction is to explain the qualitative difference and the need for qualitative change through self-transformation. *Li-chih* is constitutive of this qualitative change, from *hsiao-t'i* ("natural growth of the partial man") to *ta-t'i* ("the meaningful existence of the fully integrated whole man").[9] Hence, *li-chih*, the establishment of the will toward self-transformation signifies a qualitative change for humanization that involves one's ethicoreligious authentication and psychophysical cultivation.

In Confucianism, this cannot be conceived without one's lived concreteness. Its "spatiotemporal dimension" is emphasized in the structure of *li-chih*.[10] Hence, sociopolitical conditions are regarded as a significant part of the human situation, the locus of the humanizing process. Wang's life was an example in which he practiced faithfully this dimension. In his expression, it was experiences of "a hundred deaths and a thousand hardships." As a junior official in Peking, Wang had struggled with the gap between Neo-Confucian ideals and the Ming socio-political realities. He believed that the fullest meaning one acquired from one's dynamic inner search can be achieved only through its embodiment in practice and in a reorientation toward the world. Wang presented a memorial to the throne in protest of imperial injustice, by virtually attacking the powerful eunuch Liu Chin (1506). Because of the memorial, he was imprisoned, flogged in public, and banished to remote Lung-ch'ang (1506), where he achieved enlightenment. His establishment of the will (*li-chih*) to spread the true Confucian Tao (1502) demanded not "cheap" but "costly" Confucian discipleship, in terms of Dietrich Bonhoeffer.[11]

Chih-hsing ho-i (The Unity of Knowing and Acting)

Li-chih is the basis for Confucian *Tao* and an unequivocal requirement for the Confucian discipleship. And *li-chih,* the establishment of the will, signifies "the directionality of the mind" in the Mencian sense.[12] In Confucianism, the directionality of mind-and-heart cannot be separated from its bodily constitution. Thus Wang called his teaching the "learning of the body and mind" (*shen-hsin chih hsüeh*).[13] This leads to his famous doctrine of *chih-hsing ho-i* (the unity of knowing and acting).[14]

Tu explained the unity in relation to *li-chih*. First, *li-chih* involves *knowing*. But it is more than a cognitive knowing, and rather a "transforming self-reflection:" "as a form of introspective examination, knowing simultaneously transforms one's present existence into a state of being projected toward the future ideal."[15] Second, *li-chih* involves *acting* which "reorders one's existential situation and affects the whole dimension of one's life."[16] While *li-chih*, as knowing, causes fundamental changes in one's life, *li-chih*, as acting, brings new depth to one's perception. Therefore, in the structure of *li-chih*, knowing and acting form a unity, as the two dimensions of one process. Wang said:

> knowledge [*chih*] is the direction for action and action [*hsing*] the effort of knowledge (CSL: 11).

> Knowledge is the beginning of action and action is the completion of knowledge. Learning to be a sage involves only one effort. Knowledge and action should not be separated. (CSL: 30)

Wang's confuciology began to correct Chu Hsi's interpretation of *ko-wu*, which caused "a rupture between *hsin* (heart-mind) and *li*."[17] However, this correction with the plea to "return to *hsin*" resulted in a greater discovery of the Confucian truth, the substance of knowledge and action in original unity (see CSL: 94). Furthermore, it reveals the original nature (*pen-t'i*) in which both knowing and acting are in unity. Beyond serving as a "medicine" to the doctrinal "disease," this doctrine uncovers the ontology of original nature. Wang said:

> But people today distinguish between knowledge and action and pursue them separately, believing that one must know before he can act. They will discuss and learn the business of knowledge first, they say, and wait till they truly know before they put their knowledge into practice. Consequently, to the last day of life, they will never act and also will never know. The doctrine of knowledge first and action later is not a minor disease and it did not come about only yesterday. My present advocacy of the unity of knowledge and action is precisely the medicine for that disease. The doctrine is not my baseless imagination, for it is the original substance of knowledge and action that they are one. (CSL: 11-12)

While true knowing involves "the actual transforming effects," real acting entails "the real deepening effects" of self-knowledge.[18] Then, how can they look in reality divided? Wang's answer was that selfish desires are the source of evil which separates the unified condition of knowing and acting:

. . . I [Hsü Ai] said, "For example, there are people who know that parents should be served with filial piety and elder brothers with respect but cannot put these things into practice. This shows that knowledge and action are clearly two different things."

The Teacher said, "The knowledge and action you refer to are already separated by selfish desires and are no longer knowledge and action in their original substance. There have never been people who know but do not act. Those who are supposed to know but do not act simply do not yet know. . . . Seeing beautiful colors appertains to knowledge, while loving beautiful colors appertains to action. However, as soon as one sees that beautiful color, he has already loved it. It is not that he sees it first and then makes up to love it. (CSL: 10)

Owing to selfish desires, there appears the dualistic gap between knowing and acting. Nevertheless, one can still experience their unity in the process of love. Likewise, in the process of true learning, there is no idle time for intellectual inquiry and persuasion by the division of knowing and acting.

Study, inquiry, thinking, sifting, and practice are all ways of learning. No one really learns anything without carrying it into action. Take the learning of filial piety. One must relieve his parents of the burden of toil, serve and care for them, and personally put the principle of filial piety into action before one can be said to be learning filial piety. Can merely talking about it in a vacuum be considered as learning? . . . In all the world, nothing can be considered learning that does not involve action. Thus the very beginning of learning is already action. To be earnest in practice means to be genuine and sincere. That is already action. It is to make the action sincere and the effort continuous without stop. In learning, one cannot help having doubts. Therefore one inquires. To inquire is to learn; it is to act. As there is still doubt, one thinks. To think is to learn; it is to act. As there is still doubt, one sifts. To sift is to learn; it is to act. As the sifting is clear, the thinking careful, the inquiry accurate, and the study competent, one goes further and continues his effort without stop. This is what is meant by earnest practice. It does not mean that after study, inquiry, thinking, and sifting one then takes steps to act. (CSL: 100)

Chu Hsi's doctrine of *ko-wu* involves an epistemological overtone under a cognitivist dualism, focusing on a rigorous intellectual pursuit for self-realization. Chu Hsi presupposes that human knowing in itself is incomplete and that "enlightenment is the end result of long study" in such a way as *ko-wu*. Hence, Chu Hsi held the view of "gradual attainment" of enlightenment.[19] However, Wang's doctrine of the unity of knowing and acting shows a different view, even with an anti-intellectual overtone. For Wang, Confucian learning is "primarily a moral ideal rather than a principle of epistemology."[20] Unlike Chu Hsi, Wang believed that, since enlightenment is at hand, it happens suddenly and spontaneously. Nivison argued that with this doctrine Wang attempted to resolve "Neo-Confucian dualisms—not only the dualism of 'knowledge' and 'action' but likewise that of 'essence' and 'function,' 'principle' and 'matter,' mind and body, the observer and the observed."[21] The doctrine of the unity of knowing and acting shows Wang's paradigm shift from Chu Hsi's doctrine of *ko-wu*, even more saliently than the doctrine of the identification of the mind-and-heart with principle. Tu succinctly summarized this paradigm shift:

> First, *ko-wu* perceives the subject and object as two independent entities; they come into contact when the subject makes conscious efforts to approach the object. *Chih-hsing ho-i* rejects such an artificial dichotomy and points to a dynamic process of self-relization in which man's subjectivity becomes real experience rather than an abstract concept. Second, *ko-wu* puts too much stress on the tangible forms of self-cultivation, which tends to objectify moral decision into a "goal" of self-efforts. However, *chih-hsing ho-i* "bridges" the gap between the inner and outer by focusing on the linkage between thought and practice. Third, *ko-wu* inclines to quantify morality into a series of discrete deeds; as a result, external manifestations take precedence over inner transformations. *Chih-hsing ho-i*, on the other hand, keeps moral consciousness awake in all situations so that even the motion of the "incipient activation" (*chi*) of the mind will not be overlooked. Fourth, *ko-wu* tends to subsume moral principles under the rubric of empirical knowledge, whereas *chih-hsing ho-i*, by centering around intentionality, underscores the inner dimension of ethicoreligious cultivation. Finally, it seems that a sense of urgency is lacking in *ko-wu*, for it assumes that the process of self-realization is necessarily a gradual one. By focusing on the directionality of will, *chih-hsing ho-i* speaks to moral self-cultivation in a sense of immediacy. The question of the gradual versus the sudden process of self-realization becomes secondary, for the central concern is *how* to manifest the inner sage here and now, rather than by *what* process the inner sage will eventually be manifested.[22]

Ch'eng (Sincerity): A Concrete-Universal Approach

For Wang, this inseparability does not imply so much a closed system in the unity of two static concepts, as a dynamic process interrelated to real life situations. Authentic self-knowledge can not be attained unless it is concretely embodied into the ethicosocial context. Confucianism emphasizes that the realization of the true self must be executed in the network of human-relatedness. The locus of Confucian self-cultivation is the shared praxis in the world of everyday life, as Fingarette's idiom, "the secular as sacred," suggests.[23]

As we have seen, the eightfold process of the *Great Learning* authenticates the *concrete-universal approach*, both external and internal. The external task of self-realization must be executed from the concrete locus and universally extended through the sequence of four primal relationships: cultivation of self, harmony in the family, order in the state, and peace in the world. Consequently, a concept such as "universal love," which Mo-tzu (468-376 B.C.E.?) postulated, is an unrealistic abstraction for Confucians. Rather, the practicality of love requires its implementation from the closest network of human relatedness. If the father-son (parent-child) relationship is regarded as the first primal tie, the process of becoming authentically human must begin with the concrete practice of filial piety, rather than the care for abstract neighbors.

At the same time, the concrete-universal approach is considered as "the most authentic way of entering into universal communion with the cosmos." Tu explained, "The deeper one goes into the ground of one's own being, the closer one gets to the spring of common humanity and the source of cosmic creativity."[24] This implies also the Confucian way to go beyond one's anthropological structure. Mencius stated, "For a person to give full realization to his heart is for one to understand one's own nature, and a person who knows one's own nature will know Heaven."[25] Tu explained further: "The inner experience of a concrete person serves as the real basis of generalization" This implies the concrete-universal approach, through which we can achieve the unity of our ultimate humanity and the all-embracing cosmos, the status of the great personhood. Thus, Wang stated: "the great man [person] regards Heaven, Earth, and the myriad things as one body."[26]

Each process of the concrete-universal approach requires *li-chih* in which knowing and acting are in unity. This is "the only access to the

ontology of [humanity]."²⁷ And it is related to one of the fundamental
Neo-Confucian concepts, *ch'eng* (sincerity). Etymologically, *ch'eng*
means "completion, actualization, or perfection," and includes always
positive connotations such as "honesty, genuineness, and truth."²⁸ *The
Doctrine of the Mean* (Chung-yung)²⁹ said:

> What Heaven (*T'ien*, Nature) imparts to man is called human nature.
> To follow our nature is called the Way (Tao). Cultivating the Way is
> called education. The Way cannot be separated from us for a moment.
> What can be separated from us is not the Way. Therefore the superior
> man [profound person] is cautious over what he does not see and
> apprehensive over what he does not hear. There is nothing more visible
> than what is hidden and nothing more manifest than what is subtle.
> Therefore the superior man is watchful over himself when he is alone.³⁰

This passage claims that human nature is a heavenly endowment,
which implies the oneness of humanity and Heaven, in Tu's term,
"anthropocosmic" unity. This unity of the human and Heaven is the
principal presupposition of the Confucian faith. It is the foundation of
one's authentic possibility for self-realization. Hence, one must seek
one's approach to Heaven none other than in the structure of one's own
nature. However, the profound person must transcend his or her
anthropocentric proclivity. Nevertheless, the only way to transcend
oneself is "through a process of 'humanization,' which in this specific
context means a return to one's sincere nature."³¹ The most sincere
person is a sage, ultimate humanity, who is unified and identified with
Heaven. Therefore,

> Sincerity [*ch'eng*] is the Way of Heaven. To think how to be sincere is
> the way of man. He who is sincere is one who hits upon what is right
> without effort and apprehends without thinking. He is naturally and
> easily in harmony with the Way. Such a man is a sage. He who tries to
> be sincere is one who chooses the good and holds fast to it.³²

According to Chan, *ch'eng* in *The Doctrine of the Mean* implies
"not just a state of mind, but an active force that is always transforming
things and completing things and drawing man and Heaven (*T'ien*,
Nature) together in the same current."³³ *The Doctrine of the Mean*
further stated:

Only those who are absolutely sincere can fully develop their nature. If they can fully develop their nature, they can then fully develop the nature of others. If they can fully develop the nature of others, they can then fully develop the nature of things. If they can fully develop the nature of things, they can then assist in the transforming and nourishing process of Heaven and Earth. If they can assist in the transforming and nourishing process of Heaven and Earth, they can thus form a trinity with Heaven and Earth.[34]

Sincerity enables a person to develop one's own humanity to the utmost. "For being absolutely sincere (genuine, truthful, and honest) entails the ability to actualize, complete, and perfect one's true nature."[35] The absolutely sincere person is capable of extending the task of self-realization to the cosmos as a whole, because one's true nature and that of others, of things, and of the universe are ontologically in unity. The sage not only transcends egocentric structure through self-transformation, but also forms a organismic (triadic) unity with the cosmos through self-realization. In this anthropocosmic vision, self-realization and self-transformation are inseparable. Therefore, in sincerity "being" cannot be distinguished from "becoming." Tu said:

To be sincere is to realize oneself through self-transformation; to engage oneself in self-transformation is simultaneously a necessary expression of being sincere. Since self-transformation is a process of becoming, and sincerity is usually thought to be a state of being, it means that the ordinary distinction of becoming and being is no longer applicable in this case. To define man as a self-transforming and self-realizing agent is to characterize his becoming process.[36]

Hence, sincerity is the creative source of all processes for transformation. *The Doctrine of the Mean* explains the process in detail.

Sincerity necessarily leads to visibility. From visibility it leads to manifestation. From manifestation, it leads to illumination (or enlightenment). Illumination entails activity. Activity entails change. And change leads to transformation. Only he who is absolutely sincere can eventually transform."[37]

Sincerity is both "the creative process by which the existence of things becomes possible, and the ground of being on which the things as they really are ultimately rests."[38] Tu said, "Sincerity means the

completion of the self, and the Way is self-directing. Sincerity is the
beginning and the end of things. Without sincerity there would be
nothing."[39] The absolutely sincere person, being in a complete unity
with Heaven, "transcends anthropological restrictions, embodies the
most authentic humanity, and participates in the great cosmic
transformation itself."[40] *The Doctrine of the Mean* said:

> Only those who are absolutely sincere can order and adjust the great
> relations of mankind, establish the great foundation of humanity, and
> know the transforming and nourishing operations of heaven and earth.
> Does he depend on anything else? How earnest and sincere—he is
> humanity! How deep and unfathomable—he is abyss! How vast and
> great—he is heaven! Who can know him except he who really has
> quickness of apprehension, intelligence, sageliness, and wisdom, and
> understands the character of Heaven?[41]

Since human nature is imparted by Heaven, the creative,
transcendent power is inherent and immanent in the very structure of
human being. Hence, the final advice of *The Doctrine of the Mean* to
be fully human, is to be sincere. "For humanity in its ultimate sense is
the fullest manifestation of sincerity. Accordingly the sage participates
in cosmic creativity simply by his humaneness. Being absolutely
sincere, the sage humanizes in the spirit of cosmic creativity."[42] Being
the utmost endowment of sagehood, sincerity it is the root-metaphor of
humanization, that is the ultimate foundation of the Confucian
"concrete-universal" approach. Tu summed up:

> If one intends to become an authentic man, one must establish the will
> to become a whole man, which means the fulfillment of both human
> corporality and spirituality. The establishment of the will as an inner
> decision is itself both *knowing* and *acting*. Only in the unity of
> knowing and acting can the true nature of inner decision be found,
> because the root of self-realization is inherent in the very structure of
> man. Self-realization, however, is not a process of individuation; it is
> primarily a course of universal communion. The more one sinks into
> the depth of one's being, the more he transcends his anthropological
> restriction. Underlying this paradox is the Confucian belief that the true
> nature of man and the real creativity of the cosmos are both "grounded"
> in *sincerity* [*ch'eng*]. When one, through self-cultivation, becomes
> absolutely sincere, one is the most authentic man and simultaneously
> participates in the transforming and nourishing process of the cosmos.
> To do so is to fulfill one's human nature.[43]

Chapter 3

•

The Humanity Paradigm

Root-Paradigm: *Liang-chih*

With the doctrine of *hsing chi li* (the nature [*hsing*] is the principle[*li*]), Chu Hsi's method of cultivation focused on the attitude of reverence (*ching*)[1] and rigorous engagement in the investigation of principles. This reduced the status of mind-and-heart (*hsin*) to something inferior to nature (*hsing*). However, with the doctrine of *hsin chi li* (the mind-and-heart is the principle), Wang asserted that mind-and-heart and nature are identical and "coextensive."[2] The *hsin* itself has a innate or original ability to discern the Heavenly Principle (*T'ien-li*) and know the good. Borrowing the term from Mencius, Wang defined this primordial faculty of *hsin* as *liang-chih* (innate knowledge of the good).[3] Then *liang-chih* became "the great principle" of Wang's whole Neo-Confucian thinking.[4] Wang said:

> My idea is that it is incorrect to interpret the investigation of the principles of things to the utmost as we come into contact with them to mean . . . devoting oneself to external things and neglecting the internal. If an unenlightened student can really carefully examine the Principle of Nature in the mind in connection with things and events as they come, and extend his innate or original knowledge of the good [*liang-chih*], then though stupid he will surely become intelligent and though weak he will surely become strong. The great foundation will be established and the universal Way [in human relations] will be in operation. (CSL: 103)

Like *hsin, liang-chih* has both affective and cognitive dimensions. It is a primordial feeling "prereflective and spontaneous"[5] like the natural feeling of "alarm and commiseration" when we see a child about to fall into a well.[6] At the same time, it is "nothing other than the Principle of Nature [*T'ien-li*] where the natural clear consciousness reveals itself. Its original substance is merely true sincerity and commiseration." (CSL: 176) It is a "revelation"[7] of the Heavenly Principle (*T'ien-li*) in human original consciousness." It is the foundation of all knowledge, and "the great basis of learning and the first principle of the teaching of the Sage" (CSL: 150). It is the inherent moral "standard" (or "the inner forum")[8] to judge right and wrong, which is the "true secret" of the Confucian project of self-cultivation.

> Your innate knowledge[9] is your own standard. When you direct your thought your innate knowledge knows that it is right if it is right and wrong if it is wrong. You cannot keep anything from it. Just don't try to deceive it but sincerely and truly follow it in whatever you do. Then the good will be preserved and evil will be removed. What security and joy there is in this! This is true secret of the investigation of things and the real effort of the extension of knowledge. (CSL: 193)

Wang also compared *liang-chih* to the "spiritual seal" of the Buddha-mind which can assure the truth, like "a gold-testing stone," a mariners' "compass," or "a wonder medicine" of Taoist alchemy, "one touch of which will turn iron into gold" (CSL: 194). Therefore, Tu Wei-ming rendered *liang-chih* as "primordial awareness." The primordial awareness, as "an innermost state of human perception wherein knowledge and action form a unity" or the "'humanity of the heart,' creates values of human understanding as it encounters the world."[10]

Liang-chih is acquired not by a deliberate learning of a coded ethical knowledge, but naturally through an experiential realization (CSL: 156). However, when it encounters the world, deliberate efforts are also required to refine and clarify its meaning in the concrete context (CSL: 226). Such efforts are in fact essential to acquire our sensitivity and increase its precision toward *liang-chih*. They entail a serious hermeneutical engagement in Confucianism.

Wang illustrated this by using two intriguing examples of Shun and Wu (CSL, pp. 109-110). Sage-Emperor Shun married the two daughters of Emperor Yao without his parents' consent, which violated the conventional Confucian norm of filial piety. Sage-King Wu of Chou launched a military expedition against the house of Shang before burying his own father, which was also against the conventional practice of filial piety. However, Mencius approved their deeds as legitimate because of their greater motives which surpassed ordinary social conventions. For Shun, installing proper descendants was more essential than trying to obtain impossible permission from his parents. For Wu, saving the people, who suffered under the tyranny of King Chou of Shang, was more immediate than his father's funeral. Wang argued that they could do these unusual deeds according to the direction of *liang-chih* (CSL: 110).

Wang constituted *liang-chih* as the hermeneutical principle for the Classics. Wang's mature thought was *liang-chih*-centered. The Classics are merely "histories of *liang chih* in action."[11] They are valuable only as paradigmatic records of the work of *liang-chih* in historical contexts (CSL: 23). Wang endorsed Lu Hsiang-shan's statement: "If in learning I understand what is fundamental, all the Six Classics are my footnotes."[12] Furthermore, sages are worthy as living paradigms of *liang-chih* in action. They illustrate the trajectory of *liang-chih* as "passing shadows." Wang said, "The thousand sages are all passing shadows; *Liang chih* alone is my teacher."[13]

Wang warned against literal interpretations of the Classics and of the deeds of the sages. The Classics and the sages were history, "and no more" (CSL: 23). Although they can show examples of *liang-chih* in action, they are not the ends of self-cultivation, only *liang-chih* is the goal. *Liang-chih*, as the hermeneutical principle, surpasses even the authority of Confucius (CSL: 159).

Wang created a "hermeneutical circle," holding *liang-chih* as the foreconception (*Vorgriff*) of his interpretative structure.[14] Wang appeared to engage in a project of demythologization, like that of Rudolf Bultmann. Demythologizing the values of the Classics and the sages, Wang emphasized the existential application of *liang-chih* here and now.[15] Wang wrote a poem.

Each and every human mind has Confucius within,
But afflicted by hearing and seeing,
they become confused and deluded;
Now I point to your true original face,
It is none other than *liang chih*—have no more doubts.[16]

Liang-chih is the inner sage or "sagehood," naturally endowed in all people.[17] Every person has *liang-chih*, whether a sage, worthy, or stupid. The difference among sage, worthy and ordinary people is not in quality but in quantity like that among "the sun in the clear sky," "the sun in the sky with floating clouds," and " the sun on a dark, dismal day" (CSL: 228). Since even a sage cannot extend *liang-chih* perfectly, everybody is ultimately the same. Every person has an innate power to strive to be an authentic human (there is the sun even in the dark sky). Wang's notion of *liang-chih* shows a strong egalitarianism. He discussed this with his student.

> The Teacher said, "There is the sage in everyone. Only one has not enough self-confidence and buries his own chance." Thereupon he looked at Yü-chung and said, "From the beginning there is the sage in you." Yü-chung rose and said that he did not deserve it. The Teacher said, "This potentiality originally belongs to you. Why decline?" Yü-chung said again, "I do not deserve it." The Teacher said, "Everyone has this potentiality. How much more is that true of you, Yü-chung! Why be so modest? It won't do even if you are modest." (CSL: 194)

Self-Transcendence

The Doctrine of the Mean states:

> While there are no stirrings of pleasure, anger, sorrow, or joy, the mind may be said to be in the state of EQUILIBRIUM. When those feelings have been stirred, and they act in their due degree, there ensues what may be called the state of HARMONY. This EQUILIBRIUM is the great root *from which grow all the human actings* in the world, and this HARMONY is the universal path *which they all should pursue.* [18]

Accordingly, Ch'eng Yi defined *hsing* (nature) as the state of equilibrium (*chung*) before the rise of feelings (*wei-fa*), but *hsin* (the mind-and-heart) as the state after the feeling are aroused.[19] Chu Hsi also followed this distinction.[20] But Wang rejected this differentiation between nature and mind-and-heart, and rather identified *hsin*-in-itself (*hsin-chih-pen-t'i*, literally the original substance of the mind-and-heart) with *liang-chih*: "The equilibrium before the feelings are aroused is innate knowledge" (CSL: 136). The *hsin*-in-itself is a primordial, ontological state, in which any existential, ontic distinction of before and after, equilibrium and harmony, internal and external, or activity and tranquility becomes obsolete. It is a being-in-itself, analogous to Heidegger's notion of *Dasein*.[21]

As the mind is neither before nor after any state, is neither internal nor external, but is one substance without differentiation . . . The state before the feelings are aroused exists in the state in which feelings have been aroused. But in this state there is not a separate state which is before the feelings are aroused. The state after the feelings are aroused exists in the state before the feelings are aroused. But in this state there is not a separate state in which the feelings have been aroused. Both are not without activity or tranquility and cannot be separately character-ized as active or tranquil. (CSL: 137)

Liang-chih as the *hsin*-in-itself is a dynamic Being-in-itself which penetrates and transcends such distinctions: "but innate knowledge makes no distinction between doing something and doing nothing" (CSL: 136). It is bright and transparent like the "shining mind" (CSL: 139f.) and the "bright mirror" (CSL: 148f.). Wang identified *liang-chih* with the Heavenly Principle (*T'ien-li*). Wang said, "Innate knowledge is where the Principle of Nature is clear and intelligent. Therefore innate knowledge is identical with the Principle of Nature." (CSL: 152) Furthermore, Wang identified *liang-chih*-in-itself (*liang-chih pen-t'i*, the original substance of *liang-chih*) with the Great Vacuity (*T'ai-hsü*),[22] the Neo-Confucian expression of the Ultimate Primordiality. Like the Great Vacuity, *liang-chih*-in-itself is absolutely self-transcendent:

The vacuity of innate knowledge is the Great Vacuity of nature. The non-being of innate knowledge is the formlessness of the Great Vacuity. Sun, moon, wind, thunder, mountains, rivers, people, and things, and all things that have figure, form, or color, all function and operate within this formlessness of the Great Vacuity. None of them has become an obstacle to nature. The sage merely follows the functioning of his innate knowledge and Heaven, Earth, and all things are contained in its functioning and operation. How can there be anything to transcend innate knowledge and become its obstacle? (CSL: 220)

Furthermore, *liang-chih* as self-transcendence is the creative Spirit. It is "the spirit which creates all things, Heaven, Earth, ghosts, and gods. 'It is that to which there is no opposite [or equal].'"[23] *Liang-chih* as the creative Spirit capacitates cosmic differentiations through permeating all things and warrants them into the anthropocosmic identification. *Liang-chih* substantiates the unity among diversities and the cosmic interpenetration through the work of its *ch'i* (material force):

The Innate knowledge of man is the same as that of plants and trees, tiles and stones. Without the innate knowledge inherent in man, there cannot be plants and trees, tiles and stones. This is not true of them only. Even Heaven and Earth cannot exist without the innate knowledge that is inherent in man. For at bottom Heaven, Earth, the myriad things, and man form one body. The point at which this unity is manifested in its most refined and excellent form is the clear intelligence of the human mind. Wind, rain, dew, thunder, sun and moon, stars, animals and plants, mountains and rivers, earth and stones are essentially of one body with man. It is for this reason that such things as the grains and animals can nourish man and that such things as medicine and minerals can heal diseases. Since they share the same material force [*ch'i*], they enter into one another. (CSL: 221f.)

The Confucian Root-Paradigm

Liang-chih as *hsin*-in-itself is the life-giving true self:

Basically the original substance of the mind is none other than the Principle of Nature, and is never out of accord with propriety [*li*]. This is your true self. This true self is the master of the body. If there is no true self, there will be no body. Truly, with the true self, one lives; without it, one dies. (CSL: 80f.)

Tu Wei-ming enunciated *liang-chih* as "subjectivity," which means the true self or genuine humanity.[24] However, subjectivity is distinguished from subjectivism (egocentricism) or solipsism.[25] *Liang-chih* as subjectivity designates "the innermost and indissoluble reality" of humanity, never to be completely lost.[26] It signifies "radical humanity," in which radical means "of or from the root" (*radix*) or "going to the foundation."[27] By *liang-chih*, Wang was able to articulate the Confucian root-paradigm of humanity (and humanization), comparable to the humanity of Christ in Christianity.

Liang-chih as subjectivity has both internality and universality. *Liang-chih* as internality has two meanings: the "clear illumination" (*chao-ming*) and "spiritual awareness" (*ling-chüeh*) of the Heavenly Principle. The clear illumination means "the penetrative insight that grasps the ultimate reality by a self-generative 'intellectual intuition.'" And the spiritual awareness signifies "an all-embracing sensibility that embodies the whole universe by a self-sufficient 'anthropocosmic feeling.'"[28] However, *liang-chih*, as intellectual intuition and anthropocosmic feeling, must be extended beyond anthropocentric subjectivism.

Liang-chih as universality is dynamic and self-transcendent, hardly localizable, but universally inter-penetrating. Hence, the great person who possesses radical humanity is defined not merely by the internal possession of *liang-chih* but also by its realization in the universal extension. In this respect, Wang articulated the doctrine of *Wan-wu yi-t'i* (literally, the Oneness of All Things):

> The great man regards Heaven, Earth, and the myriad things as one body. He regards the world as one family and the country as one person. As to those who make a cleavage between objects and distinguish between the self and others, they are small men. That the great man can regard Heaven, Earth, and the myriad things as one body is not because he deliberately wants to do so, but because it is natural humane nature of his mind that he do so.[29]

The great person who possess radical humanity has "spiritual sensibility and loving care" of the cosmos as a whole.[30] This cosmic spiritual communion is possible because radical humanity is ontologically in an organismic unity with Heaven, Earth, and the myriad things. This vision of the "cosmic togetherness"[31] is well expressed in Chang Tsai's *Western Inscription*:

> Heaven is my father and Earth is my mother, and even such a small creature as I finds an intimate place in their midst. Therefore that which fills the universe I regard as my body and that which directs the universe I consider as my nature. All people are my brothers and sisters, and all things are my companions.[32]

The Paradigm of Humanity: *Jen*[33]

The Chinese character, *jen*, a cardinal Confucian virtue, is composed of a graph which means human being and two strokes that mean two. Etymologically, the word means two human beings, or togetherness of human beings. Thus, Peter A. Boodberg translated it as "co-humanity," "ço-human," or "co-humanize."[34] As we saw in the passages already quoted, Wang not only expanded this togetherness dimension of *jen* to the cosmic level as Chang Tsai's *Western Inscription* had, but also developed further an ontology such as the doctrine of the Oneness of All Things.

Forming one body with Heaven, Earth, and the myriad things is not only true of the great man. Even the mind of the small man is no different. Only he himself makes it small. Therefore, when he sees a child about to fall into a well, he cannot help a feeling of alarm and commiseration. This shows that his humanity [*jen*] forms one body with the child. It may be objected that the child belongs to the same species. Again, when he observes the pitiful cries and frightened appearance of birds and animals about to be slaughtered, he cannot help feeling an "inability to bear" their suffering. This shows that his humanity forms one body with birds and animals. It may be objected that birds and animals are sentient beings as he is. But when he sees plants broken and destroyed, he cannot help a feeling of pity. This shows that his humanity forms one body with plants. It may be said that plants are living things as he is. Yet, even when he sees tiles and stones shattered and crushed, he cannot help a feeling of regret. This shows that his humanity forms one body with tiles and stones. This means that even the mind of the small man necessarily has the humanity that forms one body with all. Such a mind is rooted in his Heaven-endowed nature, and is naturally intelligent, clear, and not beclouded.[35]

Jen (humanity) as the paradigm of radical humanity (*liang-chih*) implies not only a manifested structure of radical human subjectivity but also a spiritual medium through which reconciliatory communions are made possible. Thus, *jen* is both cosmic togetherness--"The man of humanity regards all things as one body" (CSL: 226)--and the life-giving spirituality—the "principle of unceasing production and reproduction" (CSL:. 56).[36] For this reason, *jen* is also predicated as the "clear character" (*ming-te*), the first root metaphor of *the Great Learning*. However, in terms of the substance-function relationship, this predication defines its substance (the ontological structure). It requires that we put its functional counterpart (the ethicoreligious realization), i.e., "loving the people" (*ch'in-min*),[37] the second metaphor, to universal extension:

To manifest the clear character is to bring about the *substance* of the state of forming one body with Heaven, Earth, and the myriad things, whereas loving the people is to put into universal operation the *function* of the state of forming one body. Hence manifesting the clear character consists in loving the people and loving the people is the way to manifest the clear character. Therefore, only when I love my father, the fathers of others, and the fathers of all men can my humanity really form one body with my father, the fathers of others, and the fathers of all men. When it truly forms one body with them, then the clear character of filial piety will be manifested. . . . Everything from ruler, minister, husband, wife, and friends to mountains, rivers, spiritual beings, birds, animals, and plants should be truly loved in order to realize my humanity that forms one body with them, and then my clear character will be completely manifested, and I will really form one body with Heaven, Earth, and the myriad things. This is what is meant by "manifesting the clear character throughout the world." This is what is meant by "regulation of the family," "ordering the state," and "bringing peace to the world." This is what is meant by "full development of one's nature."[38]

Wang's notion of loving the people has dynamic sociopolitical implications, by dynamically recovering the original structure of radical humanity. However, this love is prereflective and spontaneous like the feeling of commiseration. Its extension must follow the order of this natural feeling in social relations, e.g., the family, the society at large, and the world, and the universe (concrete-universal approach). But he argued against an ideal concept, like the Mohist's universal love, because it has a weak starting point and is vulnerable to the abuse of "leveling" natural affections and responsibilities.[39] Wang interpreted the notion of "relative importance" in *The Great Learning* to signify a built-in structure of order in the paradigm of radical humanity. According to this structure, he redefined four other cardinal Confucian virtues: righteousness (*i*), propriety (*li*), wisdom (*chih*), and faithfulness (*hsin*):

What *the Great Learning* calls relative importance means that according to innate knowledge there is a natural order which should not be skipped over. This is called righteousness. To follow this order is called propriety. To understand this order is called wisdom. And to follow this order from beginning to end is called faithfulness. (CSL: 223)

In Wang's Confucian anthropology, human beings,[40] as bearers of *liang-chih*, are the mind-and-heart [*hsin*] of the universe (CSL: 166), or "the psychic center of the universe."[41] Etymologically human being, *homo*, (*jen*) is the same word as the common Chinese vocable *jen* (humanity).[42] Human beings in themselves are self-transcendent with innate spiritual powers for self-realization and have dynamic capacities for self-transformation. Human beings, alone in the cosmos, are capable of creative hermeneutics; they name things, understand, interpret, and make existential decisions. They permeate the whole universe through the dynamic force of their *ch'i*. They act as servants[43] of the sovereign *liang-chih*. Their luminous spirits (*ling-ming*) are at the same time the masters of the universe. In short, human beings are the cosmic hermeneutical principle. Wang said:

> My luminous spirit [*ling-ming*] is the master of Heaven-and-Earth and all things. If Heaven is deprived of my luminous spirit, who is going to look into its height? If Earth is deprived of my luminous spirit, who is going to look into its depth? If spiritual beings are deprived of my luminous spirit, who is going to distinguish between their good and evil fortune, or the calamities and blessings they will bring? Separated from my luminous spirit, there will be no Heaven, Earth, spiritual beings, or myriad things, and separated from these, there will not be my luminous spirit. They are all permeated with one material force [*ch'i*]. How can they be separated?[44]

The Problem of Evil:[45] Selfish Desires

In its original state, mind-and-heart is full of the Heavenly Principle and empty of all human selfish desires. It is the state of the highest good and the transcendent state beyond the empirical distinction between good and evil. However, evil ensues when one deviates from this state, breaking the equilibrium or harmony of mind-and-heart by the rise of emotions. Wang said, "The highest good is the original substance of the mind. When one deviates a little from this original substance, there is evil." (CSL: 202) A deviation from the original state disturbs the unity of one's mind-and-heart with the Heavenly Principle, and makes a person's mind-and-heart lose its original substance. Then, evil comes into being:

> Someone said, "All people have this mind, and this mind is identical with principle. Why do some people do good and others do evil?"
> The Teacher said, "The mind of the evil man has lost its original substance." (CSL: 33)

However, evil is not ontologically a separate entity in opposition to good: "It is not that there is a good and there is also an evil to oppose it. Therefore, good and evil are one thing." (CSL: 202) Wang did not believe in a radical dualism between good and evil. Nor did he believe that human mind-and-heart is a battleground in which two opposite supernatural forces of good and evil are executing spiritual warfare.

There is no evil in the mind-and-heart-in-itself; the primordial mind-and-heart is beyond good and evil, and it is neither good nor evil. However, one's personal interest and preference constitute arbitrarily the distinction of good and evil:

> Such a view of good and evil is motivated by personal interest and is therefore easily wrong. . . . The spirit of life of Heaven and Earth is the same in flowers and weeds. Where have they the distinction of good and evil? When you want to enjoy flowers, you will consider flowers good and weeds evil. But when you want to use weeds, you will then consider them good. Such good and evil are all products of the mind's likes and dislikes. (CSL: 63)

The distinction of good and evil depends on one's perspective. For example, Wang illustrated the famous debate between Mencius and Hsün Tzu about human nature:

> When Mencius talked about nature, he discussed it directly from the point of view of its source and said only that generally speaking [nature is originally good]. Hsün Tzu's doctrine that nature is originally evil was arrived at from the point of view of its defects and we should not say that he was entirely wrong, only that he did not understand the matter perfectly. As to ordinary people, they have lost the original substance of the mind. (see CSL: 237).

In other words, on the one hand, Mencius's perspective was ontological and focused on the *t'i* (substance) of the mind-and-heart.[46] From the ontological perspective, Mencius concluded that human nature is good. On the other hand, Hsün Tzu's perspective was existential and focused on the defects which arise in the state of *yung* (function). From the existential perspective, Hsün Tzu contested that human nature is evil. Although they produced opposite conclusions because of their different perspectives, they in fact described two dimensions of the same thing, self-cultivation.

Selfish Desires

Evil occurs when one's will (or intention) is motivated by selfish attachment. Any attachment becomes a source of evil. Personal desires make one's mind-and-heart imbalanced by attaching to something. These perturb *liang-chih* and obscure radical humanity. Hence, evil is a consequence of "a dysfunctional mind."[47] The more one's *kung-fu* (practice) of self-cultivation becomes refined, the more difficult it is to describe and explain this phenomenon in words, because the work of *liang-chih* is so subtle and delicate. In the advanced stage of self-cultivation, attaching to any personal ideas will ruin the entire effort of *kung-fu*.[48] Even good intention can be, in the final analysis, a form of attachment. Therefore, good thoughts and efforts are also hazardous, like "gold or jade dust in the eye:"

> The Teacher once told the students, "Not a single idea should be allowed to attach to the original substance of the mind, just as not the least dirt should be allowed to stick to the eye. It does not take much dirt for the whole eye to see nothing but complete darkness." He further said, "This idea need not be a selfish idea. Even if it is good, it should not be attached to the mind. If you put some gold or jade dust in the eye, just the same it cannot open." (CSL: 256-257)

Although Wang appreciated the profound contributions from Taoist and Buddhist efforts, his criticism is based on this point. Taoists and Buddhists search for personal salvation in terms of personal immortality and emancipation from *samsara* (the sea of suffering). However, both of them are in fact motivated by personal desires. They violate the true condition of *liang-chih*.

> Taoist seekers of immortality have reached the conclusion of the vacuity [of the mind]. Is the sage able to add an iota of reality to that vacuity? The Buddhists have reached the conclusion of non-being [of the mind]. Is the sage able to add an iota of being to that non-being? But the Taoist talk about vacuity is motivated by a desire for nourishing everlasting life, and the Buddhist talk about non-being is motivated by the desire to escape from the sorrowful sea of life and death. In both cases, certain selfish ideas have been added to the original substance [of the mind], which thereby loses the true character of vacuity and is obstructed. The sage merely returns to the true condition of innate knowledge and does not attach to it any selfish idea. (CSL: 219-220)

The fundamental error Buddhists made is that they pollute the purity of the mind-and-heart-in-itself by obscuring *liang-chih* with unnecessary attachments. As mentioned in the previous chapter, *liang-chih*-in-itself is the Great Vacuity, the Great Purity; any attachment, however good it is, is a trespass like "jade or gold dust in the eye."[49]

However, Wang's criticism of religion focused on his own tradition, Neo-Confucianism. He was first and foremost self-critical. Buddhism and Taoism were not the main source of problems of his time.[50] He thought that the real source of evil was degenerated Confucians, perverted by "the four schools of recitation and memorization, the writing of flowery compositions, the pursuit of success and profit, and textual criticism" (CSL: 41). These four schools became the root cause of evil in the world of his time. They defiled the Confucian *Tao* by seeking form rather than content. They forgot that the final goal of Confucian learning is not in academic techniques or the accumulation of information, but rather in ethicoreligious realization. The pursuit of fame and profit is nothing else than selfishness, and it is the root cause of those errors.[51]

Breaking the unity of the mind-and-heart and the Heavenly Principle, selfish desires interfere with the equilibrium of the mind-and-heart, obscure *liang-chih*, and sever the original unity, inducing a separation between knowing and acting. Selfish desires are the source of all kinds of dualism which are evil.

The Mind of the Way (tao-hsin) *and the Human Mind* (jen-hsin)

Existentially, human desires contradict the Heavenly principle. Wang employed the classical distinction between *tao-hsin* (the mind of the Way) and *jen-hsin* (the human mind). The *tao-hsin* is the mind-and-heart in the original state of equilibrium or harmony. The *jen-hsin* is the mind-and-heart in the limited condition after disturbed by human desires. The former can be called the ontological mind, and the latter the existential mind. However, they are not mutually independent and co-existing.   Ontologically, there is only the mind of the Way. Nevertheless, existentially, the human mind appears when the mind-and-heart is mixed with a fixation or selfish desires.

> There is only one mind. Before it is mixed with selfish human desires, it is called the moral mind [*tao hsin*], and after it is mixed with human desires contrary to its natural state, it is called the human mind [*jen hsin*]. When the human mind is rectified, it is called the moral mind: When the moral mind loses its correctness, it is called the human mind. There were not two minds to start with. . . . The Principle of Nature and selfish human desires cannot coexist. (CSL: 16-17)

In the original sense, selfish desires are not part of humanity at all. They are inhuman things. They are something added to radical humanity (*liang-chih*). However, selfish desires can obscure the transparency of radical humanity and *jen* (cosmic togetherness). They alienate one's mind-and-heart from its original substance, obstruct and distort one's true intention, and paralyze one's Heavenly endowed nature. Since physical desires darken and obscure radical humanity, one loses one's innate cosmic inclusiveness and ultimate impartiality.

> There is no human nature that is not good. Therefore there is no innate knowledge that is not good. Innate knowledge is the equilibrium before the feelings are aroused. It is the state of broadness and extreme impartiality. It is the original substance that is absolutely quiet and inactive. And it is possessed by all men. However, people cannot help being darkened and obscured by material desires. Hence they must study in order to get rid of the darkness and obscuration. (CSL: 134)

Wang does not view *ch'i* (material force) as evil *per se*. But *ch'i* can interfere with the original disposition of the human nature. When *ch'i* is disturbed, the distinction of good and evil appears: "The state of having neither good nor evil is that of principle in tranquility. Good and evil appear when the vital force [*ch'i*] is perturbed. If the vital force is not perturbed, there is neither good nor evil, and this is called the highest good." (CSL: 63-64) Similarly, feelings are natural to mind-and-heart and not evil *per se*, but a selfish attachment to them also produces a distinction of good and evil.

Nevertheless, *liang-chih* as the primordial awareness naturally reveals these erroneous movements and discerns good and evil. *Liang-chih* has an innate power to remove the obscuration and restore the original substance.[52] However, this must be accompanied by one's disciplined practices of attentive self-exertion, such as the investigation of things (which, in the final analysis, is the extension of *liang-chih*, a theme of the next chapter). In his famous but controversial doctrine in Four Axioms, Wang summarized:

> In the mind-and-heart-in-itself (*hsin-chih-t'i*),
>   there is no distinction of good and evil (*wu-shan wu-ô*).
> When the will becomes active (*yi-chih-tung*),
>   there presents good and evil (*yu-shan-yu-ô*).
> The faculty of innate knowledge (*liang-chih*) is
>   to know good and evil (*chih-shan chih-ô*)
> The investigation of things (*ko-wu*) is
>   to do good and remove evil (*wei-shan ch'ü-ô*).[53]

Chapter 4

•

Humanization:
Self-Cultivation as *Chih Liang-chih*

Ch'eng-i (the Sincerity of the Will)

Wang affirmed that the very structure of the self is sufficient for the actualization of the inner sage. However, he does not mean that practical efforts are useless. Continuous self-cultivation is required to manifest the inner sage. Although he formulates the doctrine of the unity of knowing and acting to correct Chu Hsi's mistake in interpreting *ko-wu* (the investigation of things), Wang did not abdicate the practice of *ko-wu*. But Wang understood the 'sincerity of the will' (*Ch'eng-i*) as the real issue of *ko-wu*:

> The teaching in the *Doctrine of the Mean* that "Without Sincerity there would be nothing," and the effort to manifest one's clear character described in the *Great Learning* mean nothing more than effort to make the will sincere. And the work of making the will sincere is none other than the investigation of things. (CSL: 14-15)

Tu pointed out that Wang's anthropology consisted of the "four correlations," body (*shen*) and mind (*hsin*), mind and intention (*i*), intention and knowledge (*chih*), and intention and thing (*wu*).[1] Among these four elements, the intention (or the will) is central. The body is a temporal space where "the thing" dwells. The mind is the master of the body, though they are inseparable. The will is the function of the mind, and it never operates "in a vacuum." The knowledge is the original substance of the will. And "the thing" is its intended object. The will, as "the directionality of the mind," links the knowledge (its original substance) and "the thing" (its directed object):[2]

> The ears, the eyes, the mouth, the nose, and the four limbs are parts of the body. But how can they see, hear, speak, or act without the mind? On the other hand, without the ears, the eyes, the mouth, the nose, and the four limbs, the mind cannot see, hear, speak, or act when it wants to. Therefore if there is no mind, there will be no body, and if there is no body, there will be no mind. As something occupying space, it is called the body. As the master, it is called the mind. As the operation of the mind, it is called the will. As the intelligence and clear consciousness of the will, it is called knowledge. And as the object to which the will is attached, it is called a thing. They are all one piece. The will never exists in a vacuum. It is always connected with some thing or event. Therefore if one wants to make his will sincere, he should rectify (*ko*) it right in the thing or event to which the will is directed, get rid of selfish human desires, and return to the Principle of Nature. Then in connection with this thing or event the innate knowledge will be free from obscuration and can be fully extended. This is the task of making the will sincere. (CSL: 189)

These four kinds of correlation are related to the four inner dimensions of self-realization (the cultivation of the body) in the *Great Learning*: the rectification of the mind, the sincerity of the will, the extension of knowledge, and the investigation of things. However, for Wang, the sincerity of the will is the central issue. For "the sincerity of the will refers to a process through which the intention becomes truthful to the genuine directionality of the mind." This process entails "the rectification of the intended object" (*ko-wu*) and the "penetration of the original substance" (the extension of the knowledge). At the same time, it also involves the regulation of the mind and the cultivation of the body (*hsiu-shen*). Focusing on the sincerity of the will, Wang conceived "*ko-wu* as a dynamic process through which man's [one's] ontological being is manifested in his [one's] existential becoming."[3]

Wang specified this task in terms of two inseparable procedures: *ts'un t'ien-li* (the preservation of the Heavenly Principle) and *ch'ü jen-yü* (the extirpation of human desires).[4] *T'ien-li* refers to "the ultimate basis on which man can become what he ought to be" and to "the ontological reality of human nature and the inner sage in the mind is 'naturally so.'" However, human desires tend to obstruct and distort this process of becoming what human beings ought to be. Obstruction implies "a passive limitation," and distortion means "an active falsification."[5] To preserve the Heavenly principle means to realize the ontological reality, and to extirpate human desires is to avoid the limitation of the full realization of one's authentic self and the falsification of one's original intention.

These two procedures are "inseparable aspects of the same process." The preservation of the Heavenly Principle is to "protect the genuineness of one's ontological being" ("establish sincerity" [*li-ch'eng*]).[6] It inevitably involves one's effort to eliminate human desires. Ontologically, the Heavenly Principle is the original substance of the mind-and-heart. However, existentially, when the mind encounters a thing, it is vulnerable to become attached to the intended object. If such an attachment occurs, the mind is "materialized" (*wu-hua*) and loses its dynamic creativity. Although the inseparability of the mind and the Heavenly Principle is the ontological reality, the vulnerability of the mind-and-heart through the influence of human desires is the existential human condition. Therefore, *ko-wu*, now as a rectification of the intention (or the sincerity of the will), involves a continuous process of the preservation of Heavenly Principle and the extirpation of human desires.

Chih Liang-chih (the Extension of *liang-chih*)

Wang's teaching of self-cultivation culminated in the doctrine of *chih liang-chih*. He regarded this doctrine of the extension of innate knowledge as "the great basis of learning and the first principle of the teaching of the Sage" (CSL: 150). This doctrine is "the height of learning. Even a sage can do no more" (CSL: 213). And every person can do it. The difference between the sage and the ordinary people lies only in the ability to demonstrate it:

> Only the perfect sage in the world has quickness of apprehension, intelligence, insight, and wisdom. How deep and mysterious this formerly seemed! But as we look at it today, we realize that these qualities are common to all men. Man's ears are by nature quick of apprehension, his eyes intelligent, and his mind and thought have insight and wisdom. The sage is the only one who can demonstrate them with one effort. What enables him to do so is his innate knowledge, and the reason ordinary people cannot do so is that they do not extend their knowledge. How clear! How simple! And how easy! (CSL: 225-6)

It is such a "clear," "simple," and 'easy" method for attaining sagehood. Nonetheless, it also needs serious practice. Julia Ching argued that the word *chih* (extend) requires special attention. Wang's semantic shift, from Chu Hsi's formula of the extension of knowledge (*chih chih*) to the extension of the knowledge of the good (*chih liang-chih*), is intended both to emphasize the meaning of the word *chih* (extend), "self-exertion," and to strengthen its ethical nuance by substituting *liang-chih* for *chih* (knowledge). Hence, the extension of *liang-chih* entails one's sincere efforts of "self-exertion, discipline, attentiveness."[7]

However, though he was much concerned about the meaning of *liang-chih*, Wang said little about how it is to be extended. Ching argued, "one angle from which Yang-ming contemplates the works of extending *liang-chih* is that of purifying *hsin*."[8] To purify the mind-and-heart requires the precept of the preservation of the Heavenly Principle and the extirpation of human desires:

> The determination to have the mind completely identified with the Principle of Nature and devoid of even an iota of selfish desire is the task of becoming a sage. But this is not possible unless selfish desires are prevented from sprouting and are subdued at the time of sprouting. To do this is the task of being cautious and apprehensive as taught in the *Doctrine of the Mean* and of the extension of knowledge and the investigation of things as taught in the *Great Learning*. There is no other task outside of this. (CSL: 140)

By the preservation of the Heavenly Principle and the extirpation of human desires, *liang-chih* "will be free from obscuration and can be fully extended" (CSL: 189). To remove selfish desires one must be "single-minded," so as to "get rid of all desires for fame and profit and other interests", and one must completely free from one's anxiety about life and death (CSL: 223). Wang warned against pride (egocentrism), because it is "the chief of all vices." He advocates that humility (selflessness) is "the foundation of all virtue:"

> A great defect in life is pride. The proud son is sure not to be filial, nor the proud minister loyal, nor the proud father affectionate, nor the proud friend faithful. . . . You gentlemen should always realize this personally; the human mind is in fact the natural principle. It is refined and clear without an iota of defilement or selfish attachment. It is just a non-ego. One must not harbor any egoism in the mind. To do so means to have pride. The many good points about ancient sages are but

selflessness. Being selfless, one is naturally humble. Humility is the foundation of all virtues, while pride is the chief of all vices. (CSL: 259)

For Wang, harmony refers to "a natural state of the mind-and-heart, free from any affection or insincerity." Criticizing Chu Hsi's over-emphasis on the role of stillness, Wang focused on activity. For him, the mind-and-heart is "a dynamic principle of moral activity."[9] Mencius said, "Always be doing something."[10] It is "a positive manner of stating the negative imperative, 'Do away with your selfish desires.'"[11] Specifically, it means the "accumulation of righteous deeds" (*chi-yi*).[12] Thus, Wang equated this Mencian notion of the accumulation of righteous deeds with *chih liang-chih* which includes the whole task of self-cultivation described in the *Great Learning*:

> "One must always be doing something" means merely the accumulation of righteous deeds, and the accumulation of righteous deeds means merely the extension of innate knowledge. To talk about accumulating righteous deeds does not immediately reveal the basis, but as soon as we talk about the extension of innate knowledge there is right away a concrete basis on which to engage in this task. I therefore advocate solely the extension of innate knowledge. To extend innate knowledge in daily affairs as they occur is to investigate things. To extend innate knowledge in a genuine and earnest way is to make the will sincere. To extend innate knowledge in a genuine and earnest way without the least arbitrariness of opinion, dogmatism, obstinacy, or egotism is to rectify the mind. . . . If one accumulates righteousness in and through his own mind every hour and every minute, the substance of innate knowledge will be absolutely clear and it will spontaneously see right as right and wrong as wrong, neither of which can escape from it in the least. (CSL: 174-175)

For Wang, self-cultivation focused on "inward transformation rather than outward imitation."[13] Students must "recognize the feeling and expressions of a sage" (CSL: 127). One can have this feeling only through one's personal experience of *liang-chih*.[14] Therefore, some-times, a sage's behavior went beyond the conventional standards of Confucian virtues, as in the famous examples of Emperor Shun's marriage and the military expedition of King Wu of Chou. But they were right because they simply followed the direction of *liang-chih*, free from self-deception. Ultimately, self-cultivation is summarized in only one effort, *chih liang-chih*:

In the countless changes in his dealings with others, the superior man acts if it is proper to act, stops if it is proper to stop, lives if it is proper to live, and dies if it is proper to die. In all his considerations and adjustments he does nothing but extend his innate knowledge to the utmost so that he can satisfy himself. (CSL: 153-54)

Iki argued that Wang's teaching of the extension of *liang-chih* aimed to correct mistakes of the two most powerful modes of thinking of his time, the Chu Hsi school and Buddhism.[15] On the one hand, Chu Hsi emphasized an external, empirical, and gradual dimension of self-cultivation, as we have discussed. For Wang, *liang-chih* is innate, inborn, and spontaneous. This resonates with the Ch'an Buddhist notion of sudden enlightenment. The extension of *liang-chih* is not merely self-effort, but self-realization of the innate ontological power. On the other hand, Buddhists pretended to realize the Way by the act of separation from the primal ties such as the family and the state. Wang criticized this as a subjectivism, seeking "self-satisfaction of the great ego." *Liang-chih*, the "great root of the world" must be extended in the concrete-universal way.[16] Wang thought that the true significance of our lives does not lie simply in being absorbed into Nothingness. *Liang-chih*, as "being the Nothingness, realizes the Being, and at the same time, being the Being, it always returns to Nothingness." Wang understood that "life transcends human beings and at the same time is immanent in social life. And the only way left is to follow life's movements, which are immanent in social life, while at the same time transcending it." [17] While *liang-chih* is an immanent transcendence,[18] at the same time it is the true foundation of social solidarity, political governance, and cosmic communion:

If gentlemen of the world merely devote their effort to extending their innate knowledge they will naturally share with all a universal sense of right and wrong, share their likes and dislikes, regard other people as their own persons, regard the people of other countries as their own family, and look upon Heaven, Earth, and all things as one body. When this is done, even if we wanted the world to be without order, it would not be possible. When the ancients felt that the good seemed to come from themselves when they saw others do good, when they felt that they had fallen into evil when they saw others do evil, when they regarded other people's hunger and drowning as their own, and when they felt that if one person's condition was not well adjusted it was as if they had pushed him into a ditch, they did not purposely do so in order to seek people's belief in them. They merely devoted their effort to extending their innate knowledge and sought to satisfy themselves. The Sage-emperors Yao and Shun and the Three Kings spoke and all people believed them, because in speaking they extended their innate knowledge. They acted and all the people were pleased with them, because in acting they extended their innate knowledge. Therefore their people moved around and were contented. Though these rulers punished the people by death, the people did not complain, and when the rulers benefited the people, the people did not think of the ruler's merit. . . . Why? Because all people have the same innate knowledge. Alas, how simple and easy was the way of sages to govern the empire. (CSL: 167)

Identification of Subjectivity and Ontological Reality

As mentioned early, Tu interpreted *liang-chih* as subjectivity which must be universally extended beyond anthropological subjectivism. Tu said, "The uniqueness of man [human being] is defined not merely by his possession of *liang-chih* but also by his ability to extend his *liang-chih* to embody the universe as a whole." At the same time, ontologically, humanity as the cosmic togetherness is "in an organismic unity with the cosmos as a whole." This anthropocosmic communion is the ontological reality of *liang-chih*, the radical subjectivity of humanity. *Chih liang-chih* is to actualize the inner sage, or to manifest one's radical humanity; in short, radical humanization. This radical humanization requires a concrete-universal approach of self-realization. Such an approach entails the external steps of self-realization through concrete human networks and involves the inner steps of humanization, like the eight developmental stages in the *Great Learning*. The danger is one's attachment or fixation to any thing. Hence, real humanization is possible only through freeing oneself from selfish desires. Then, one's humanity can be "expanded' to its full potential."[19] *Liang-chih* is the ultimate foundation for the human capability to transcend the negative forces of subjectivism.

In the final analysis, the doctrine of *chih liang-chih* implies the identification of radical subjectivity and ontological reality, which Tu suggested as a defining characteristic of Wang's mode of thought. *Chih liang-chih*, as a process of transcending subjectivism, involves a circular (more precisely, a spiral) movement of identification. Ontologically, *liang-chih* as radical subjectivity is identical with the Heavenly Principle. Existentially, however, selfish desires obstruct this unity and form a false polarity between the ontological reality and existential situation. Nevertheless, *liang-chih*, as an irreducible reality, engenders the dynamic, creative power to transcend the polarity. By the full extension of radical subjectivity, we can restore the original unity, and our mind-and-heart manifests the Heavenly Principle. Hence, *chih liang-chih* as the identification of subjectivity and ontological reality entails radical subjectification. Tu summarized:

> . . . It may therefore be suggested that the identification of subjectivity (*liang-chih*) and ontological reality (*t'ien-li*), as a defining characteristic of Yang-ming's mode of thinking, seems to have been deeply rooted in a unique type of anthropocosmic experience.
>
> In such an experience, subjectivity is fundamentally different from subjectivism. A series of assumptions are involved: (1) As the inner sagehood and true selfhood, subjectivity symbolizes genuine humanity. (2) Although existentially its concrete manifestations can be obstructed and distorted, genuine humanity is in an ontological sense an irreducible reality. (3) Despite its self-sufficiency, the irreducible reality can always generate dynamism and creativity. (4) Even though the dynamic and creative power does not produce something *ex nihilo*, it entails a process of self-realization. (5) Practical difficulties notwithstanding, the process of self-realization ultimately leads to the complete manifestation of the Heavenly principle. (6) In the last analysis, the Heavenly principle as an ontological reality is the original substance of the mind. And the original substance of the mind as pure subjectivity must be extended to manifest the Heavenly principle.[20]

Summary Remarks

Self-cultivation, the Confucian paradigm of "how to be fully human," is the center of the Confucian enterprise. It proposes a radical humanization, an ethicoreligious authentication of full humanity (sagehood). It involves both a serious self-realization of the ontology of humanity (being) and a creative cosmic transformation in a concrete-universal way (becoming). All these are grounded in sincerity (*ch'eng*), the root-metaphor of the Confucian Way. As the natural endowment of sagehood, sincerity is the ultimate source of anthropocosmic creativity and transformation,

Shifting the Neo-Confucian focus to the mind-and-heart from Chu Hsi's occupation with principle, Wang Yang-ming identifies human mind-and-heart with principle (*hsin chi li*). He insists on the unity of knowing and acting (*chih-hsing ho-i*), in both the ontological state and the ethical process of self-cultivation. He advocates a concrete-universal approach, commencing the task with concrete existence and ending in universal extension, as the Confucian way to attain sagehood in the anthropocosmic vision.

Wang's greater achievement is his Neo-Confucian articulation of *liang-chih* (the innate knowledge of good, primordial awareness, pure subjectivity, or radical humanity), the root paradigm of the Confucian immanent transcendence. This formulation substantiates the Mencian faith in the authentic human possibility of self-transcendence. It expanded the paradigm of humanity, *jen*, to the anthropocosmic dimension; namely, cosmic (organismic) togetherness. With this discovery, self-cultivation as radical humanization can be summarized as *chih liang-chih*, the actualization of primordial awareness, the full manifestation of radical humanity, the identification of subjectivity and ontological reality, or radical subjectification.

Since the locus of self-cultivation is the concrete human situation, the network of human relatedness, *chih liang-chih* as radical humanization involves a serious sociopolitical hermeneutics. Wang argued that the Confucian point of departure is an ethicoreligious commitment to the Confucian *Tao (li-chih)*, rather than an intellectual inquiry. In this context, Confucianism can be conceived as faith in original humanity's ontological possibility of self-transcendence and self-realization toward creative anthropocosmic transformation.

Nevertheless, existentially, this possibility is obstructed and distorted by anthropocentric and selfish desires, which is the Neo-Confucian definition of evil. Therefore, self-cultivation as radical humanization requires two inseparable dimensions, a sincere self-realization according to the anthropocosmic vision of radical humanity (*pen-t'i* [e.g., the preservation of the Heavenly Principle]) and a corresponding ethicoreligious practice of concrete-universal self-transformation (*kung-fu* [e.g., the extirpation of human desires]).

PART II

THE CHRISTIAN PARADIGM

KARL BARTH'S THEOLOGY OF SANCTIFICATION

Chapter 5

•

Prolegomena

Karl Barth's Theology
In the Context of the Wider Ecumenism

Ever since Hendrik Kraemer published his book *The Christian Message in a Non-Christian World*,[1] Barth's theology has been regarded as the chief problem which impedes Christian dialogue with other religions. Barth's critics contend that Barth's theology is too negative toward non-Christian religions to facilitate a fruitful interfaith dialogue and is responsible for the general disinterest of contemporary theologies in "the wider ecumenism."[2]

Alan Race classified Christian attitudes toward other religions in the three categories of exclusivism, inclusivism, and pluralism.[3] Race identified Barth's theology as "the most extreme form" of exclusivism.[4] Paul Knitter developed a fourfold typology of attitudes of twentieth-century theologies toward other religions: (1) "the conservative Evangelical Model" (one true religion), (2) "the mainline Protestant model" (salvation only in Christ), (3) the Roman Catholic model" (many ways, one norm), and (4) "the theocentric model" (many ways to the center).[5] Knitter took Barth as the foremost representative of the first type.[6] John Cobb identified the failure of the World Council of Churches on interfaith dialogue as a legacy of Barth's theology which dominated mid-twentieth-century theologies.[7] Cobb said that Barth's theology was mainly responsible for diluting the important task of interfaith dialogue.

However, these arguments are ill-grounded.[8] First of all, the critics did not properly consider the context for which Barth made theological affirmations (which continued to shift throughout his career). They often referred to Barth's *"Nein!"* to Emil Brunner on the issue of natural theology[9] and to "The Revelation of God as the Abolition of Religion," a well-known section of Barth's *Church Dogmatics* (I/2: 280-361). But they neglected the context of these writings in which Barth engaged in a political hermeneutics with European Christianity which had been threatened by the demonic power of Hitler's National Socialism. This was the period when Barth was involved with the Confessing Church and wrote the Barmen Declaration.[10] His declaration of "No" to natural theology was intended to close the door against the entry of the Trojan horse of Hitler's natural theology. At that time, other world religions were not the issue with which he was primarily concerned. The statements about Barth's attitude toward non-Christian religions based on these writings, having failed to understand their context, missed the point.

Secondly, the primary concern of Barth's theology always was in the radical "self-examination"[11] of Christian communities of faith and their necessary on-going transformation (*Ecclesia semper reformanda*) under the dynamic effect of the Word of God. First and foremost, his theology was engaged in that task for communities of faith at that time, especially in Europe. While, in one sense, it was a limitation of Barth's theology, in another his theology addressed its depth in his criticism of the "religion" of contemporary European religio-cultural imperialism. When he said "religion as unbelief,"[12] the religion referred to was primarily European middle class civil religion rather than world religions or religion in general. The issue of world religions was not the focus of Barth's theology at that time.

Thirdly, Kraemer's missiology was based on Barth's early writings from which Barth himself had departed. Unlike his early writings, the later Barth positively regarded other religions as "true words . . . *extra muros ecclesia* [outside the walls of the church]," or "lights in the world," or "parables of the kingdom of heaven." (IV/3/1: 110; 136-7; 114). Furthermore, Barth's "free theology of culture"[13] does not limit the freedom of theologians of other cultures to express their doxology in their distinctive ways. When South East Asian theologians asked Barth how they also could do theology, Barth wrote a letter, titled "No Boring Theology!"

In my long life I have spoken many words. But now they are spoken.
Now it is your turn. Now it is your task to be Christian theologians *in
your new, different and special situation* with heart and head, with
mouth and hands. . . .
. . . Yes, do that: say that which you have to say as Christians for God's
sake, *responsibly and concretely with your own words and thoughts,
concepts and ways*! The more responsibly and concretely, the better,
the more Christian! You truly do not need to become "European,"
"Western" men, not to mention "Barthians," in order to be good
Christians and theologians. You may feel free to be South East Asian
Christians. Be it! Be it, neither arrogantly nor faint-heartedly with
regard to the religions around you and the dominant ideologies and
"realities" in your lands! Be it all openness for the problems which are
so burning in your region, and for your own, special and unique
fellowmen; but be it above all in the freedom which is given and
allowed to us. . . .[14]

Lochhead is correct to say: "The theology of Karl Barth, in spite of
what many critics have claimed, is not a theology that is closed to
dialogue with communities of other traditions."[15] On a deeper level,
Barth's theology bestows the freedom to say "No" to a religion and a
culture, precisely because it is already endowed with the freedom to say
even greater "Yes" to them, corresponding to God's big "Yes" to the
human race and the world.[16] In fact, Barth's theology is an inclusive
theology that is "open to an affirming of *any* dialogue with the world."[17]
However, what he disliked was that "dialogue" often becomes a liberal
game of intellectual speculation and theological abstraction. Before
going into a dialogue, Barth seriously requested faithfulness, integrity,
concentration, and commitment-for-transformation among the dialogue
partners.

Barth's uncompromising theology of "concentration" is necessarily
"one-sided," but not exclusively.[18] At a superficial level, this one-
sidedness appears to be problematic for any dialogue; however, at a
deeper level, it enables a real freedom to be open in any dialogue. For
example in his relation to Roman Catholic theology, he appeared to be
irreversibly un-ecumenical. He attacked the Roman Catholic doctrine
of *analogia entis* as "the invention of anti-Christ," an even harsher
criticism than his comment about religion as unbelief (I/1: xiii).
However, the history of theology has shown a positive result. His

theology has been regarded by some as a most significant contributor to "the possibility of a new *ecumenical theology*."[19]

In fact, many Roman Catholic theologians have responded affirmatively to his theology.[20] Assimilating Barth's theology, Hans Urs von Balthasar contended that Barth's antithesis between *analogia entis* and *analogia fidei* was a false problem.[21] Hans Küng further argued that, if properly understood, there is a fundamental agreement between Barth and the Roman Catholic Church on the doctrine of justification as a whole.[22] "From this perspective [Küng claimed] there was no further basis for a schism between Protestants and Catholics."[23]

Even though one-sided in some senses, Barth's theology was "never one-dimensional."[24] Looking only at this angle of one-sidedness, one might condemn Barth's theology as obsolete and anachronistic, as his critics contend. However, grasping another angle of this multi-dimensionality, one finds his theology helpful in opening new possibilities for dialogue. Thus Küng called Barth "the chief initiator of a postmodern paradigm in theology." Nonetheless, his theology is only *a* paradigm which has both strengths and weaknesses. Barth is "not the perfecter" but an initiator of the postmodern theological paradigm.[25] Barth himself said: "I understand . . . [my] *Church Dogmatics* not as the conclusion but as the opening of a new common discussion."[26]

In his review of the legacy of Barth's theology, Küng has proposed "a critical-sympathetic rereading of Barth" as "a constructive approach in bringing the grand themes and enormous richness of this theology into the contemporary scene, and in dealing freshly with them in the context of the world's religions and regions."[27] One can simply call this a *creative rereading* of Barth in the context of the wider ecumenism. This creative rereading of Barth, especially in the context of interfaith dialogue, may necessitate a *theological bracketing*, i.e. a "bracketing off of the theological dimension."[28] Robert Palma noticed that Barth "intermittently excludes the theological dimension"[29] in his theology of culture, which Hans Frei called Barth's "secular sensibility."[30] To develop a dialogue between Barth's theology and "non-theistic"[31] East Asian religions, in particular, may require expanding such theological bracketing of secular sensibility even further. In this regard, Lochhead's proposal of "faithful agnosticism"[32] is well-taken and helpful. Faithful agnosticism means the refusal to evaluate a priori claims of other faiths for interfaith dialogue. Hence, it suggests the need of *a priori bracketing*, i.e., a bracketing off of a priori dimensions of the faith traditions in dialogue with other religions.[33]

Paradigm Shift: Gospel and Law

The Word of God, believed as the revelation of God, is the source and foundation of the Christian faith and constitutes the point of departure for Christian theology. Martin Luther distinguished the Word of God in the sequence of law and Gospel, a sequence that has been generally accepted. However, this sequencing entailed theological dualism and anthropological narrowness. Barth reversed it to that of Gospel and law, one of the significant paradigm shifts for Barth's dogmatic theology which constitutes his assertion of the unity of theology[34] and ethics.[35]

Luther's Doctrine of Law and Gospel

Luther argued that the distinction between law and Gospel is "the highest art of Christendom that we should know:"[36] And "There is no better method of preserving and handing on pure doctrine than to follow this method, that is, to divide Christian doctrine into two parts: law and gospel."[37] Without this distinction, the Word of God can be confused, either Gospel into law or law into Gospel. Luther saw two examples of such a confusion in the doctrines of his contemporary Roman Catholicism and of the Radical Reformers.

On the one hand, Roman Catholic theology had confused the Gospel with the law. The sale of indulgences was a clear example of Roman Catholic distortion against the truth of the good news. Salvation is simply a gift of God, and justification cannot be achieved by deeds, but by faith alone. Nevertheless, Roman Catholic theology suppressed the irreducible Gospel into a code of law. On the other hand, Radical Reformers such as Thomas Müntzer (ca. 1490-1525) confused the texts in the Bible pertaining to the law with those of the Gospel. For example, the word of God that commanded David to wage war cannot apply to the preacher in the pulpit whose duty is to proclaim the Gospel. Luther argued that, since the law in the Bible, including the Ten Commandments, always has a specific context to which a particular command applies and a particular person to whom a specific command is addressed, the distinction of law and Gospel is the "hermeneutical criterion"[38] for true Christian theology.

Luther differentiated law and Gospel in terms of activity and passivity. In the law, since God commands us to act, we are active doers. In the Gospel, since God alone acts, we are merely inactive recipients of God's action. His problem lies in the existential question of which Word of God is directed to me here and now. According to his experience, the law declares its sovereignty through the conscience. Through the power of conscience, the law accuses us as sinners and leads us to despair. Furthermore, the law can interfere with the Gospel so that the story of Jesus Christ is reduced into a code of law.

The central issue which Luther addressed, nevertheless, is that the true reality is not this law but the Gospel, the good news of salvation.[39] The Gospel alone has the power to facilitate the right distinction between law and gospel. The Gospel, as the warrant of this distinction, clarifies the limitation of the law. Luther advocated the use of the law to two levels: the first use of the law (political), to govern and restrain the world; and the second use of the law (theological), to awaken us as law-breakers and sinners.[40] However, this doctrine of law and Gospel entails an unfortunate implication for the doctrine of God. One must distinguish between the God of wrath in the law and the God of Grace in the Gospel. Of course, law and Gospel can attain their unity in God. However, according to Luther, it is a dialectical unity.

Barth's Reversal of Gospel and Law

Barth was primarily concerned not with the right distinction between law and Gospel, but with the right relationship between them.[41] In Barth's mature theology,[42] the ethical imperative as the command of God presupposes the dogmatic question of God's existence and activity. The knowledge of God's existence and activity which can be acquired only from the Gospel. Therefore, the law, as the command of God, actually originates from the Gospel. This logic consists in Barth's reversal of the traditional order of law and Gospel into the sequence of Gospel and law. In his article "Gospel and Law," Barth said,

anyone who really and earnestly would first say Law and only then, presupposing this, say Gospel would not, no matter how good his intention, be speaking of the Law of *God* and therefore then certainly not of *his* Gospel. This usual way is, even in the most favorable case, enveloped in ambiguities of every sort.[43]

Grace, as a free and unmerited gift to humanity, is the content of the Word of God in all circumstances.[44] The duality of the Word of God as Gospel and law can be properly expressed only in the context of their unity (Grace). Barth feared that the contrast between the two modes of the Word of God inevitably leads to a dualism within God's own being; for example, a conflict between the God of grace and the God of wrath and between God revealed and God hidden. Luther's doctrine of law and Gospel has dangerously created such a dualistic tendency which Jüngel calls "the dualist peril."[45] Contending that the God of the law is none other than the God of the Gospel, Barth rejected this dualism and reversed the traditional order to that of Gospel and law.

The reversal of the traditional order to Gospel and law became salient in Barth's doctrine of sin. In the doctrine of reconciliation (CD IV), Barth subordinated the three forms of sin, pride, sloth, and falsehood to Christology, the Lord as Servant (IV/1), the Servant as Lord (IV/2), and the true Witness (IV/3). In the history of dogmatics, this formulation marked a revolutionary shift. Traditional dogmatics usually locate the doctrine of sin before Christology. However, human beings cannot know the reality of their evilness, without revelatory knowledge in the Gospel: "Access to the knowledge that he is a sinner is lacking to man because he is [already] a sinner" (IV/1: 360-1). A law, apart from the Gospel, apart from Jesus Christ, inevitably leads to a concept of God which is apart from the revelation of God in Jesus Christ through the Gospel. "This god and his law are not by any means harmless fictions, for in them the real God is dishonored and His real Law is emptied of content" (IV/1: 365). The real knowledge of sin can be grasped only by the knowledge of God through the Gospel of Jesus Christ, but not by natural law: "Where the grace of God encounters him, there his sin is revealed, and the fact that he is a sinner" (IV/2: 381).

Only when Gospel and law have been properly ordered, can we see the reality that "sin deceives us with the Law and therefore about the Law." In this deception, the good law becomes "the 'Law of sin and death' (Romans 8:2), and the executor of divine wrath (Romans 4:15)." Nevertheless, the good news is that "the *Law* is and remains the Law of God even though dishonored and emptied by our lust." If the Gospel of God enters and if the law becomes a true part of the Gospel, in spite of the reality of sin, the Gospel performs its function as "the really *glad* tidings for *real* sinners." Sin can obscure the unity of Gospel and law, but it can not destroy the unity. Exposing such a covering of sin, the unity in the true relationship of Gospel and law enables the law to perform its real function as a form of the Gospel. Barth's point was that "the Law is nothing else than the necessary *form of the Gospel*, whose content is grace."[46]   Barth used the spatial image of the Art of the Covenant to describe this relationship: "The Gospel itself, as the good news of human liberation by and for the free God, has also the character and form of the true Law of God, the promise of the grace of God containing God's no less gracious claim, as the ark of the Old Testament covenant contained the tables of the Decalogue" (IV/3: 369).[47]

God and human beings have a relationship of covenant, according to the divine disposition. God as Lord of the covenant not only promises salvation to human beings who are really sinners, but also grants salvation through His[48] judgment on Jesus Christ, the incarnated Son of God. This is the Gospel which has the character and the form of law. The point of departure for Barth's theology is the divine self-attestation to the human race. Then, Gospel and law as basic predicates of God become anthropologically relevant. However, Luther first regarded law and Gospel as categories which describe human existence in front of God. Barth could not accept this, saying that the human being is in the presence of God, prior to saying that God is in front of humanity. God in front of humanity first brings a human being in the presence of God and constitutes the 'primal history' of the existence of humanity in God's presence. Luther focused on the proper distinction between law and gospel, more oriented to the dialectic of human existence. However, Barth focused on the dynamic relationship of the law with the Gospel, primarily concerned with the unity in the ultimate reality of God's being, will, and activity and, thus, the unity among the modes of the Word of God, the concrete beginning of theology.

For Barth, God's law is first and foremost the embodiment of God's gracious will to the human race. God's "loving attitude claims and demands a corresponding human attitude toward God."[49] Barth called the doctrine of the election of grace, which is a part of the doctrine of God, "the sum of the Gospel" (II/2: 3). In this context, "the Law as the form of gospel" means the norm of "the sanctification which comes to man through the electing God" (II/2: 509). Hence, Jüngel says,

"Barth's treatment of gospel and law is supralapsarian."[50] Traditionally, dogmatics treat the doctrine of sanctification merely as a consequence or an implication of the doctrine of justification. However, in Barth's theology, God's gracious election is prior to justification, and "sancti-fication already belongs to election."[51] Barth saw that sanctification is God's loving and gracious gift universally endowed to the whole human race, not just Christians. The dis-position of God's gracious election culminates in God's revelation in Jesus Christ (the Gospel), who is both the electing God and the elected humanity. This disposition as the gift of God also claims and demands a corresponding human action (the law).

Since theology is a special discourse about God, the logic in Barth's theology comes from the action of God. The action of God, God's eternal election of the human race, precedes all human disposition, and thus God establishes God's claim to humanity. Therefore, discourse about humanity, in correspondence to God, is an inseparable part of the special theological discourse. In the doctrine of the election of grace, Barth included the foundation of theological ethics as a part of the doctrine of God. As long as election, as the sum of the Gospel, is an inclusive concept, sanctification (which belongs to election) is not exclusively for the regenerated, but an inclusive concept. Since election is to enable us to be and become fully human as God's covenant partners, sanctification is none other than our corresponding action to realize our true nature, i.e., humanization. The law demands us to live in correspondence to our election (the sum of Gospel), that is our sanctification.

The Unity of Theology and Ethics

Barth's reversal of the traditional sequence of the two modes of the Word of God to Gospel and law led to his inclusion of theological ethics as a part of dogmatics. While God, as Lord of the covenant, turns to and encounters the human race in the Gospel, God also claims humanity for Himself (the law). While God surrenders Himself to humanity through the incarnation and the crucifixion of Jesus Christ (theology), God demands the corresponding surrender from the human side (ethics).

Furthermore, there is an axiomatic motif in Barth's thought that content always precedes form.[52] The law as the form of the Gospel cannot be prior to its content, the Gospel. This has a significant anthropological implication. Barth perceived a human being in correspondence to his understanding of divine being; namely, "a 'being in action,' as active being, as activity."[53] Barth says, "To exist as a man means to act. And action means choosing, deciding" (II/2: 535). Barth formulated human being as "a Doer of the Word" (I/2, 18.1) who "does not subsist of itself, but only in a specific doing on the part of the subject" (I/2: 369). Human being is "constantly realising its existence in acts of free determination and decision;" therefore, its essence is "the very self-determination without which he would not be a man" (I/2: 364).[54]

Barth used the human analogy in relationship between Gospel and law. If the Gospel is related to the "determinateness of the inward . . . aspects of human life," the law ties with the "determinateness of the . . . outward aspects" (I/2: 369). The Word of God compels our self-determination in the unity of the inwardness and the outwardness. Jüngel explained, "The 'inner' is already apparent in the 'outer;' human being is apparent in human doing; human existence is apparent in self-determination; . . . one's person is apparent in one's activity."[55] The true meaning of being Christians as hearers of the Word is to become doers of the Word. To be and become authentic Christians presupposes the unity of hearing (being) and doing. Barth rejected the anthropological dualism between the inner and the outer, and affirmed the inseparability of being and acting in the analogy of the unity of human being. "In this doing of the Word, which is true hearing, we are saved and blessed, the object of the divine good-pleasure—not otherwise" (I/2: 366).

This is a dimension which Luther's theology did not have. Otto Weber called this Luther's "anthropological narrowness."[56] In the emphasis on salvation by hearing and believing alone, Luther diminished a necessary dimension of doing works. For Luther, a person can be justified merely as a recipient of God's activity, prior to one's being as a doer of works. Barth agreed that there can be "no 'cooperation on the part of our will in our conversion.'"[57] However, the Holy Spirit is working on our humanity, as the Formula of Concord stated. A person becomes the object of the divine action through the renewing power of the Holy Spirit. The work of the Holy Spirit is not "coercion or compulsion, because the converted man spontaneously does that which is good." Barth understood this spontaneity "not only as the result of divine action, but also as based on an ontological characteristic of the person who is transformed by God into a rational, self-determining, acting creature."[58]   Our self-determination is not a coercive result according to our encounter with the action of God, but rather ontologically a corresponding matter of being "determined in the act of our self-determination in the totality of its possibility" (I/2: 266).

Luther understood the Gospel only in terms of human passivity and receptivity, for he said that the Gospel "snatches us away from ourselves and places us outside ourselves."[59] For Luther, such a snatched condition is the basic paradigm for humanity as the hearer of the Word. However, Barth argued for a different paradigm. Since human being is defined by action and self-determination, his theological anthropology immediately authenticates the Gospel to be transformed into the form of the law that commands human action. The efficacy of the Gospel is not so much a snatch or leap that allows no space for human activities, but rather a real corresponding action from the human side as "the doing of the Word, which is true hearing" (I/2: 366). Luther viewed the Gospel as unambiguous and the law as ambiguous. Barth rejected this point. Jüngel commented on Barth's position, "The unambiguous gospel that brings life and salvation also brings with it an already unambiguous law. And this law has the function of leading us to a decision which corresponds to God's primal decision of election."[60] In Luther's theology, only God acts, and we just receive. However, in Barth's theology, precisely because God acts, we must respond with a corresponding human action. The Gospel initiates a new humanity in action according to a "human self-determination which corresponds to this [divine] determination" (II/2: 510).

If the Gospel points to a new humanity according to the action of God, the law aims at a corresponding human action. Hence, ethics, as the doctrine of the law or the command of God, is inseparable from dogmatics and theology.   Since human beings act as doers in correspondence with God's action, the theme of the goodness of human conduct becomes a part of the doctrine of the command of God. Therefore, theological ethics is a part of dogmatics. Barth rejected theological ethics as an independent discipline, because an independent ethics makes theology a predicate of anthropology: "Since independent ethical systems are always in the last resort determined by general anthropology, this inevitably means that dogmatics itself and theology as a whole simply become applied anthropology" (I/2: 783). However, Barth's inclusion of ethics within dogmatics does not mean a delimitation of ethics in favor of dogmatics, but, on the contrary, its full recognition. The Word of God makes human existence theologically relevant. Since a human being is understood as a being in action, dogmatics that deals with the Word of God "raises the ethical question or rather recognizes and treats it as its most characteristic problem" (I/2: 793). Therefore, "dogmatics itself must be ethics," and "ethics can be only dogmatics" (I/2: 795). Barth said:

> (1) the separation [between dogmatics and ethics] must be merely technical in character, not based on principle and method; (2) dogmatics thus separated from ethics must be pursued in thoroughgoing relation to ethical problems; (3) ethics thus separated from dogmatics must be pursued in thoroughgoing subordination to dogmatics. (I/2: 795)

In the subsequent *Church Dogmatics*, Barth put this proposal into practice. He subordinated ethics as a part of the doctrine of God, including ethics as the doctrine of the command of God at the concluding part of each volume.[61] The doctrine of God (content) constitutes the material basis of theological ethics (form). The divine disposition claims the corresponding action from the human side. Concretely, in God's gracious election, God has made Himself responsible to humankind. The election is the essence of the divine attitude and thus the sum of the Gospel. Accordingly, God demands humankind a corresponding action to accomplish the law—the form of the Gospel—which was completely fulfilled in Christ. Including an ethical chapter at the end of each volume concerning doctrines of creation, reconciliation, and redemption, i.e., the command of the Creation, the Reconciler, and the Redeemer, Barth made a clear shift of emphasis "from the commanding position of God to the commanded position of humankind:"[62]

In this structure, the law as the norm of sanctification and ethics as the embodiment of sanctification become important tenets of Barth's theology. Such an inclusion of ethics within dogmatics is the basic reason why Barth's theology has made "a political impact such as has scarcely been the case since the Reformation."[63] It is not surprising to see that Barth's uncompromising dogmatic theology has produced a powerful political theology, as we have already seen the similar case in the ecumenical dialogue in which Barth's thoroughgoing Reformed theology is also received as a catholic theology.

This chapter may be regarded as a prolegomenon of the following chapters which will deal with Barth's actual theology of sanctification. For the Word of God is the only concrete point of departure for Barth's theology, Barth's paradigm shift of Gospel and law and his assertion of the unity of theology and ethics constitute the basic framework for his doctrine of sanctification. In coming chapters, we will see Barth's continuous struggles with this tension between his theological affirmations and secular sensibility. While endlessly moving back and forth between the doctrinal polarities (justification and sanctification, faith and love, etc.), he overcame dualism by holding fast to the Christological foundation of their unity.

Sanctification and Justification

Barth formulated the doctrine of sanctification as a part of the doctrine of reconciliation which consists in a trinitarian structure of justification (CD IV/1), sanctification (CD IV/2), and vocation (CD IV/3). In accordance with the sequence of Gospel and law, Barth began his theology of reconciliation with Christology; following hamartialogy, soteriology, ecclesiology, and finally Christian ethics in an architectonic structure.[64]

Barth regarded sanctification as "the second theme and problem" of the doctrine of reconciliation (IV/2, 64.1 and 66.3). [65] The event of reconciliation includes both justification, i.e., "wholly and utterly a movement from above to below, of God to man," and sanctification, i.e., "wholly and utterly from below to above, the movement of the reconciled man to God" (IV/2: 6).

Whereas modern Protestant theologies tend to overlook it, he argued that the doctrine of sanctification must be treated "with no less attention than that which we devoted to the first [justification]" (IV/2: 7). Warning that an excessive opposition to anthropomonism can be an "opposite error" of a "no less abstract theomonism" (IV/2: 10), he argued that the Bible does "not put God abstractly at that heart of the message, but man with God" (IV/2: 10). While God's promise "I will be your God" refers to our justification, the other promise "Ye shall be my people" indicates our sanctification. "The imperative: 'Ye shall be holy' [Lev. 19:2] is simply the imperative indication of the irresistible dynamic of the indicative: 'I am holy,' i.e., I am holy, and act among you as such, and therefore I make you holy—this is your life and norm" (IV/2: 501).

For Barth, there are four mutual relationships between justification and sanctification. First, sanctification is not "a second divine action" which follows justification, but a different moment of the "unitary" divine action of reconciliation in Jesus Christ (IV/2: 501). Justification and sanctification must be grasped as "the one totality of the reconciling action of God, of the one whole and undivided Jesus Christ, and of His one grace" (IV/2: 502).[66]

Secondly, however, they are neither "identical" nor "interchangeable" (IV/2: 503). They cannot merge into each other.[67] John Calvin articulated justification and sanctification in terms of *duplex gratia* (the double grace) which we receive in the *participatio Christi* (the participation in Christ).[68] On the one hand, justification cannot be reduced merely as a process of sanctification. Our faith in Jesus Christ—the Judge judged in our place—cannot be identified with an obedience of an anthropocentric discipleship.[69] On the other hand, sanctification cannot be "swallowed up in justification." A "monism of the *theologia crucis* and the doctrine of justification" can "obscure in a very suspicious way the existential reach" of reconciliation (IV/2: 504).

Thirdly, justification and sanctification "do belong inseparably together." Without their mutuality, we would fall into either "an indolent quietism" (cf. "cheap grace")[70] or "an illusory activism." While justification describes the way from sin and death to life in which "*God* goes with man," sanctification shows that "it is really with *man* that God is on this way as He reconciles the world with Himself in Jesus Christ" (IV/2: 505).[71]

Fourthly, there is no temporal and material order between the two (see IV/2: 507). Their relationship is neither monistic or dualistic. But "In the *simul* of the one divine will and action justification is first as basis and second as presupposition, sanctification first as aim and second as consequence" (IV/2: 508). Barth calls John Calvin "the theologian of sanctification," arguing that Calvin put "a strategic precedence" on sanctification over justification (IV/2: 509).[72] Endorsing Calvin's primacy of sanctification, Barth argued for the significance of sanctification.

Chapter 6

•

The Humanity Paradigm

In biblical Greek, "to reconcile" (*apokatallassein*) means "to exchange" (IV/2: 21). Hence, the basic meaning of reconciliation is the exchange of the divine abasement and the human exaltation in Jesus Christ.). Barth established the foundation of sanctification on this exaltation of Christ; metaphorically, "the return home of the Son of Man" in the parable of the prodigal son (Lk. 15:11-32 [see IV/2: 21-25]).

Jesus Christ is both *vere Deus* (true divinity) and *vere homo* (true humanity), the formula used by traditional theology to fight against the docetic Gnosticism. *Vere homo* involves God's complete assumption into humanity, making "a man as distinct from God, angel or animal, his specific creatureliness, his *humanitas*" (IV/2: 25). Different from a naturalist, idealist, or existentialist anthropology, Christian anthropology is first and foremost based on the *humanitas Christi* (the humanity of Christ). And Christology offers the basis for understanding anthropology. Barth said, "A genuine knowledge of man in general, a theological anthropology, and therefore a theological doctrine of the sin and misery of man, can be based only on the particular knowledge of the man Jesus Christ, and therefore on Christology" (IV/2: 27).

Root-Paradigm: *Humanitas Christi*

Humanitas Christi signifies not "an angel, a middle being, a demi-god," but "totally and unreservedly" a human like us (IV/2: 27). The exaltation of Jesus in the New Testament means neither "a destruction or alteration of His humanity" or an absolution of "His likeness with us, emptying it of its substance" (IV/2: 28), but "the exaltation of our essence with all its possibilities and limits into the completely different sphere of that totality, freedom, correspondence and service" (IV/2: 30). The humanity of Jesus Christ, "the basis and power of the atonement" (IV/2: 28)[1] involves this upward movement in which the servant becomes the lord. Hence, the theology of glory is as legitimate as the theology of the cross: "We cannot stop at an abstract *theologia crucis*, for this is full already of a secret *theologia gloriae*" (IV/2: 29).

Humanitas Christi consists in three doctrines: (1) the gracious election of God, (2) the event of the incarnation, and (3) the resurrection and ascension of Christ (see IV/2: 31). (1) <u>Election</u>. *Humanitas Christi* "was and is and will be the primary content of God's eternal election of grace." For "God's eternal election of grace is concretely the election of Jesus Christ." Hence, the humanity of Christ is "not merely of *a* but *the* purpose of the will of God" (IV/2: 31), "the primary object and content of the primal and basic will of God" (IV/2: 33).

(2) <u>Incarnation</u>. According to God's eternal election of grace, true humanity was historically fulfilled and actualized through the incarnation of God in the *humanitas Christi*. The incarnation is the ontic and noetic foundation of the Christology, "the *ratio essendi* and *ratio cognoscendi*, the ground of being and ground of knowledge" (IV/2: 37). In the event of incarnation, "without ceasing to be God" (IV/2: 40), Jesus Christ "becomes and is *also* true man" (IV/2: 41). Incarnation is one mode of "the work of the whole Holy Trinity" (IV/2: 44), *opera trinitatis ad extra sunt indivisa*, being as the Son.[2] As a moment of the "intra-trinitarian life of God," the *assumptio carnis* takes places radically and totally and has opened a new "frontier" for humanity.

Incarnation involves four doctrinal aspects: (a) Jesus' becoming human; (b) His existence as human existence; (c) the unity of divine and human essence in Him; and (d) the exaltation of human essence to divine essence through Him. (a) The incarnation, that "The Word became flesh," signifies "the becoming and being of God the Son in human essence." It is an event, a God's own act, "a being which does not cease as such to be a becoming" (IV/2: 46). The efficacy of this *assumptio carnis* is inclusive, related not merely to "one man, but [also to] the *humanum* of all men, which is posited and exalted as such to unity with God" (IV/2: 49).

(b) The incarnation implies that the existence of the Son of God is that of a human being, a fellow person of the human race. "God Himself acts and suffers when this man acts and suffers as a man . . . just because God Himself is its human subject in His Son." Barth endorsed the traditional doctrine of the hypostatic union, i.e., "the union made by God in the *hypostasis* (the mode of existence) of the Son" that is "the basis and power of the *nativitas Jesu Christi*," i.e., the conception and birth of Jesus through Mary (IV/2: 51).

(c) The incarnation indicates that "in the One Jesus Christ divine and human essence were and are united" (IV/2: 60). This unity must not be understood "*in abstracto*, not in a vacuum, not as the assertion of a general truth;" but "*in concreto*, in the encounter with this one Subject, in the acknowledgment and recognition and confession of its particular truth" (IV/2: 61). The hypostatic union must not be conceived as an a priori possibility but as an *a posteriori* actuality.[3] The union of the two natures in Christ is "not itself a unity, but a union in that two-sided participation, the *communio naturarum*" (IV/2: 63). In this participation, Barth affirmed the Chalcedonian definition of Christological union; without confusion, change, division, and separation (see IV/2: 63-65).

(d) The incarnation signifies our exaltation; "as the Son of God became and is man, as He caused His existence to become that of a man, as He united divine and human essence in Himself, He exalted human essence into Himself" (IV/2: 69). The mutual participation of divine and human essence in and by Jesus Christ involves the "twofold differentiation" (IV/2: 70) in both downward and upward directions. This mutual participation has a threefold meaning of impartation: the communication of attributes relates to the impartation of the human essence to the divine and the divine to human in Jesus Christ; the communication of grace refers to the fact that the human essence in Jesus Christ is totally determined by grace; and the communication of operations pertains to "the common actualization of divine and human essence" (the union as act, not state) in Jesus Christ (IV/2: 104). This operation is "not just a divine *novum*, nor just a human;" On the contrary, "at one and the same time it is the great divine and the great human *novum*" (IV/2: 115).

(3) <u>Resurrection and Ascension</u>. The *novum*, which is both divine and human, actualizes and establishes "the knowing human subject" (IV/2: 120) in which the Holy Spirit is "the *doctor veritatis*" (IV/2: 126). The resurrection and ascension of Jesus Christ are revelatory

events of His self-declaration. Together, they are one "coherent" *event* (IV/2: 142) which has "a concrete element in human history at large," consists in "a series of concrete encounters and short conversations between the risen Jesus and His disciples" (IV/2: 143), and is "the concretely historical event of the self-manifestation of Jesus after His death" (IV/2: 146).

The resurrection and the ascension are "two distinct but inseparable moments in one and the same event" (IV/2: 150). If the resurrection refers to the *terminus a quo*, (the beginning), the ascension means the *terminus ad quem* (the end). "The resurrection of Jesus Christ is the point of departure, the commencement of this history of revelation," signifying that Jesus came from the dead and rose again (IV/2: 151). "His ascension is the terminating point of this history of revelation," revealing that Jesus went to heaven (IV/2: 153): "He goes to the place of origin of all the dominion of divine power and grace and love. It is not only God who is now there, but as God is there He, this man, is also there." (IV/2: 154) In this way, Jesus has opened an ontological space for humanity in heaven, which is the good news.

Barth's deliberations on *humanitas Christi* can be summarized in terms of the threefold concrete-universal act of God. First, the *humanitas Christi* is the concrete-universal manifestation of God's gracious election for the human race. Second, the *assumptio carnis* (incarnation) of the Triune God in the particular person Jesus is the historical, and thus the concrete, fulfillment of God's salvific love for the human race. Third, the resurrection and ascension of the particular humanity of Jesus in heaven has opened the ontological basis for the redemption of all humanity and, thus, the universal foundation for the exaltation of the human race. Through the events of election, incarnation, and resurrection and ascension which consummate the divine-human transformation of turning the most concrete into the most universal, God accomplished His gracious will to humanity as His covenant partner once and for all. Thus, the *humanitas Christi* manifests the most concrete-universal way through which God includes humanity within His intratrinitarian history and substantiates the ontological space of sanctification for humanity. The *humanitas Christi*, the foundation of sanctification, is *the most concrete-universal.* Barth further elaborated the nature of *humanitas Christi* as the root-paradigm of radical humanity in his Christology of the royal man.

Royal Humanity

Barth enunciated four aspects of Jesus Christ as royal man (traditionally Christ's kingly office [*manus regium*]); (1) the distinctive presence of royal humanity, (2) royal humanity's likeness to God, (3) the accomplished life-act of royal humanity, and (4) the significance of the cross for royal humanity.

(1) The presence of the royal man Jesus was distinctive and irrevocable. Jesus was present as a human being in encounter with others (IV/2: 156). In this encounter, Jesus demanded decision (IV/2: 157). His presence, as the presence of the Kingdom of God, was unforgettably distinctive (IV/2: 159). And He was "present irrevocably—in a way in which His existence was not compromised or broken by His death," not only as the Son of Man but also as the Son of God (IV/2: 163).

(2) The royal man in one mode of God's being (see IV/2: 126) exists as an eschatological revolutionary, heralding the Kingdom of God. Sharing "the strange destiny which falls on God in His people and the world" (IV/2: 167), the royal man "ignored all those who are high and mighty and wealthy in the world in favour of the weak and meek and lowly" (IV/2: 168). Barth would agree with the idiom of liberation theology "the preferential option for the poor."[4] He said, "In fellowship and conformity with this God who is poor in the world the royal man Jesus is also poor, and fulfils this transvaluation of all values, acknowledging those who are in different ways poor men as this world counts poverty" (IV/2: 169). The royal man's attitude to the established orders is genuinely revolutionary. Setting "all programmes and principles in question" (IV/2: 172), the royal man deals with the world in His royal freedom,

> not in principle, not in the execution of a programme, but for this reason in a way which is all the more revolutionary, as the One who breaks all bonds asunder, in new historical developments and situations each of which is for those who can see and hear—only a sign, but an unmistakable sign, of His freedom and kingdom and over-ruling of history (IV/2: 173).

The "passive conservatism" (IV/2: 173) the royal man showed was "provisional." He did not ignore the temple, the order of family, the law, or provoke any direct conflict with economic and political relationships. However, "there is also no trace of any consistent recognition [of the relationships] in principle" (IV/2: 175). In fact, He assaulted radically and comprehensively not only the order of family and the prevailing religious order, but also the industrial, commercial, economic, and political *status quo*. He advocated a new bottle for a new wine, i.e., the invading kingdom of God: "the radical and indissoluble antithesis of the kingdom of God to all human kingdoms, the unanswerable question, the irremediable unsettlement introduced by the kingdom of God into all human kingdoms" (IV/2: 177). As the new cloth destroys the old garment, Jesus actualized and fulfilled the new thing, completely ignoring and transcending the old order. Nevertheless, the royal man is "not against men but for men—even for men in all the impossibility of their perversion" (IV/2: 180). The decisive point is:

> the royal man Jesus is the image and reflection of the divine Yes to man and his cosmos. It is God's critical Yes, dividing and disclosing and punishing with all the power of the sword. . . . But, like the Yes of God, it is really a Yes not a No, even though it includes and is accompanied by a powerful No. (IV/2: 180)

Hence, the New Testament beatitudes do not speak of "an empty paradox," but the declaration of Jesus the royal man—Lord of all humanity. They proclaim that earthly suffering, suffering actions, and voluntary suffering for His sake are not in vain. The beatitudes are "not merely a promise and proclamation, but the present impartation of full salvation, total life and perfect joy" (IV/2: 192).

(3) The life-act of the royal man Jesus is the root-paradigm of being human in the unity of being and acting: "His life *was* His act, and it has therefore the character of history" (IV/2: 193). Classical Christology divides the person and the work of Christ. However, in the life-act of royal humanity, the person and the work of Christ are not dualistic but identical. Moreover, His life-act shows the history of a Word in unity with deed, as the proto-paradigm of "human being as the doer of the Word" (CD I/2, 18.1). The life-act of the royal man Jesus also manifests the unity of knowing and acting *par excellence*.

> If we are to think of the speaking of Jesus as understood in the Gospel tradition, we must abandon completely the current distinctions between *logos* and *ethos*, or speaking and action, behind which there usually lurk the differentiations of knowledge and life, theory and practice, truth and reality (IV/2: 194).

The Word in the life-act of Jesus is the powerfully evangelizing, teaching, and heralding Word, but also a concretely, comprehensively, and a wholly *human* word (see IV/2: 194-209). His concrete speech "always" accompanies His concrete activity. In His life-act, words and actions are in unity; "as His life-act was wholly His Word it was also wholly His activity, . . . His activity was as it were the kindling light of His speech—the light of the truth of His speech kindling into actuality" (IV/2: 209). His speaking constitutes an activity in a word, but neither remain to be "only" a word or an event in the spiritual sphere. The concrete speech accomplishes the corresponding concrete changes in the material and physical sphere of the world. "Not merely in part, but totally, His Word makes cosmic history" (IV/2: 209f.).[5]

> As a Word, therefore, it is also an action—an individual, concrete action as an individual, concrete indication of the fact that as a Word it is spoken in power. As an action it points to the fact that it is a Word which is spoken in fulfilled time by the One who fulfils it, so that it is no longer a promise, but itself that which is promised; a definitive Word in the unequivocal form of a definitive action. (IV/2: 210)

The acts of Jesus have an extraordinary, miraculous nature such as exorcism and healing. The miracles of Jesus (see IV/2: 216-8) are "absolutely new and different' from all other usual, unusual, or super- natural occurrences (IV/2: 215). But they are mighty actualizations of "God's conclusive action, the coming of the new aeon" (IV/2: 219). The miracles imply God's radical blessing, election of humankind as His covenant-partner, and solidarity with humankind, and manifest the freedom of grace as the basis for human liberation.

In this context, faith is the necessary and corresponding "anthropo- logical counterpart" to the free grace of God (IV/2: 243). Faith leads us to comprehend the miracles as signs of the coming kingdom and Jesus as the cosmic savior. Faith becomes the true basis of human freedom to communicate with God. In faith, those who attain the freedom of being God's partner become beings of unconditional and unlimited capacity. But Christian faith is not always identical with the general Christian concept of *credo*. Christian faith is specific, because the Christian encounter with Jesus Christ is "not like the sunrise illuminating a wide landscape from above, but like a single ray of light focused on one point and piercing at this point what is otherwise an abyss of darkness" (IV/2: 246). The metaphor of a single ray for Grace clearly describes the concrete-universal approach latent in Barth's theology. Christian faith works in a concrete-universal way, starting with the particular for the sake of the universal, corresponding to the freedom of grace which works like a single ray of light (in high density, specificity, and concentration).

> It is not just applied to all men equally. It is applied specifically to these particular men. In this particularity it is not merely a divine promise and therefore divine truth for all men here and now. As a sign for all men, but a sign set up then and there, it is a promise which is divinely fulfilled and truth which is divinely actualised. (IV/2: 246)

Grace has the total freedom to accomplish specific, and thus real, deliverance here and now; yet it concerns the whole human race in a most universal way.

(4) The cross is the sign that "controls and penetrates and determines this whole" existence of the royal man (IV/2: 249). The cross is not alien, but central to the royal life of Jesus "whose story is finally the story of His passion" (IV/2: 250). Paradoxically, the crucifixion of Jesus on the cross as the "final negative" signifies the foundation of all "positivities." In other words, the final negativity of the cross is the most concrete point which opens the new aeon of universal positivities. The most concrete point in the Christian faith is this dangerous memory of the Crucified God-man in this final negativity, His innocent sufferings and voluntary death. However, the memory of the cross reveals and introduces the other inseparable, dangerous memory—the resurrection of royal humanity—the most universal point in Christian faith.

> In His passion the name of the God active and revealed in Him is conclusively sanctified; His will is done on earth as it is done in heaven; His kingdom comes, in a form and with a power to which as a man He can only give a terrified but determined assent. . . . In the deepest darkness of Golgotha He enters supremely into the glory of the unity of the Son with the Father. In that abandonment by God He is the One who is directly loved by God. . . . And it is not a new and specific secret. It is the secret of the whole. Nor is it a closed secret. It is a secret which has been revealed in the resurrection of Jesus. (IV/2: 252)

The crucifixion of Jesus on the cross was not just "the frightful paradox of a radical contradiction and destruction of the Son of Man," but, in fact, "the radical affirmation," the "overwhelming" "victory of the new actuality over the old." The disciples realized that it was the "coronation" of Jesus as the royal man (IV/2: 254). His cross was no longer the symbol of hopelessness, but had become the solid basis and sign of both the eternal and temporal hope. His passion, including His prediction, is not "an anti-climax, but the climax of their witness" (IV/2: 255). All the witnesses of the Synoptics, John's Gospel, Pauline theology, and the first century Christians (cf. IV/2: 255-8) are congruent in understanding the cross as "a decisive redemptive turning point." The cross has four implications: (a) The deeper dimension of death is "a more precise form of a readiness and willingness" (IV/2: 258). (b) The cross is the "must" for Jesus Christ according to both His voluntary self-determination and the predetermined divine order (IV/2: 259). (c) This "free but divinely ordained" giving-up actualized the finale to Israel's history and God's "handing over" to the people outside Israel in which "the Messiah of Israel becomes the Saviour of the world" (IV/2: 260). (d) "The 'must' of His passion extends to them [disciples] too" (IV/2: 263). The cross of the royal man becomes the light, power, glory, liberation, and hope for His disciples. Correspondingly, disciples must carry their own individual crosses, suffer their own afflictions, and bear the definite limitation of death so as to go after Christ and follow 'in his steps;' that is the secondary theology of the cross.[6]

To conclude, the royal man Jesus, both in genuine humanity and one mode of God's being, has a revolutionary attitude to the established order with the preferential option for the poor. His life-act is the history of Word in unity with deed. While the incarnation of the *humanitas Christi* refers to the concrete-universal embodiment of God's sincerity toward humanity in the anthropocosmic history, the life-act of the royal man Jesus represents the paradigm of radical humanity in the unity of being and acting. The life-act of royal humanity manifests the paradigm of humanity *par excellence* in the unity of knowing and acting and of theology and ethics. Therefore, *humanitas Christi* reveals the most concrete-universal of the divine-human drama of reconciliation, and illustrates, as the royal man, the root-paradigm of radical humanity in action. The miracles of Jesus Christ manifest the unity *par excellence* of human speech and cosmic transformation. The cross, as the most concrete signpost of the Christian faith, opens the new aeon of universal actualities. While the most concrete point of the Christian faith is the dangerous memory of the Crucified God-man in the final negativity, the dangerous memory of the resurrection of the Crucified, its inseparable end, is the most universal point of the Christian faith. On the cross, the royal man Jesus reveals the root-paradigm of radical humanity in utterly self-giving love (*agape*) and consummates the concrete-universal drama of the Triune God with the world.

Real Human Nature: *Imago Dei*

Barth argued that *humanitas Christi* as the root-paradigm of humanity illuminates the specificities of sin (Christ and sin). In the context of the exaltation of royal humanity, sin is understood as sloth, and the human condition as misery, i.e., the predicament of the untransformed human state (IV/2, 65). In this analysis, Barth used four structural relationships of a human being: relation to God, relation to fellow-human, relation to self, and relation to time. Barth had used the same fourfold structure when he delineated the nature of humanity under the rubric of the doctrine of creation (III/2). This is Barth's theological anthropology of real human nature. From this vantage point, sin as sloth is none other than lack of sincerity in becoming and being true, authentic (in Barth's term, real) human nature.

At this juncture, it is important to note that Barth already had given up his early claim "God is everything, humanity is nothing."[7] He agreed that such a position not only "fails to give God His due" but also "denies humanity its due."[8] Later, Barth more explicitly asserted the "humanity of God." The living God becomes the dialogical and ontological partner of the human in God's "sovereign togetherness." God's deity, which already has "the character of humanity," "includes" our humanity:

> Indeed—and this is the point back of which we cannot go—it is matter of *God's* sovereign togetherness with man, a togetherness grounded in Him and determined, delimited, and ordered through Him alone. . . . It is a matter, however, of God's *togetherness* with man. Who God is and what He is in His deity He proves and reveals not in a vacuum as a divine being-for-Himself, but precisely and authentically in the fact that He exists, speaks, and acts as the *partner* of man, . . . He who does *that* is the living God. And the freedom in which He does *that* is His deity. It is the deity which as such also has the character of humanity. In this and only in this form was—and still is—our view of the deity of God to be set in opposition to that earlier theology. There must be positive acceptance and not unconsidered rejection of the elements of truth,

which one cannot possibly deny to it even if one sees all its weakness. It is precisely God's *deity* which, rightly understood, includes his *humanity*.[9]

In the *Church Dogmatics*, III/2, Barth articulated the nature of human being (or the real human nature) as (1) "real" human being (Sec. 44), (2) "humanity" (Sec. 45), and (3) "whole person" (Sec. 46).[10] (1) Real Human Being (human-to-God). Here again, Barth took Jesus Christ, who is a human being *for* God and God *for* human being, as the basis for defining real human being. Hence, Christology determines the formal and material dimensions of real human being. Formally, real human being consists in the right relationship with God, because human being is "*from, to,* and *with* God."[11] Materially, real human being is defined in four levels. (a) Real human being is "a being with Jesus [which] rests upon the election of God . . . [and] consists in the hearing of the Word of God" (III/2: 142). (b) Being a human "is a history" in a dynamic movement, but not a condition or a finished state (III/2: 157). (c) Human being is "a being in gratitude" (III/2: 166). Only as beings in gratitude are we to be real human beings in our own action, "not only the object but the subject of history" (III/2: 168). In this status, we are not only the object of God's grace in which God is the subject, but also the subject who responds with our thanksgiving to God as object. In other words, "the intersubjectivity of the interaction of grace (*charis*) and thanksgiving (*eucharistia*)" constitutes the content of human being.[12] (d) Real human nature is a being engaged in active responsibility to God. Real human being is the "subject in pure spontaneity" to the grace of God as well as its "object in pure receptivity" (III/2: 174). Human being in responsibility before God entails four inner notes: the knowledge of God, the obedience to God, the invocation of God, and the freedom which God imparts to us. At this point, Barth's theological anthropology moves toward a more inclusive understanding of human nature beyond the Christian terminology.[13]

(2) Humanity (human-to-human). Jesus, the root-paradigm for humanity, is a human being for other human beings. Barth argued that, in the light of *humanitas Christi*, "humanity [*Menschlichkeit*] is to be described unequivocally as fellow-humanity [*Mitmenschlichkeit*]." The life-act of Jesus manifests that "man is the cosmic being which exists absolutely for its fellows" (III/2: 208). The paradigm of humanity as *Mitmenschlichkeit* is nothing but a copy [*Nachbild*] of the intra-trinitarian life of the Triune God.[14] Between the being of God and the being of human, "there is correspondence and similarity;" that is to say,

"There is an *anologia relationis*" (III/2: 220). The inner-trinitarian co-existence, co-inherence, and reciprocity in the eternal I-Thou relationship repeats and reflects in humanity as co-humanity. This *analogia relationis* has been completely fulfilled in the *humanitas Christi*, the root-paradigm of humanity.

Furthermore, the humanity of Jesus is the image of God, the *imago Dei* (III/2: 219). The *humanitas Christi* as the *imago Dei* indicates, attests, and reveals the paradigm of humanity as *Mitmenschlichkeit* in the *analogia relationis* to the inner being of God. Barth said,

> Man generally, the man with the fellow-man, has indeed a part in the divine likeness of the man Jesus, the man for the fellow-man. As man generally is modeled on the man Jesus and His being for others, and as the man Jesus is modeled on God, it has to be said of man generally that he is created in the image of God. He is in his humanity, therefore in his fellow-humanity. God created him in His own image in the fact that He did not create him alone but in this connexion and fellowship. For in God's action as the Lord of the covenant, and even further back in His action as the Creator of a reality distinct from Himself, it is proved that God Himself is not solitary, that although He is one in essence He is not alone, but that primarily and properly He is in connexion and fellowship. It is inevitable that we should recall the triune being of God at this point. God exists in relationship and fellowship. As the Father of the Son and the Son of the Father He is Himself I and Thou, confronting Himself and yet always one and the same in the Holy Ghost. God created man in His own image, in correspondence with His own being and essence. . . . Because He is not solitary in Himself, and therefore does not will to be so *ad extra*, it is not good for man to be alone, and God created him in His own image, as male and female. This is what is emphatically said by Gen. 1:27, and all other explanations of the *image Dei* suffer from the fact that they do not do justice to this decisive statement. . . . God is in relationship, and so too is the man created by Him. This is his divine likeness. When we view it in this way, the dispute whether it is lost by sin finds a self-evident solution. It is not lost. But more important is the fact that what man is indestructibly as he is man with the fellow-man, he is in hope of the being and action of the One who is his original in this relationship." (III/2: 323f.)

Barth identified the image of God as togetherness, the plurality of the I-thou relationship. In his *Table Talk*, Barth further said:

Image in Genesis I means that like God, who is living but not isolated (*Elohim* denotes plurality), there is plurality in man. Man has plurality like God, who is plural. Being man means being in togetherness: man [Adam] and wife [Eve]. . . . 'Living God' means 'togetherness'. . . . Image has a double meaning: God lives in togetherness with Himself, then God lives in togetherness with man, then men live togetherness with one another.[15]

Since the basic form of humanity is determined as the "being with others," being human entails "a determination" of being with others (III/2: 243). The statement "I am" presupposes the condition "I am in encounter" (III/2: 247). Barth put this relationship into the formula, "I am as Thou art" (III/2: 248), meaning a dynamic and essential encounter between two histories of two beings of I and Thou. In short, humanity is determined as the historical actualization of the being-in-encounter, in which the statement "I am as Thou art" is being realized. Humanity as being-in-encounter means "two-sided openness" (III/2: 251), a reciprocal intercommunication, and "mutual assistance in the act of being" (III/2: 260) in the history of encounter between I and Thou. Barth used the analogy of a fish which needs water to argue for this awareness of sociality as the structure of humanity (III/2: 263). Humanity as being-in-encounter stands for joyful co-humanity (*Mitmenschlichkeit*).[16] This common joy realizes "the freedom of encounter" from the ontological freedom of being a human as a creature (III/2: 272).[17] Human nature or the nature of humanity involves "freedom in the co-existence of man and man in which the one may be, and will be, the companion, associate, comrade, fellow and helpmate of the other" (III/2: 276).[18]

(3)   The Whole Person (human-to-self). The *humanitas Christi* is the paradigm and norm of the whole person in the unity and proper order of soul and body. The basis of human soul and body is the Spirit. The foundation of human being as soul and body is the action of God's Spirit as the Creator, the Preserver, and the Redeemer. In other words, the Spirit is its irresistible and irreversible context and background to being authentically (in Barth's term, naturally) human. In this context, human being as a spirit has a space to be a subject as a natural human being, but not merely as an absorbed substructure of the divine being. To protect this human subjectivity, Barth made a distinction between the Spirit as Redeemer and the Spirit as the Creator and the Sustainer. In the Spirit as the Creator and Sustainer, Barth underscored the

primordial ties of human beings in general with God and with other human beings prior to redemption.

Finally, Barth discussed general psychology.[19]   Human nature is constituted as an interconnected unity within which there is an antithesis; namely, between "creaturely life" and "creaturely being" (III/2: 367).   The creaturely life which refers to the soul designates a *living* being, i.e., a person's temporal existence, whereas the creaturely being, the body, is a living *being*, i.e., one's spatial form.   Barth rejected the dualistic understanding of body and soul, refuting both extreme spiritualization and extreme materialization.   The soul, the inner movement in time, perceives, experiences, thinks, feels, and decides; however, its full enactment necessitates the body, the outer movement in space.   The freedom of "natural" human being signifies self-determination.   However, human being cannot function as a subjectivity with this capacity and freedom, apart from its material body.   The soul and the body can be distinguished, but cannot be separated.   They are completely interconnected so that a denial of this interconnectedness means a distortion of human nature.

Human nature is both a percipient being and an active being. Perception consists of a compound act of awareness (outer) and thought (inner).   Although the former is distinctively related to the body and the latter to the soul, perception is an inseparable, single act of the whole person.   But awareness and thought are primarily the acts of the soul, and secondarily those of the body.   Action also consists of a compound act of desire (outer) and will (inner).   In a similar manner to perception, desire and will are an inseparable single action, though desire is distinctively bodily and will soulful.   They are also primarily of the soul and secondarily of the body.   By willing, we can choose, determine, and make up our mind as to our desire.   Being a whole person requires a discipline to preserve the order of human nature as the soul of the body.

Sin in the Light of the *Humanitas Christi*

The human situation determined by sin can be fully exposed in the light of the *humanitas Christi*.   Since we are corrupt even in our self-knowledge, we know the nature of sin only from the knowledge of Jesus Christ, root-paradigm, under the direction of the Holy Spirit (the topic of the next chapter).   It is "basically impossible" for us to perceive our "aberration" as "destruction" of our peace with God, neighbors, and ourselves (IV/2: 380). Genuine knowledge of sin can be acquired by genuine knowledge of God through the revelation of and faith in the existence of the royal man Jesus. In His humanity, the human situation has been altered to a new humanity from a prior state.[20] Barth said,

> the life of a new man lived by Jesus is preceded by the dying of an old man suffered by Him, the rising of the true man in His existence and death by the destruction of a false and perverted, His being as the royal man by the accepted and conquered being of the enslaved, His life in the spirit by the vegetating and passing flesh in which He willed to be like us, to be one of us. God has had mercy on the man who even in the form of that old, perverted man, even as that slave, even as flesh, is still the good creature which He elects and loves. (IV/2: 384)

Interestingly, Barth connected this realization of sin to shaming. God has received us "so basically and radically" that God was ready to make Himself our Brother in His own Son, to share our situation, and to bear our shame (IV/2: 384). The humanity of Christ elicits our serious, radical, and total shaming, the disclosure of actual shame in our life-act like the shaming of Peter (IV/2: 387f.). In the light of royal humanity, corruption, failure, and the lost state of our humanity are exposed. No matter how holy and brilliant we are, we are in a situation of shamefulness. When confronted by royal humanity both in His abasement and exaltation, we cannot escape being shamed. Every attempt to escape being shamed only confirms our actual shame. Royal humanity exposes one's disqualification as a sinner. Since there is no "alibi" (IV/2: 396) for this, no one can be a Christian without being totally shamed by Him. Sin cannot be fully grasped by a systematic or metaphysical conception, but only through the knowledge of the cross, the ultimate shaming. Free grace encounters us with the shattering event of the cross, the "total disqualification" of any system in which we can find refuge (IV/2: 402). *Humanitas Christi* as the most concrete-universal of the free grace is the most radical humanity and thus the most affirmatively critical self-judgment of humanity.

The Sloth of Human Being

From the standpoint of *humanitas Christi*, sin is understood as "sloth", i.e., "sluggishness, indolence, slowness, or inertia." In the context of justification, sin is pride which is a "heroic, Promethean form of sin."[21] In the context of sanctification, sin has not merely an heroic form of pride, but also the "unheroic and trivial form" of sloth. Whereas sin as pride is the counter-movement to divine condescension, sin as sloth is "the counter-movement to the elevation" of real and royal humanity (IV/2: 403).

In spite of the divine direction for a definite action, sloth refuses and fails to follow the direction given to us and to "trust in the One who demonstrates and maintains His faithfulness" (IV/2: 405). Hence, sloth is sin in a form of disobedience, unbelief, and ingratitude. Sloth is crystallized in the rejection of the royal man Jesus. "As the rejection of the outstretched hand of God [and] the refusal of His grace" (IV/2: 408), sloth makes us neglect our own calling, be untrue to our own cause, and go out into the void. In sloth, hence, we become human beings "in contradiction" (IV/2: 409). Sloth as the self-confrontation distorts the fourfold relationship of the real human being: with God, fellow-human, the created order, and time. Although the self-contradiction in these four primordial ties is interrelated, each will be discussed individually.

(1) In relation to God, sin as sloth is folly and stupidity. Sloth is inaction, refusal to act in accordance with divine knowing. Folly has nothing to do with education or scholarship. Rather, in the biblical sense, it means refusal to be enlightened by the revelation of God. This is why Anselm of Canterbury did not describe folly "as *ignorans* but as *insipiens* (=*insapiens*)" (IV/2: 412). While folly propagates an autonomous life, stupidity is practical atheism which has no adequate safeguard. Nevertheless, Barth authenticated the relative value of human wisdom:

> And because even in his folly man is always the good creature of God it is inevitable that in all its forms . . . his own wisdom . . . should exhibit positively significant and impressive elements and aspects which enable it to commend itself both to him and to others. The wisdom of the world or of men is not, therefore, something which we must rate too low. In many cases it may have a very high value. It is never simply and unequivocally devilish. Within its limits, it is often worthy of the most serious respect. (IV/2: 417)

But, in reality, this worldly wisdom tends to "serve as a covering, to provide an alibi, for stupidity" (IV/2: 417). Folly sees the wisdom of God, the cross of Christ, as foolishness (1 Cor. 1:18). In and with the rejection of God, folly makes us lose the three other relationships: inhumanity (a rejection of our basic character as co-humanity), a disintegration of the whole person (a dualism between soul and body), and a perversion of the right timing (Eccl. 3). For God alone is the guarantee of all these relationships.

(2) In relation to fellow human beings, sloth results in inhumanity. We are inactive when we ought to move toward others. Nothing can oppose or alter the reality that in Jesus we all are "elected and created and determined for fellow-humanity, for neighbourly love, for brotherhood" (IV/2: 433). There is the ontological connection in Jesus among all people, and thus no person can "withdraw into a final isolation" or "sabotage this fellowship" (IV/2: 434). Nevertheless, we act sloth, the impossible against the gracious will of God in His incarnation. The genuine human life is a "life in fellowship" (IV/2: 435). Otherwise, it is lived in inhumanity. Inhumanity violates the other relationships with God, self, and time. First, inhumanity, as a violation of our bond with others, also endangers our bond with God. Barth said, "True Christianity cannot be a private Christianity" (IV/2: 442).[22] A person who wills and chooses inhumanity is not dealing with the Christian faith, but with the faith of pure illusions and myths.

> Without one's fellow-man, God is an illusion, a myth. He may be the God of Holy Scripture, and we may call upon Him as the Yahweh of Israel and the Father of Jesus Christ, but He is an idol in whom we certainly cannot believe" (IV/2: 443).

Further, inhumanity leads to "a collapse of the structure and order of his human nature," because "I cannot and will not be an I without a Thou" (IV/2: 443). Furthermore, inhumanity extends to human life as "limited temporal duration" (IV/2: 444). Time is really ours only when it is shared with others and when we live, experience, and actualize, and suffer together with others. Our history consists in our co-operation not only with our contemporaries, but also with generations of the past (the dead) and of the future (those yet to come).

(3) In relation to self, sin as sloth involves dissipation. The life of Jesus Christ is the "normalisation" of human nature. In this light of *humanitas Christi*, we confront the truth of our nature, the sanctity, dignity, right and glory of human life. Our human nature is normalized and even glorified once and for all in the royal man Jesus. If we receive His Spirit, we know that in the truth of His human nature we are elected, created, and determined for "an authentically human life" (IV/2: 452). However, sloth leads us to "a life of dissipation" that divides, confronts, and inverts the order of human nature in soul and

body. In other words, it makes us "unnatural." For our soul and body must be in their original unity and in their natural order in which the soul guides the body. Dissipation is a "declining to make use of the freedom" to be a whole person and a "contracting out of the purifying and sanctifying and reforming movement" directed by Jesus (IV/2: 453). Hence, sloth, as dissipation, is a form of "indiscipline" (IV/2: 454). To live as an authentic person is to keep oneself disciplined. Disintegrating the three other relations, dissipation lead us to fall into a vicious circle of unbelief, inhumanity, and anxiety.

(4) In relation to time, sin as sloth involves futile human anxiety. Evil originates from our unwillingness to accept the limitations of our existence. We struggle against nature and destiny. However, the limited duration of our existence is the good order of God, the gracious, merciful, and invincible Creator. Hence, our excessive anxiety is an "empty and futile" self-contradiction of the good order of God. Anxiety fears the "frontier, which is the good order of God" (IV/2: 469). It acquires historical forms such as exploitative activity (Westerners) and contemplative passivity (Easterners [see IV/2: 473f.]). Sloth as anxiety or care also breaks the three other relations: Anxiety results in the ignorance of God. It destroys genuine human fellowship, isolating us from our fellows, atomizing human society. And it jeopardizes our being and becoming whole persons, disintegrating the unity of human being as the soul of one's body.

The Misery of the Human Condition

The *humanitas Christi*, manifested in the royal freedom of Jesus, is the paradigm of true human existence, as the exalted and sanctified person. In this light, our false and inauthentic existence is uncovered as status of *corruptionis*. Barth called this state "the misery" of humanity. As slothful beings or sinners, we fall into the exiled state of stupidity, inhumanity, dissipation, and anxiety. Nevertheless, even in this status we are not "outside the sphere of influence of divine grace" (IV/2: 484). For God does not cease to be the God who is the Creator and our Covenant-partner. Despite all our slothful actions and the miserable condition, we do not cease to be God's creatures and covenant-partners. However, as perverters of our human creaturliness and covenant-breakers, we "must suffer the grace of God as His disfavour and wrath and judgment" (IV/2: 485). Our misery consists in our "ill-founded insufficiency," "inexcusable shame," and "self-contradiction which cannot be smoothed over." The *humanitas Christi* illuminates this exiled state of misery in three forms: (1) the boundlessness of misery, (2) the misery of the old being, and (3) the bondage of the will.

(1) Since the liberation of humanity from misery can be achieved only by the crucifixion of Jesus, misery is seen as "boundless" (Luther). It is the state of exile (*Elend*). However, it is not that of "destruction," but the state of "perversion" (IV/2: 488). Even in this misery we are "not half a man, but a whole man." Although being still the good creatures of God, We are "wholly and utterly caught up in this history" of corruption and perversion.[23] Hence, it is "futile" to discuss that a "relic of goodness" is in the faculty of reason or that the religious or moral a priori remains in humanity yet as a sinner. The goodness which remains in human nature as a sinner is "not merely a 'relic' but the totality of His God-given nature and its determination" (IV/2: 489). In the same totality, our total beings exist in the history of the perversion, being caught up in the miserable movement from above to below. The New Testament expresses this perversion in the term of "flesh" which denotes "his being in the history of the division of his ego, his self-alienation and self-contradiction."

(2) Jesus brings in our new humanity, and shows the misery of the old being. Liberated from misery, we become "a new man as the subject of new and different acts which are obedient and well-pleasing to God" (IV/2: 490). However, old humanity has "a life of its own in which it continually confirms and renews itself in an endless circle." The original sin (*peccatum originale*) in the old being gives rise to actual sins (*peccata actualia*). We are not only sinners, but also commit sin. Apart from our new beginning and new birth in Jesus Christ as the subject of new and different acts, we cannot end the vicious circle of misery. Barth rejected the distinctions between mortal and venial sins and between voluntary and involuntary sins, because he views every sin as mortal, regardless of how small it is. In this respect, Christians cannot boast of themselves as being superior to the un-regenerate.

(3) Since Jesus Christ has liberated us from misery, misery constitutes the bondage of the will. His salvific action is "the act of free will, the decision of *liberum arbitrium*" (IV/2: 493). However, in our liberation by Him, we learn of "the determination of our will as *servum arbitrium*." This bondage of the will in sin can neither be "proved or disproved by empirical findings or *a priori* reflections," but comprehended only in Christ. However, the bondage of the will does

not involve a determinism, but "the perversion of the human situation which results from the sloth of man in his relationship with God." It does not mean that we are deprived of *arbitrium* so that we cannot will and act at all. If this were the case, we would no longer be human beings, but parts of "a mechanism moved from without." From this vantage point, freedom does not refer to an abstract choice to will and decide "like Hercules at the cross-roads" (IV/2: 494).

> Freedom is not an empty and formal concept. . . . It speaks concretely of the fact that man can be genuinely man as God who has given him this capacity can in His freedom be genuinely God. The free man is the man who can be genuinely man in fellowship with God. (IV/2: 494)

It is wrong to describe freedom as the possibility of sin (in the traditional distinction of *posse peccare* and *posse non peccare*) offered to us by God. Genuine freedom, i.e., freedom to be genuinely human, excludes this possibility of sinning. Rather, Barth expressed this true freedom in terms of *non potest peccare* (not being able to sin). We can sin only when we renounce this capacity and make no use of freedom. Sloth as stupidity, inhumanity, dissipation, and anxiety consists in our failure to make use of this true freedom. In fact, we are "turning" to an inactuality, "grasping" an impossibility, and "choosing" a "dreadful negation of this genuine choosing." As sinners, we have "decided against his freedom to be genuinely man." The sinful, slothful person is in a state of *non potest non peccare* (not capable not to sin). Sin excludes freedom, just as freedom excludes sin. "There is no middle position" between the two (IV/2: 495). The slothful person who takes the first alternative chooses a path toward the corruption of the person's will and ceases to be genuinely human: "This is the bondage of the human will which is the bitterest characteristic of human misery" (IV/2: 496).

However, this bondage has its limitation with respect to the liberation accomplished by *humanitas Christi*. This limitation is set by the sanctification of humanity, the topic of the next chapter. Jesus brings to us a new birth, conversion, freedom in a new creation. In Him, we are free from sinning and set for faith, obedience, and gratitude so that we can become genuinely free. Since we are constrained by the limitation of sin, we need sanctification. To this extent, we are not free, but in the bondage of the human will, in the old humanity. Even as Christians, we are still stupid, inhuman, dissipated, and discontented. We never seem to choose the right, but only the wrong. In us, freedom and bondage clash with each other: freedom as new humanity in Jesus and in the Holy Spirit conflicts with our bondage in the old humanity of the flesh. They are a totality, not a reconcilable dualism.[24] For there is,

> no *tertium*, no bridge, no mediation or synthesis between them, but only the antithesis of that conflict, life in sanctification, the *militia Christi*. No co-operation, then, between the two! For how can there be co-operation between total freedom and total bondage? How can the Spirit give assistance to the flesh, or the flesh to the Spirit? (IV/2: 497)

Then, in this condition of misery and conflict—in terms of Luther, the *simul justus et peccator* (simultaneously justified and sinful)--how can we be and become genuinely and radically human? The next chapter will deal with Barth's doctrine of sanctification to answer this question, a main issue of this book.

Chapter 7

•

Sanctification under
the Direction of the Holy Spirit

Barth articulated sanctification as the Christian response to the direction of the Son of Man, in the power of the Holy Spirit. The exaltation of *humanitas Christi* is the objective basis of sanctification. Although every person has *de jure* an ontological connection with Jesus, the ontological reality is *de facto* unrecognized. This necessitates the process of recognition of the Christ's event of universal redemption. Becoming and being a Christian, being radically human, is based on the power of transition from Jesus Christ (the Holy One) to us (the potential saints) that is the action of the Holy Spirit. Hence, sanctification constitutes a participation in the work of Christ, walking under the direction of the Holy Spirit. Under the sapiential direction (*Weisung*), Christians, being defined as disturbed sinners, involves the process of sanctification: discipleship, conversion, works, and the bearing of the cross.[1]

The Direction of the Son

Barth articulated the basic presupposition of sanctification in terms of "the direction [*Weisung*] of the Son" (IV/2: 265). The direction of divine power and authority was given to us by the One who is both the Son of the eternal Father and the Son of Man as real and royal humanity. The Christmas message (God with us) signifies that our "abstract and subjective and therefore corrupt humanity is corrected and rectified by His true humanity" (IV/2: 272). In this real, royal, and radical humanity, we are not only regenerated and converted but also already engaged in turning to God as Christians. Hence, our being in the Son involves both our justification and our sanctification.

The exaltation of Jesus as the Son of Man is the objective basis of our sanctification (see IV/2: 274-280). The history of the royal man Jesus (grace) includes the history of all humankind (thanksgiving).[2] This means "ontological connexion" between the being of the human Jesus and the human race (IV/2: 275). In the history of Jesus Christ which is both God's history and human history, God transforms history into the history for all humanity. The New Testament and the Heidelberg Catechism declare this ontological reality for all human beings.

> . . . It [the New Testament witness] was an ontological declaration about their own being under His sovereignty, as those who were righteous and holy before God in Him, as those who belonged to God's covenant which in Him was kept and fulfilled from the human side as well as the divine. . . . It belongs to the distinctive essence of the Jesus Christ of the New Testament that as the One He alone is He is not alone, but the royal Representative, the Lord and head of many. . . . It is this ontological connexion between the man Jesus on the one side and all other men on the other, and between active Christians on the one side and merely virtual and prospective on the other, which is the basis of the fact that in the New Testament the gathering and upbuilding of the community, of those who know Him, is depicted as a necessity grounded in himself, and that this community is sent out, again with a necessity grounded in Himself, and entrusted with the task of mission in the world. . . . This ontological connexion is the legal basis of the *kerygma* which forms the community and with which the community is charged. And this ontological connexion is also the basis of the fact that the *kerygma* does not indicate possibilities but declares actualities. (IV/2: 275)

Christians' hope rests on "an immutable foundation" (Heb. 6:17-20) of this ontological connection with Jesus. The Johannine writings express the ontological connection in terms of the mutual "abiding" (*menain*) of Jesus and disciples, i.e., the disciples in Jesus and Jesus in them (John 15:4f.). This abiding presupposes obviously "a being: not just an experience that we have, nor a disposition, not an attitude of the will or emotions, nor a possibility that is available but has still to be realised; but our truest reality, in which we are to see and understand ourselves in truth" (IV/2: 276). This abiding is also in accordance with

Paul's ontological confession; "it is no longer I who live, but it is Christ who lives in me" (Gal 2:20). This 'in Christ' is the a priori of all Pauline instructions: "To be a Christian is *per definitionem* to be *én Christo*" (IV/2: 277). Paul eloquently described the "impregnability" of the ontological connection in Christ between God and human beings in Rom. 8:37ff (IV/2: 280). This ontological connection of humanity with Jesus Christ is universal.[3] In Christ, humanity as a whole has been affected by this ontological relationship with God as His covenant-partner (IV/2: 282).

However, our being in Jesus Christ is *de facto* concealed, and we actually demonstrate ourselves against this ontological reality. This concealment is not merely because of human errors, defects, and sin. Nor is the concealment "a metaphysical mishap" (IV/2: 289). Again, this points to royal humanity under the sign of the cross: "Everything moved towards this cross" (IV/2: 290). His cross was both the most concrete-universal enactment of divine-human reconciliation and His coronation as the royal man. The cross as "the dominating characteristic of His royal office" (IV/2: 292) fulfills the secret of incarnation, the abasement, self-humiliation, and condescension. Jesus genuinely took on Himself our situation and radically altered and transformed it at the cross. His determination for death on the cross is not merely for "the controlling sign" or "the dominating fact," but has "the character of an act of God" (IV/2: 294). All human and creaturely (cosmic) life "moves towards death to take its full form in death" (IV/2: 295). The crucified is also the Victor resurrected from death. In the final analysis, the concealment rests on the mystery of His cross. The cross has a critical character, but it is "positively critical, not negatively" (IV/2: 296).

We need to recognize the ontological dignity of our being in Christ as a corresponding determination of being a Christian (IV/2: 297). This reality of ontological connection is power: "this reality and its truth—the being of Jesus Christ, and our being in Him, in the concealment of His crucifixion—are power. They are not just static power, but active; not just latent, but manifest." (IV/2: 298) Jesus declares Himself as the royal man in the "distinctive sovereignty as a human person" and in the "divine proximity of His attitudes and decisions" so that He actualized the kingdom of God on earth and interceded for us in His death. The New Testament tells us that His resurrection is not merely "the *datum*," but "the event" (IV/2: 299). In the event that the crucified is also risen, the power of transition appeared to us (IV/2: 302). What is imparted to us is the power of conversion to become and be Christians.

It is also the freedom of conversion "to see and understand and recognise, the freedom of love, the freedom to be Christians" (IV/2: 306). This is the power of Christ's self-disclosure in His resurrection for our new and exalted humanity. It is the power of beginning and ever-refreshing conclusion. It is "the power of the inconceivably transcendent transition from what is true and actual in Jesus Christ to what is true for us, or even more simply from Christ to us as Christians." Remember that we already have acquired all the necessary conditions in Jesus Christ: "In Jesus Christ a Christian has already come into being, but in himself and his time he is always in the process of becoming" (IV/2: 307). This process of becoming a Christian involves a "leap," a discontinuous human response to irresistible grace, i.e., repentance.

This transitional power from Christ to Christians has the characteristics of light, liberation, knowledge, peace, and life. (1) The transitional power has the character of light, "shining from the darkness of His crucifixion, of the exalted and new and true man who is now seated at the right hand of God" (IV/2: 310). It brings out "the definite illumination" as the *mysterium tremendum et suprendum* as well as *numinous in person* (IV/2: 311). (2) It is "the power of our liberation accomplished already in the freedom of Jesus Christ: our liberation from the compulsion of continuing in our disobedience . . . and our liberation for a life" (IV/2: 311f.). (3) It has the character of knowledge in the correspondence to the irresistible self-disclosure of the divine knowledge. Therefore, it has "a rational character" (IV/2: 312).

> The power of the transition is the power of this particular divine seeing and thinking and speaking. . . . It is a receiving in which the divine seeing and thinking and speaking in Jesus Christ finds its response in a human, Christian seeing and understanding and knowing, in an awakening and enlightenment of the reason. . . . Where it is at work, it always means light for the mind too, . . . The man in whom it is at work becomes a scholar. He begins to learn and think. He acquires a conscience, i.e., he becomes a *consciens*, one who knows with God. He will not be silent, or stammer or babble, but speak. He will speak in new and foreign tongues, but he will really speak. His faith will not be "introverted" but "extroverted." He is ordained to speak what he knows, to be a witness. When the apostles had to do with this power, its work found expression as a *fides explicita*. They were not incited

and summoned either to an enthusiasm or a sacred silence, but to *theology*. It was for this that they were equipped. This power may be very great and wonderful, but it has a clear and unmistakable affinity with sound reason. It puts this in its right limits. (IV/2: 313)

(4) The power of transition has the character of peace. It originated from God's will for the reconciliation and thus peace with the world, which was fulfilled on the cross. This peace which finally means salvation manifests itself in the resurrection of Jesus Christ from the dead. It is the power "to spread on earth the peace which is resolved in heaven" (IV/2: 314). It is "the peacemaking power of the resurrection of Jesus Christ" (IV/2: 315) which removes the "antitheses" in the actual human condition between God and humanity, between a person and one's fellow human being, and between a person and oneself.

(5) Finally, the transitional power has the character of life. The power establishes "genuine human life, i.e, a true life which is lived in harmony with the will of God and therefore unspotted, inviolable, incorruptible and indestructible" (IV/2: 315f.). The power produces "seeds" of "eternal life." Freeing us "from self-centered greed and anxiety," it directs us to the "determination to be life with God" and "aims at an enlightened, liberated and understanding life which is at peace in all dimensions." This power of the resurrection "snatches" us "upwards" (IV/2: 316). However, the snatch does not merely refer to a dubious, abstract, spiritual life of pure inwardness, but a human life in its totality including its material, outward life. The power sows "a seed which is not only psychical but physical, and give[s] nourishment which is not only spiritual but material—a whole preservation of the whole man" and a "total life-exaltation" (IV/2: 317). To be a bearer of this seed of life is to live a life that, while yet fleeting and transitory assailed by the shadow of death and discontinuity, is incorruptible and indestructible in virtue of promise and unity.

Becoming and being a Christian is possible by the operation of this sovereign power of transition from Jesus Christ to us. The transitional power works to deliver and establish our being in a new determination, through our election in Him, His humiliation as the Son of God for our justification, and His exaltation as the Son of Man for our sanctification. It does not work "to destroy our earthliness, but to give to it a new determination" (IV/2: 318f.). It distinctively operates with reference to a human being: "not to an ideal man or super-man; but to man as he is there in his earthliness before God and his fellows and himself." The

Christian does not mean "a second Christ, but a man like others" (IV/2: 319). The only difference is that the person participates in the exaltation of humanity as it has taken place in the humanity of Christ, in spite of His limited, assailed, and oppressed existence. In short, being Christian means "being radically human."[4]

The Direction of the Holy Spirit

The New Testament witnesses the operation of this transitional power as the outgoing, receiving, presence, and action of the Holy Spirit. The Holy Spirit creates, commissions, controls, and empowers us not only to be and become Christians, but also to gather, upbuild, and go out as a Christian community. Hence, an individual Christian and a Christian community are by definition "pneumatic" (IV/2: 321). In the power of the Spirit, the royal man went to His death and was raised again from the dead. The power of the Spirit is the power of this revelation of Jesus Christ. The Holy Spirit is the Spirit of the Son "whom the Father has sent forth into our hearts" (IV/2: 323). The outpouring of the Spirit as the proceeding from the Son manifests Himself as the Holy Spirit of God. The Spirit establishes and fashions the form of Christian life as the gift of a beginning of new hope. The Spirit not only differentiates Christians from non-Christians, but also unites Christians with non-Christians. The Holy Spirit authenticates and sanctifies Christians as really and radically Christian and human beings as really and radically human.

According to Barth, there are three decisive factors in this history of transition: the royal man Jesus as the basic and controlling factor, the community as the goal of this history, and the one which links Jesus and the community as the power of the transition. In these three moments, we find God's own presence and action. None of us belongs to God, but now we discover ourselves in God, "really ourselves, not *a priori* but *a posteriori*" (IV/2: 338). To know God in this history is to know ourselves in God, and vice versa (Rom. 11:36). This history directs us to the Holy Trinity, in whom the outpouring of the Holy Spirit makes this transition and recognition possible. God, present and active in this history, is the triune God. The three factors of history coincide with three modes of being of God as a reflection of a *vestigium trinitatis*. The third and middle factor unequivocally relates to the divine power of the transition from Christ to Christian communities, in the mode of being of God as the Holy Spirit. It is not only the divine power mediating between Christ and His community, but also a mode of the divine being which unites the Father and the Son. Barth stated explicitly that the Holy Spirit is "the true theme of this section [the Direction of the Son]" (IV/2: 339).[5]

There is the problem of distinction and confrontation in the history between the royal man Jesus and us. The Holy Spirit is not a magical third party mediating this problem between Jesus and us, but God Himself who acts in His own most proper cause. What the Holy Spirit makes between Jesus and us is the transition in that distinction, the mediation in that confrontation, the communication in that encounter, and the history in that partnership (of the Father and the Son). "God is twice one and the same, in two modes of being, as the Father and the Son, with a distinction which is not just separation but positively a supreme and most inward connexion." The Father and the Son are "with one another in a love which is divine love the one does not merge into the other nor can the one or the other be alone or turn against the other" (IV/2: 344).

Barth called this relationship "history in partnership," but not "the history of an isolated individual." For "God was never solitary. . . . [but] always a Partner." God's partnership does not mean "merely a first and static thing which is then succeeded by the history as a second and dynamic" (IV/2: 344), but the occurrence of history which means "the eternal rise and renewal of the partnership" (IV/2: 345). In dealing with this history of the eternal partnership, Barth made an intriguing statement "There [in this history] is no rigid or static being which is not also act" (IV/2: 345). The Holy Spirit, in the third moment of the triune life, concretizes this history in partnership, that is the transition in the distinction, the mediation in the confrontation, and the communication in the encounter. The history between the Father and the Son culminates in the concrete history of the Holy Spirit. God is self-sufficient and self-transcendent as the Holy Trinity.

> [The Trinity] does not lack in Himself either difference or unity in difference, either movement or stillness, either antitheses or peace. In the triune God there is no stillness in which He desires and must seek movement, or movement in which He desires and must seek stillness. (IV/2: 346)

The Holy Spirit is "the basis of the riddle" of the existence of Jesus Christ, an antithesis in the humiliation of the Exalted and the exaltation of the Humiliated (IV/2: 348). The antithesis in the humiliation of the Son of God manifests a transcendent differentiation in God's one, but twofold mode of will, action, and being. The Holy Spirit, as the Spirit of Jesus Christ, witnesses the power of the crucifixion of the Son of God and the resurrection of the Son of Man. The riddle in His exaltation of the Son of Man rests on the same divine act of the Father and the Son. His existence as the royal man has not only the humiliation and concealment but also the exaltation and revelation. Accordingly, in addition to a theology of the cross, we need a theology of glory of the new humanity actualized in Jesus Christ who triumphs as the Crucified (IV/2: 355). The antithesis is not merely a paradox; rather it is based on the *doxa* (glory) of God in the trinitarian life of God. The Holy Spirit not only kindles Christian faith and confession (theology of the cross), but also summons the Christian community to joy and thankfulness (theology of glory).

The *telos* of the riddle of Jesus' antithesis is Christian freedom in the power of the Holy Spirit:

> the freedom with which the Christian community believes in Jesus Christ triumphant in His crucifixion, in the life of the Son of Man which is not destroyed but maintained in His real death, in the grounding of the life of all men in the dying of this One, in the fulfilment of their election in the fulfilment of His rejection, in their glory in His shame, their peace in His chastisement; the freedom with which it may therefore confess that Jesus is Victor, believing that we also are victorious in Him (IV/2: 356).

The Holy Spirit stimulates and empowers the Christian and the community to the second step in this freedom, which is the goal of the first. In fact, the riddle of the existence of Jesus Christ is "the dynamic and teleology of the divine life." In the first step (before Jürgen Moltmann),[6] Barth affirmed the actual suffering of God even though the suffering is not His own: "No, there is a *particula veri* in the teaching of the early Patripassians. This is that primarily it is God the Father who suffers in the offering and sending of His Son, in His abasement." (IV/2: 357) In the second step, the glory of God lights up the riddle of the existence of Jesus Christ. The puzzling existence of Jesus Christ attests neither paradox, nor juxtaposition of a divine No and Yes: "It attests a No which is spoken for the sake of the ensuing Yes" (IV/2:

359). In that greater context, the Holy Spirit is the power that authenticates the transition from Jesus to us and our participation in the exaltation of the Son of God, i.e., our becoming and being radically human.

Then, how does the Spirit work? What does it mean to "receive" or "have" the Spirit? What does it mean to "be" and to "walk" in the Spirit? According to Barth, the Holy Spirit gives a concrete direction (*die Weisung*). The person in the direction of the Holy Spirit should be a wise person who should think, will, and act with exemplary wisdom. Here Barth played with the German word *Weisung* (direction) which has the same root as the German words *Weisheit* (wisdom) and *weise* (wise and *way*) (See IV/2: 362). Therefore, the *Weisung* designates precisely the Way in wisdom. The *Weisung* of the Holy Spirit is "not one possibility among many, nor is it merely the norm, but it is the only reality" (IV/2: 362). Barth understood that the direction (*Weisung*) refers to a sapiential (*Weisheit*) and definite ("a way without crossroad") Way (*Weise*) of life. The Holy Spirit as the Spirit of the Son of God does not give us a gloriously ideal example or a loftily abstract teaching, but a real and dynamic direction for our being and action as testified in the Book of Proverbs. To receive and have the Holy Spirit is not to romanticize a being, but to receive and have His direction as the *Way*. To be or walk in the Spirit is to be under His direction; we may call this the Christian Way. What distinguishes the work of the Holy Spirit from other spiritual experiences is that it gives a concrete direction which proceeds from the man Jesus. According to Barth, the *Weisung* of the Holy Spirit indicates, corrects, and instructs.

First of all, the *Weisung* of the Holy Spirit is indication. It points us to a definite place of departure that is our real freedom. The Holy Spirit does not operate with open options, but situates us to a fixed place. In the same manner as the Way, the Spirit does not "make us an offer or give us a chance:" "The Holy Spirit does not create the ghost of a man standing in decision, but the reality of the man concerning whom decision has already been made in the existence of the man Jesus." We are to become what we are to be in Jesus. The basic indicative of the divine *Weisung* becomes an imperative to "Be what thou art" (IV/2: 363). The *Weisung* of the Holy Spirit is to bring "man back to his own beginning from which he lives and alone can live" (IV/2: 365). In short, the *Weisung* of the Holy Spirit indicates the Christian *Tao* of what it means to be human.

Secondly, the *Weisung* of the Holy Spirit is warning and correction. In contrast to our inclination toward unfreedom in the shadow, the Holy Spirit awakens us to the reality of our existence in freedom. The Holy Spirit "champions freedom against unfreedom, obedience against disobedience, our life against our death, the one possible thing against the many impossible" (IV/2: 368). The Spirit makes us grasp real freedom, select what we ought to select, and recognize the transition from Jesus to us. In terms of Bonhoeffer, Barth affirmed that this recognition and acknowledgment is by no means "a painless operation—cheap grace" (IV/2: 369). The *Weisung* is "a categorical indication" which has a corrective and radically critical character (IV/2: 370).

Finally, the *Weisung* of the Holy Spirit is instruction. Theological ethics are inclined to suggest that our discernment of the will and the command of God occurs among many possibilities. However, the Holy Spirit, who is "rather more than a professor of theological ethics," instructs the only good possibility for us here and now and assigns a concrete point for us to begin in freedom. The instruction of the Holy Spirit cannot be understood as a general law or a written code, but it demands "the most concrete obedience" (IV/2: 372). The Spirit gives definite instruction, always in a concrete context. The *Weisung* of the Holy Spirit entails a concrete-universal approach. "And in spite of the fact that He speaks so specifically and concretely, He speaks to them in common, thus creating brotherhood" (IV/2: 373). The instruction of the Holy Spirit does not "put the Christian at a point or in a position. He sets him on the way, on the march. And it is a forced march, in a movement which never ceases and in which there can be no halting." (IV/2: 376). The Spirit commands us to march in true freedom, and calls us to gather, mobilize, and concentrate our whole person in sanctification, which is not a deification but a humble subjection to God. The grace of God is *sufficient* for us. We are no longer our own but belong to Jesus Christ, the royal humanity. Since the instruction is not from us but from the Holy Spirit, it leads us to all the glory of the Father and the incarnate Son which is "powerful, effective, fruitful and victorious" (IV/2: 377). In short, the *Weisung* of the Holy Spirit indicates, corrects, and instructs us in the Christian Way of how to be really, radically, or fully human.

The Holy One and the Saints

Sanctification is based on the mutuality between the Holy One and the saints (IV/2, 66.2). Sanctification is a "transformation" or a "new determination" which has taken place *"de jure"* for the world and for all the human race (IV/2: 511). However, it is *"de facto"* grasped, acknowledged, and confessed only by those awakened to faith. The Holy One is the active Subject of sanctification and constitutes the saints in this action. "Our sanctification consists in our participation in His sanctification as grounded in the efficacy and revelation of the grace of Jesus Christ" (IV/2: 517). However, even before our *participatio Christi*, our sanctity is already achieved in the sanctity of Jesus Christ. Sanctification does not mean "a private arrangement" for a particular group of people, but for all people (IV/2: 518). For God's gracious action for our sanctification is concrete-universal:

> In their sanctification He attests that He is the Lord of all men. In all its particularity, their sanctification speaks of the universal action of God, which has as its purpose and goal the reconciliation of the world, and therefore not merely of this group of individuals in the world. . . . the great decision of God which in Jesus Christ has been made not only concerning them but concerning all the men of every time and place. (IV/2: 518f.)

Sanctification does not imply "the pride of religious self-seeking and self-sufficiency," but rather is set in "the larger sphere of the creation of God." It involves "a solidarity even with secular things with which it is contrasted." In the particular humanity of Jesus as the Son of God, He as the Son of Man has ordained the exaltation of every person. Sanctification refers to "the new impression of humanity" (IV/2: 519) in "all-embracing character" (IV/2: 520) for all children of the world. Here is a weakness of Calvin's doctrine of the *participatio Christi*. The doctrine diminishes the fact that the sanctification which comes *de facto* to the saints by their participation in Jesus Christ has already come *de jure* on all persons in Jesus Christ, not only on Christian saints but also on every other person. Barth underscored that universal sanctification has been ontologically established in Jesus Christ.

This ontological establishment is concretely realized through the *Weisung* of the Holy One (IV/2: 523). The *Weisung* signifies "the sowing and the developing seed of new life," as "it becomes their wisdom." The direction as "the power of His Word spoken with divine authority" has "illuminating fruitfulness and power." We must *hear* "effectively" the *Weisung* as "a call to obedience."

Barth called Christians "disturbed sinners" who are still sinners but disturbed by the direction of the Holy Spirit (IV/2: 524). First, this disturbance is "critical." Sinners are disturbed by the divine No to the sinful will and action of all persons. Second, the disturbance is "the limit." Since our sinful beings are limited by the power of the direction of the Holy Spirit, we are given freedom against human bondage. The direction is "not a possibility but the new actuality" of our real "freedom" and the "capacity" of our liberation (IV/2: 531).

Hence, we are "set in sovereign antithesis" to our being as sinners who are "radically assailed, but not destroyed." The freedom of the saints is not grounded on the power of our reception, but on the power of the Giver of this gift. We are free, and we can make use of this freedom, because we have been made free in Christ (Gal 5:1). This freedom under the direction of the Holy Spirit entails (a) the call to discipleship, (b) awakening to conversion, (c) praise of works, and (d) the dignity of the cross.

The Call to Discipleship

The call issued by Jesus is a call to discipleship expressed in the phrase "Follow me." The New Testament never uses the term "discipleship" in its noun form but only as a verb. This warns us that discipleship is not to be understood as "a general concept" (IV/2: 534). The call to discipleship is characterized in four ways. First, the call to discipleship means the grace of God which commands us to follow the particular form of Jesus' summons. The disobedience of this command results in the terrifying impossibility (e.g., the parable of the rich young ruler [Mk. 10:17f.]).

Second, the call to discipleship "binds" us to the One who calls us. Jesus can not be enclosed in systematic ideas such as Christology, a "christo-centric system," or a "supposedly Christian conception of a Father-God." Nor is discipleship a "recognition and adoption" of a programme, ideal, or law, or an "execution of a plan of individual or social construction imparted and commended by Jesus." Discipleship is not "something general," but a "concretely filled-out happening" between Jesus and a particular person (IV/2: 536).

Third, the call to discipleship is a summons to take "a definite first step" in faith, i.e., self-denial. The term in the New Testament does not denote "a simple denial," but "the renunciation, withdrawal and annulment of an existing relationship of obedience and loyalty." Nor does self-denial mean "merely a new and critical and negative mind and attitude" in relation to oneself; but rather "involves a step into the open, into the freedom of a definite decision and act, in which it is with a real commitment . . . having no option but to decide and act in accordance with it—cost what it may" (IV/2: 339f.). Zwingli proclaimed this in his famous statement, "For God's sake do something brave" (IV/2: 538).

Dietrich Bonhoeffer called this "simple obedience." Barth said,

> Obedience is simple when we do just what we are told—nothing more, nothing less, and nothing different. In simple obedience we *do* it, and therefore we do not finally not do it. But what we do is literally and exactly that which we are commanded to do. The only possible obedience to Jesus' call to discipleship is simple obedience in these two senses. This alone is rendered in self-denial. This alone is the brave act of faith in Jesus. (IV/2: 540).

The commanding grace of God is "quite unambiguous." The command of Jesus creates the situation in which we have to obey so that there is no need for any further waiting, consideration, or "appraisal or selection of different possibilities, but only for instant obedience." In this obedience, "we are not about to leap," because "we are already leaping." Discipleship does not demand legalistic, or arbitrarily discursive, or dialectical obedience, but it "makes history" (IV/2: 542).

Fourth, the call to discipleship makes a break with mammon. This call reveals the kingdom of God, i.e., "the *coup d'état* of God" (IV/2: 543). The break is "not a matter of our own revolt, either as individuals or in company with those likeminded," but is "a matter of the kingdom of God and God's revolution." To make this break become history, Jesus calls His disciples. Hence, discipleship is not merely a matter of saving one's own soul in the attainment of a private beatitude. On the contrary, we lose our souls and jeopardize our eternal salvations, unless we accept "the public responsibility" of discipleship. In this respect, the true meaning of the *militia Christi* is self-criticism (IV/2: 545):[7]

The *militia Christi* will arise of itself, although there can, of course, be no question of Christian contentiousness against non-Christians, let alone of violence, crusades and the like. And even the *militia Christi* will not really consist in conflict against others, but decisively in conflict against oneself, and in the fact that one is assailed, and in some way has to suffer, and to accept suffering, at the hands of others. (IV/2: 546).

Christian discipleship involves a renouncement of any "general attachment to the authority, validity and confidence of possessions, not merely inwardly but outwardly" (IV/2: 548), including honors or fame among people. The incursion of the kingdom of God concretely attests "the end of the fixed idea of the necessity and beneficial value of force" (IV/2: 549). It "destroys the whole friend-foe relationship," and "abolishes the whole exercise of force." (Hence, "we cannot be pacifists in principle, only in practice.") It dissolves "self-evident attachments" between human beings, namely, family. However, this does not mean a rejection of authentic relationships such as husband and wife, parents and children, brothers and sisters. But the danger is the "impulsive intensity," "self-sufficiency," or "imprisonment" in those relationships. We must be liberated from "this captivity to clan" (IV/2: 550). Finally, we must not confirm "the absolute *nomos* of religion." Concerning the piety of Judaism, Jesus demands his disciples to exercise it in "a new way" and to show a "better righteousness" (IV/2: 551). The call demands His disciples to take up their crosses, making a break with the "self-evident factors" of the world so as to attest to "the irruption of the kingdom of God" (IV/2: 551f.). Hence, Christian discipleship is not "cheap grace," but demands an "even more costly" way (IV/2: 553).

Awakening to Conversion

Our sanctification in the fellowship with Jesus, in the power of His call, and in the freedom given by the power of the Holy Spirit makes us look to Him and "lift up ourselves in spite of the downward drag of our slothful nature" (IV/2: 553). This lifting-up really happens to "those who waken up" (IV/2: 554). The awakening does not exclude, but includes human action, "the total and most intensive conscription and co-operation of all his inner and outer forces" (IV/2: 556). That is conversion, our awakening and rising from the dead.

Biblically, conversion means the "turning round and going in the opposite direction." Conversion is not an "improvement but alteration," nor "a reformed or ennobled life, but a new one." It means alteration and renewal like "turning on an axis" (IV/2: 560). Whereas the life of the old humanity involves movement "straight ahead" to death, the life of the converted, new humanity, implies an axis on which to turn in the opposite direction. The twofold reality, that God is for us and that we are for God, sets us in our *conversio* which is as such our *renovatio*. Barth returned to Calvin's statement "*Nostri non sumus, sed Domini* [We are not our own masters, but belong to God]" (*Institutes*, III,7,1). In this way, as in God's Yes to us and our Yes to God, we no longer belong to ourselves, but now belong to God as our Lord.

Conversion as renewal means regeneration and new birth. Human nature, in the act of conversion, is no longer the old nature, nor even a corrected and revised edition, but a new human nature. Conversion involves a movement of the whole human being. "There are in his being no neutral zones which are unaffected by it and in which he can be another than the new man involved in this process." Conversion does not include merely our relationship with God, but also our relationship with others. Barth again emphasized the definition of humanity as co-humanity, "he is not a man without his fellow-men" (IV/2: 563). For that reason, the prophets in the Old Testament challenged the practical, cultic, economic, and political conduct of Israel. Accordingly, conversion and renewal demand a radical alteration of social relationships. At the same time, conversion involves not only a collective renewing movement and activity, but also an individual person's heart, thinking, will, and disposition. Conversion implies neither only in a purely inner, religious sphere, nor exclusively in a purely cultic, moral, political, ecclesiastical sphere. A conversion is not a real conversion unless it embraces the whole human being. Conversion is not purely a private matter, but also a public matter. Our conversion is not "a far too egocentric Christianity." "The biblical individual is not selfishly wrapped up in his own concerns" (IV/2: 565). Hence, we must accept both private and public responsibility. In the Bible, the call for conversion is usually addressed to "a plurality of people" such as the people of Israel. Our conversion to God adds us as saints to the *communio sanctorum*. Furthermore, conversion is not merely a matter for one period in our lives, but an ongoing matter for our whole lives: "But sanctification in conversion is not the affair of these individual moments; it is the affair of the totality of the whole life-movement of man" (IV/2: 566).

However, as a new humanity by the direction of the powerful summons, we are still in our old nature. In other words, we are already the new people, but we are still the old.[8] Luther described this condition in terms of *simul (totus) justus, simul (totus) peccator*. The *simul* entails the coincidence of the 'still' and the 'already.' However, the *simul* does not signify a balancing or a co-ordination of two similar factors, or a positioning of two moments which are simultaneously present. The "falling-out" is the best description of this situation. It refers to "the coincidence of the 'still' and the 'already,' of the old man and the new, [and] of the *homo peccator* and the *homo sanctus*" (IV/2: 573). It indicates that one's whole will, movement, and impulse is "to fall out or to fall apart."[9] We find ourselves engaged in conversion as a "quarrel." We have not only fallen out with ourselves in totality, but also have engaged in a dispute in which we must determine to become new humanity.

Hence, conversion necessarily involves "a convulsion" of freedom (IV/2: 578). Conversion is the free act of our obedience to God, corresponding to the decision of God for us. The grace of God commands our conversion as "a radical termination and a radical recommencement." It demands us to be "the being in transition from what we still are to what we are already" (IV/2: 580). Conversion is "the enlightening work of the Holy Spirit" which points to the dignity of the cross (IV/2: 582).

Praise of Works

Barth affirmed that our sanctification does require our works. "Work" has a twofold theological meaning: God affirms and praises works, and works also affirm and praise God. Therefore, Christians are obliged to do good works in this twofold sense. Otherwise, the whole event of reconciliation becomes "futile" (IV/2: 585). However, "good works" mean primarily that "it is God who is at work" (IV/2: 587). Biblically, the work of God, standing primarily in relation to the human race, "embraces all creation, heaven, and earth and all that therein is" (IV/2: 588).[10] The royal man Jesus shows that "human works are capable of doing this" (IV/2: 589). Not only can we, as sinners in sinful actions, declare the good work of God, but also can we, as sinners in the course of sinning, do good works. Declaring only His good works, without claiming them as our merit, we participate in God's works, as His co-workers.

The Dignity of the Cross

Finally, Barth emphasized that the cross marks both the limit and goal of our sanctification which involves our participation in Christ through discipleship, conversion, and works. "The cross is the most concrete form of fellowship between Christ and the Christian" (IV/2: 599). The cross is the crown of Christians. However, this does not mean that they still have to suffer God's rejection, because it has been suffered already by Him. We rest entirely on His cross in which He alone bore the rejection. However, even though our cross cannot be a reenactment of His, we correspond to it as "bearers of dignity" (IV/2: 600). We must not evade our cross, because our special fellowship with Christ involves our participation in the passion of His cross. Although there is a great dissimilarity, His cross and ours have a similarity in terms of dignity. "The sign of the cross is the sign of the provisional character of their Christian existence" (IV/2: 605). Our cross "intercrosses" our Christian life (IV/2: 606). For the cross makes us always humble and bold enough to accept punishment, and it is a powerful disciplinary force to offer a particular verification of our Christian existence by testing, purifying, and intensifying.

Hence, the cross involves specific forms of suffering. It is primarily "persecution" (IV/2: 609), consisting in our "particular share in the tension, transience, suffering and obscurity" (IV/2: 611). It involves temptation, because we still stand under the law of sin and are afflicted with the burden of flesh. However, the suffering is not to be desired or "self-sought." And the suffering is "not an end in itself," but the direction to sanctification. In the final analysis, the cross is not ultimate but penultimate and provisional. The ultimate goal of Christian hope is the eschatological coming of eternal life to which the cross of Christ directs us in the power of His resurrection. Hence, it is a joyful thing to bear our cross: "there cannot lack a foretaste of joy even in the intermediate time of waiting, in the time of sanctification, and therefore in the time of the cross" (IV/2: 613).

Chapter 8

•

Root-Metaphor: *Agape* (Love)

Finally, Barth delineated the effect of sanctification in the power of the Holy Spirit at corporate and individual levels. Collectively, the direction and quickening power of the Holy Spirit builds up, causes to grow, sustains, and orders the Christian community as the body ('the earthly-historical form') of Christ (IV/2, 67). Individually, when placing a sinful individual in the Christian community, the direction and quickening power of the Holy Spirit grants that person the freedom of self-giving to love God and fellows (i.e., Christian love), in correspondence to the self-giving love of God for the person and fellows (IV/2, 68). Christian love (*agape*) is the sum of the Christian law, i.e., the two great commandments of Jesus Christ: "You shall love the Lord your God with all your heart, and with all your soul, with all your mind, and with all your strength," and "You shall love your neighbor as yourself" (Mk. 12:30f.). Barth advocated Christian love (*agape*) as the Christian *Way*. Barth's treatment of Christian love can be regarded as a concluding summary of his doctrine of sanctification.[1]

The Problem of Christian Love

We meet Jesus Christ in receiving His great self-giving. Christian love (*agape*), corresponding to this love, is also an act of self-giving love: "It is the act of a pure and total giving, offering and surrender corresponding to this receiving." In saying this, we are immediately faced with the problem of how we can formulate the relationship between faith and love. Obviously, Christian love as giving "stands contrasted with faith as reception" (IV/2: 730). Justification and sanctification are one undivided, simultaneous divine action, though they constitute two separate and distinguishable moments of reconciliation. Analogously, the same relationship also occurs on the human side: Faith and love, as reception and surrender, are "two indivisible but distinguishable moments of the one vital movement and act which constitutes Christian existence" (IV/2: 731). The contrast between love and faith is "only relative," for we can hardly speak of love without faith, and faith without love (IV/2: 731ff.).

Barth highlighted the whole of 1 Cor. 13 "as an answer to the question of the Christian 'way' [*Weg*]." Paul reminded the Corinthian Christians of the "more costly way" of Christian faith (*agape*) which they "ought not to have forgotten as *the* way and *the* act" (IV/2: 732). Christian love as self-giving involves a particular relationship with others. It is a movement in which a person turns away from oneself and turns to the other "purely for the sake of the other" (IV/2: 733). The realization of this freedom of self-giving is precisely its problem.

Barth demarcated Christian love (*agape*) from self-love (*eros*). *Agape* is a self-giving form of love, while *eros* a possessive or self-seeking form. The self-love does not have "its origin in self-denial, but in a distinctively uncritical intensification and strengthening of natural self-assertion" (IV/2: 734). Self-seeking *eros* and self-giving *agape* are always in conflict. We must choose one of these two ways: "Where Christian love enters, there always begins at once the unceasing controversy between itself and every other love." The Christian life exists in "the history of the distinction between these opposing types of love" (IV/2: 736). Although both of them are decisively related to human nature, they are radically divergent. First of all, *agape* is "in correspondence" and "analogue" to human nature, whereas *eros* "in contradiction" and "catalogue:"

> *agape*-love takes place in correspondence and *eros*-love in contradiction to this [human] nature; the one as its "analogue" and the other as its "catalogue;" the one as man does that which is right in relation to it, and the other as he does that which is not right in relation to it. *Agape*-love takes place in affinity, *eros*-love in opposition, to human nature. . . . In this antithetical use and character, in which the one unchanging human nature takes on form but which differ as Yes and No, being related only in respect of their object, *eros* and *agape* go their divergent ways." (IV/2: 743)

Barth's further analysis on the divergence of *agape and eros* is related to his understanding of real human nature which we have examined (see Chap. 5); i.e., the whole person (human-to-self), the real human being (human-to-God), and humanity (human-to-human). Respectively, they refer to the inner dimension, to the "vertical" or transcendental dimension (IV/2: 743), and to the "horizontal" dimension of human nature (IV/2: 745). Barth claimed that *agape* is the way to be what human beings ought to be, i.e., "natural" (or "real") humanity. The real human nature is the demarcating norm between the true and wrong ways of love: *Agape* is the right way of correspondence to human nature, while *eros* is the wrong way of contradiction.[2]

From the vertical perspective, *agape* corresponds to the real human being in the proper human-to-God relationship, but *eros* contradicts it. Although God frees the nature and essence of human being, human beings cannot alter the fact that a person can be fully human in the right relationship with God. Hence, the decisive divergent factor is "in this decision that there arises the new thing either of his *agape*-love in which he corresponds to his being from and to God or of his *eros*-love in which he contradicts it" (IV/2: 743). The crucial difference is that *agape* "transcends" human nature, while *eros* "falls short of it" (IV/2: 744).

From the horizontal perspective, *agape* corresponds to the basic form of humanity as the joyful co-humanity or being-in-togetherness, but *eros* contradicts it. A person is genuinely human as he or she is free to be a comrade, companion, or fellow to the other. *Agape* respects the essence of humanity as co-humanity. A person who loves in this way cannot oppose or neglect the other fellow people. In one's *agape*-love, there takes place the genuine encounter of I and Thou. In this respect, *agape* means self-giving; a person's giving oneself to the others "with no expectation of a return" (IV/2: 745). In this self-giving love, a person transcends his or her humanity, which is the way to be genuinely human; "he gives a true expression to human nature; he is a real man."

Whereas *agape*-love is the way to be genuinely human, Barth said, *eros*-love is "a denial of humanity." In fact, the latter is "a new thing in face of human nature," i.e., "a contingent occurrence" (IV/2: 746). The basic difference between *agape* and *eros* is in their relationship with human nature; correspondence and contradiction, or affirmation and denial. But their difference lies ultimately in their relationship with the quickening power and direction of the Holy Spirit. In *agape*-love, by the quickening power of the Holy Spirit, one can actually love in one's life-act as "a true person in this positive way:" however, in *eros*-love, in "the new thing," one arbitrarily entangles oneself in a "contradiction" with one's own creaturely nature, oneself, one's neighbors, and God. Only in *agape* can one leave the vicious circle of this destruction of *eros*. Only in *agape*-love and through one's self-giving to both God and fellows, can one be and become genuinely oneself and be really human. In this right way, a person no longer desires and seeks the freedom and glory of the self, because one has already found oneself in real freedom and glory. One has already attained what one cannot acquire by desiring and seeking, not by one's power of renunciation, but by the power of self-giving in which one responds to the love of God. We *ourselves* are the one whom God loves. We *ourselves* are those to whom God has given Himself in His Son and in the Holy Spirit. Since we are already at the place, we are "cut off from *eros*-love, and taken out of that circle" (IV/2: 747). Hence, the self-giving, *agape*-love is the way to be genuinely, really, and radically human, overcoming and reconciling the problem of antithesis. "I have only to love continually as a Christian, and therefore without regard or purpose for myself, in self-giving to God and my fellows, and I will come to myself and be myself" (IV/2: 750). In short, *agape* is the Christian way of radical humanization.

The Foundation of Christian Love

Of course, for Barth, the foundation of Christian love is the Triune God, the object of Christian faith. In the act of the Christian life as the act of faith, we believe *in* the Christian life as that of love. We love *because* we are confronted and impelled by God's prior love; "love is from God" (I Jn 4:7). The foundation of our love is the love of God that irresistibly enlightens and impels us to follow His "primary" love with our "secondary love." This primary-secondary relationship is "irreversible" (IV/2: 753). In order to establish properly the basis of love, we must begin with "its primary and ultimate foundation, namely, in the being and nature of God Himself" (IV/2: 754). Similarly to the paradigm of Gospel and law, Barth established the doctrine of God as the context of the doctrine of Christian love. Barth affirmed love as the divine essence.[3]

At a deeper level, the triune mode of being is the ultimate foundation of love. The Christian God is "not an isolated monad which as such cannot love" (IV/2: 757). On the contrary, God reveals Himself to us as the One who loves in the threefold mode of being, the Father, the Son, and the Holy Spirit.[4] Hence, the question of the basis of love is "identical with the *opus Dei ad extra*" (IV/2: 759). Christian love is defined as the human act corresponding to this trinitarian dynamic of love. The love of God as "wholly an act" (IV/2: 761) has a trinitarian character; the self-giving love of *God* in Jesus Christ, the self-sacrificial love of *Jesus Christ*, and its revelation and operation in and towards us by the *Holy Spirit* (IV/2: 765).

Barth delineated three definitions of divine love as the foundation of Christian love: electing love, purifying love, and creative love. First, it is the "electing love," which is "merely another way of saying that it is the free act of God" (IV/2: 766). It is not necessary to the natural process, but only by virtue of the eternal freedom of the divine love and action (gracious election). In His *opus ad extra*, God loves the human race by electing, willing, and determining them as His creature and covenant-partner. His electing love is His own free decision of God. Second, the love of God is "purifying love" (IV/2: 771), in relation to the perversion and corruption of human nature, i.e., sin and human condition. It is "something very radical" (IV/2: 772). It does not imply "a divine state," but "an act" of God, saying "Yes" to us but "No" to our sin. The aim of God's love in total grace and total judgment is our purification. "God utters a Nevertheless, a merciful Therefore" (IV/2: 773). Third, God's love as the foundation of Christian love is "creative, i.e., a love which causes those who are loved by Him to love" (IV/2: 776). God creates a new and different person in whom love takes place as a human act. The love of God is this liberation of us for genuine love.

By this act of God we become a different person who is free to imitate His divine love in human fashion. Barth underscored the communal dimension of Christian love in correspondence to the action of Jesus Christ that "builds His community, calling men to Himself, gathering them in it, giving them a part in its faith and mission, sanctifying them, therefore treating them as His own, as members of His body." The love of God is "the creative basis of the liberation in which men become those who love; in which they become Christians and therefore those who love, those who love and therefore Christians" (IV/2: 779).

The Way of Christian Love

Although its foundation is exclusively the love of God in the trinitarian mode of being, Barth did not diminish the involvement of human action in Christian love. On the contrary, as he did in the formula of Gospel and law, he authenticated a more radical affirmation of human love in the context of concrete divine love. Hereafter, Barth focused on the active quality of Christian love from the human side. Human being does what a person has the freedom to do so from God; as the one who is loved by God, one loves. Barth presented four characteristics of this human act of love; newness, freedom, sacrifice, and joy. First, the act of love has the character of something new, unusual, and unexpected, because it realizes "the deepest and true being of man—his determination for God and for fellow-humanity" (IV/2: 785).

Secondly, the act of love is unequivocally "a free act," i.e., "a human response, correspondence, imitation, or analogy to the love of God" (IV/2: 786). Barth gave two delimitations, which clarifies the mis-understanding of some critics of Barth's anthropology:[5] (1) Christian love is not just an extension of God's love: Barth emphatically said that Christian love is,

> not a kind of prolongation of the divine love itself, its overflowing into human life which man with his activity has to serve as a kind of channel, being merely present and not at bottom an acting subject. It is not the work of the Holy Spirit to take from man his own proper activity, or to make it simply a function of His own overpowering control. Where He is present, there is no servitude but freedom. (IV/2: 785)

Barth said that many, even the best, Christians misunderstand this fact (e.g., A. Nygren). But the work of the Holy Spirit entails human liberation for one's own act and evokes spontaneously the human act of love. Indeed, Christian love is a human act corresponding to the divine love of God; but it is also to be "distinguished from it" (IV/2: 785f.). Christian love is "an act in which man is at work, not as God's puppet, but with his own heart and soul and strength, as an independent subject who encounters and replies to God and is responsible to Him as His partner." In our human response to the divine love we have a correspondence not only in disposition, thought, and emotion, but also, more importantly, with an act. The divine act of love is the basis and creative model of true human love. Human love as the "imitation" of the divine love is also "an act, and not merely an internal but an external act, the act of the whole man." Christian love takes place concretely here and now, in the totality of human action: "Where there is love, there takes place something from God, but in space and time, 'with hearts and hands and voices.' Where there is no human act in the full sense of the term, there is no love. For there is no imitation of God" (IV/2: 786).

Thirdly, the act of love has the character of an impartation, an action of giving, especially self-giving. Since *eros* keeps and takes, it has to form a closed circle to keep and take again and again. However, Christian love breaks this circle by giving. There is no love without giving. But in the Christian sense, giving means a self-giving—a sacrifice. Those who love do not have a "part" only for themselves, but they are always together with the others whom they love and to whom they give themselves. They do not desire to include loved ones in their own beings (i.e., *eros*), but they impart their own beings to those they love. This love of impartation makes one's life "an 'eccentric' life, i.e., one which has its centre outside itself" (IV/2: 788), in correspondence to and imitation of the greater impartation of the Triune God.

Fourthly, the act of love has a character of exaltation and joy. But we must not love for the sake of this reason, because it will create at bottom a cycle of eros. However, we can say unconditionally and confidently that those who love are happy ones who are to be countlessly blessed. "God does not like an uncheerful giver" (IV/2: 789). The one who genuinely loves is a cheerful person. A person does not genuinely love unless one is a genuinely cheerful person.

Love for God. Barth described the twofold meaning of this act, or the object of Christian love; namely, love for God (vertical) and love for others (horizontal). Vertically, Christian love is the love for God, in response to the electing, purifying, and creative love of God. The covenantal relationship between God and us becomes "two-sided instead of one-sided." The gracious Word of God does not confront us with an empty space, but it evokes our word of gratitude. Christians attest to this in the act of love for God. This vertical love, as the new, free, giving, and joyful human act in the liberating power of the Holy Spirit, is "an integral element in the divinely inaugurated and controlled history of the kingdom and salvation" (IV/2: 790). The love for God as a step into open fellowship in reconciliation with God becomes our provisional goal and end, in response and correspondence to the eternal love of God to and in us. This love "from below" and on the human side is to be "at least as great" as the love from above and on the divine side (IV/2: 790). Therefore, Jesus said the first commandment is, "you shall love the Lord your God with all your heart, and with all your soul, and with all your mind, and with all your strength" (Mk. 12:30). The freedom we have for this movement is a "miracle . . . no less a miracle than the Virgin Birth of Jesus Christ or His bodily resurrection from the dead" (IV/2: 791). The love for God is identical in the New Testament with the love for Jesus. It implies an *interest* "in God, i.e., in 'God in Christ.'" This interest constrains and comprises our trust and obedience. Since God has us and is for us, we must have God and have "no option but to be for God." We must do this love "centrally" and continually in the totality of our life-act (IV/2: 793). Thus, the person who loves God is "no heaven-storming idealist," but one's interest is "in the *ens realissimum*: the cause of God on earth; His cause for and against and with the world and men and himself; His cause which is not a cause but His work, His kingdom, and in His work and kingdom He Himself, the living God, the living Jesus" (IV/2: 794).

Distinctively and particularly, Christian love for God is recognized and acknowledged as the content of the first commandment. The human liberation for the love of God carries immediately our liberation for obedience to God: "To love God is to give oneself to Him, to put oneself at His disposal " (IV/2: 798f.). In this process, our freedom for love is transformed into our freedom for obedience ("If you love me, you will keep my commandments" [Jn 14:15]). Christian obedience is the act in which one willingly and readily subordinates oneself to His commandment. We love God in freedom, on the basis of the electing, purifying, and creative love of God and in the quickening power of the Holy Spirit. But in this freedom, we inescapably discover the freedom of obedience, i.e., to give ourselves to God "in return," with "no option but to place" ourselves under the will, command, and order of God as we hear His Word. Therefore, Barth said, "Obedience is the required action of love, i.e., the action of love which is demanded by love itself, resulting directly from the fact that as man loves God he places himself at His disposal" (IV/2: 800). Although this action is required, this action is free: "A puppet does not obey" (IV/2: 801). Barth again warned against such a theomonistic misunderstanding of Christian love (e.g., A. Nygren):[6]

It is now clear why in our general consideration of the act of love we had to insist so strongly that it cannot be understood as a prolongation or effluence of the divine action, of the love of God. The apparent grandeur of this theomonistic conception must not blind us to the fact that if it is true there can be no question of a free act of human love for God, and therefore of an act of obedience enclosed in it and following from it. Nor can we describe as a covenant relationship the kind of relationship in which God alone is really at work and man is only the instrument or channel of the divine action, so that the antithesis of Creator and creature, of Savior and saved, of the One who loves and the one who is loved, has no significance. In the covenant relationship— the true relationship between God and man according to the witness of Scripture—the initiative is wholly and exclusively on the side of God. But this initiative aims at a correspondingly free act, at genuine obedience as opposed to that of a puppet, on the part of the man with whom the covenant is made. And this is the fulfillment of the covenant in the reconciliation of man with God accomplished in Jesus Christ, in so far as this has a human side and may now be considered from this lower, human aspect. As certainly as Jesus Christ is very God and also very man, it includes also the fact that there may be genuine obedience on the part of man; the obedience of man as his free act. (IV/2: 800f.)

Christian love is an action of obedience which demonstrates that love is a self-giving in the historicity of time and space. In the definite action of obedience toward God and his fellows, a Christian participates in one's own place in the history of the world with God (i.e., salvation history). Christian love is "a matter of obedience to the living God, or to the living Jesus Christ." The action of love, as an answer, a response, and an imitation of the love of God, is not related to "the setting up of a static counterpart, perhaps in the form of a way of life which is fixed once and for all according to certain standpoints and regulations" (IV/2: 801). For God who is living and still active is "not a fixed and static and rigidly determined figure which is dead for all the majesty ascribed to it." Therefore, Christian obedience requires "a continual readiness and willingness to follow His action" or "a continual subjection" to His electing, willing, and producing Word, in a complete "loosening of one's own rigidity." Christian obedience takes place in human history with God; the love for God is never dispensed with, but continually renewed in response to God's eternal love and in the power of the Holy Spirit. The Christian is the person who loves God; a Christian demonstrates one's love through rendering one's obedience, continuously corresponding to the action and the command of the living God.

<u>Love for Neighbors</u>:   Horizontally, Christian love is the love for neighbors; as Jesus said the second commandment is, "You shall love your neighbor as yourself" (Mk. 12:31). This second love is "no less indispensable and decisive" than the first. In the Bible, those whom Christians loved together with God were their fellow human beings, who stood "in a definite historical relationship or context" with them (IV/2: 802). On the biblical basis, Barth explicitly articulated that Christian love is not so much an alleged universal love as a differentiated love which chooses and differentiates:

> It may sound harsh at first, but we have to note that neither the Old Testament nor the New speaks of a love for man as such and therefore all men; of a universal love of humanity. As the Bible understands it, love both for God and for man has the character of an action. The universal love of humanity can be thought of, if at all, only as an idea which dominates man or an attitude of mind which fills him. But Christian love, as we have seen, is an act of obedience which as such, even if we think of a sequence of such acts, takes place somewhere in time and space, which does not, therefore, take place always and everywhere, but in which there is always a demarcation and limitation of its object or objects. It is the concrete and not the abstract loving of someone who is concrete and not abstract. In correspondence to the love of God, it is a loving which chooses and differentiates. (IV/2: 802f.)

Barth underscored the significance of concrete proximity as the starting point for Christian love:

> This love between men takes place on the assumption that there is between them, not an indefinite, but a very definite and specific proximity; a proximity between the one who loves and the one or many who are loved which is not general or accidental and which could not apply to all men, or indeed to any except on a particular basis. It is in this proximity that there takes place the act of Christian love. (IV/2: 803)

The biblical definition of "neighbor" is "the one who is loved apart from and side by side with God, but for the sake of love for God" (IV/2: 803). The term in the Christian sense is understood concretely in the context of salvation history.   In the Old Testament, it refers to foreigners who hold a specific relationship with the history of Israel.

Similarly, in the New Testament, those who are loved are not so much abstract fellow human beings as "the closed circle," i.e., the circle of the disciples and the saints in the particular community of faith in Jesus Christ. This does not mean that Christian love is exclusive and esoteric. Rather, it aims to establish the concrete basis for the embodiment of the real meaning of humanity to the widest extension; in other words, it biblically entails a *concrete-universal way.*

Of course, the context is the salvation history that takes place for the human race and can apply to all people through particular communities of faith. The history of salvation is "the nexus of the particular speech and action of God for the reconciliation of the world with Himself which at its centre and climax is the history of Jesus Christ." Christians respond to the divine love in the act of love as a free human act. But it is a free human act in the context of the salvation history, i.e., the history of God with His people. Therefore, one who loves God cannot be "solitary." The person cannot be a religious individual who seeks only one's own personal concerns, joy, wishes, and achievements. The one who has an active part in salvation history engages from the very outset with specific fellows—those who belong together to the people of God, fellow-partners in the covenant, or those in the "household of faith" (Gal. 6:10). Again, Barth emphasized the collective dimension of Christian love. The basis of one's love for God is not a private revelation to oneself. But a person begins to love God as a being-in-the-world, and in the context of the community, called and gathered by the Holy Spirit, which attests its "mystery to love God in return." But the life of the community is "not the functioning of a mechanism but a nexus of human relationship" (IV/2: 806):

> To love God is, then, to live at a specific point in this nexus, and at this point to be together with the men who are also called to the service . . . To love God, since it is always a question of definite action, is to stand at this point in one of the many human relationships which exist here, being united to this man or that by the fact that he too is awakened by the love of God to love God in return. (IV/2: 807)

Barth affirmed the universal extension of Christian love even beyond the baptismal restriction, but he avoids a confusion of the notion of universal love. On the one hand, "There can be no question of an extension in principle of the concept of Christian love for the neighbor into a universal love of humanity, unless we are radically to weaken and confuse it." On the other hand, "there can be no question of a restriction in principle of this concept to love for those whom we know . . . as those with whom we find ourselves in this context of the history of salvation." Although endorsing the "positive seriousness" of baptism as the concrete sign of unity with fellows, Barth rejected the exclusive understanding of baptism for salvation.[7] Barth's emphasis on a specific point of departure for Christian love in the context of salvation history does not exclude those in the "hidden presence" or "these 'foreign' children" whom Karl Rahner calls "anonymous Christians" (IV/2: 807).[8]   Barth underscored the reaching-out or widening of the circle of Christian love; a Christian concrete-universal way:

> Hence the restriction of Christian love to the circle of brothers known to me cannot be theoretical and definitive, but only practical and provisional. In any case I have to exercise love at this point, and yet all the time I have not to be closed but open to the possibility that the circle of the brothers whom I must love may prove to-morrow, or even within the next hour, to be *wider* than I now realise. . . . *In the narrower love I am always reaching out to the wider.* And since I cannot know of man that he will not prove to be my brother to-morrow, I cannot withhold from any of my fellows an attitude of openness, of expectation, of good hope and therefore of readiness for love. I love neither God nor my brothers if I do not show openly to every man without distinction the friendliness emphatically recommended and even commanded in so many New Testament passages. . . . But it certainly must be said that, *while the circle of vital Christian love for the neighbour is not the sphere of all men indiscriminately, it is not a hermetically sealed circle within this sphere, but one which continually broadens out into it.* (IV/2: 808f.)[9]

However, the love for God and the love for neighbors are distinctive but inseparable. For salvation history entails both a history between God and people and a history between a person and a person. Our liberation for God is one thing, and our liberation for our fellows is another. But, since our liberation for God includes our liberation of a people, our love for God entails our love for the fellow-members in the household of faith. Thus "the awakening to mutual love succeeds instantaneously the awakening to love for God" (IV/2: 810). The history of salvation is fundamentally this twofold history which necessitates side by side the two commandments of love; the first commandment—the love for God—and its historical fulfillment, the second commandment—the love for neighbors. The one who loves

God cannot do otherwise. If you love God, you will love your neighbor, because the person is the one whom with you is loved by God and who with you loves Him in return. The salvation history has these vertical and horizontal dimensions, a different but inseparable twofold object and direction.

One needs to proclaim this love "reciprocally" (IV/2: 813). In the common life of the people of God, none is alone and no one leaves the other alone. This is the law of the people of God, the command which is continually given to each member, that they should be witnesses to one another and thus become neighbors to one another. This is to say, in the "gracious inter-relating" among people that each becomes a witnessing neighbor of this love to the other. In the event of reconciliation and salvation, this is an essential dimension; "there is no revelation or knowledge of that great love apart from this inter-relating of man and man." The "reciprocal human action" in the horizontal level is "a reflection" or "a copy" of that in the vertical level. The reciprocal act of love will be genuine and useful, even with all their human imperfections, if there is "a true reflection and imitation" of what takes place between God and human beings (IV/2: 815). Within the limits and with all the frailties of human action, Christians do mutual love "in reality and truth" (IV/2: 816); by doing that, they fulfill the commandments (the law).

Therefore, the function of the love for neighbors in correspondence to God's love and the love for God is "the ministry of human witness in which the one guarantees to the other the turning of God's love to His people and the turning of His people to God" with a visible reflection (IV/2: 817). This ministry or service continually renews and maintains the whole life of the community of people so as to evoke the united life of Christians. While the first commandment has over-riding primacy, the fulfilling of the second commandment is a matter of confirming this primacy. At this juncture, Barth also argued against the positivism of revelation which diminishes the dimension of human action:

> As there can be no above without a below, no before without an after, so there can be no divine revelation without a human ministry of witness, no history of salvation between God and man without its reflection and repetition in a history between man and man. The one without the other would necessarily prove to be a mere mythology and illusion in the form of a "positivism of revelation." (IV/2: 818)

Christian love for the neighbor is distinctively "a self-giving which pledges and guarantees" (IV/2: 820). In this corresponding self-giving, Christians attest to the self-giving of God to humanity for human liberation:

> And I can do so only as I love him, i.e., as I interpose and give myself as their pledge, unreservedly placing myself at his disposal as such. . . . If I am to be a Christian, this is the content of my life-act as such on the plane of dealings between man and man, just as on the plane of dealings between God and man it consists in the fact that I may and must respond to the self-giving of God to me with my self-giving to Him. (IV/2: 820)

The biblical testimonies of mutual love, through the Israelite, the Christian, the people of God, or the Samaritan (Lk. 10:25f.), culminates in the royal man Jesus. The life-act of Jesus is the paradigm of the act of Christian love. Although our love is always improper in the light of His paradigm (thus we are shamed by it), the action in which we imitate and reflect the love of God is "a real action." In our concrete discipleship to Christ, we can actualize this real action, because we are already empowered to perform dynamically the acts of love in "the likeness of Christ's act of love" (IV/2: 824).

Barth concluded with the manner of Christian love as the culminating way (say, the metaphor) of Christian life. Although the New Testament describes the life-act of the Christian also as the act of faith or hope, there is no hymn of praise to the manner of faith or hope. The only hymn pertaining to the manner of Christian life in the New Testament is I Cor. 13 pertaining to Christian love. Claiming that love alone counts, conquers, and endures, St. Paul declares that love is the *way*, "the greatest of these," that Christians should do and "follow after" (IV/2: 827). Finally, Barth said that Christian love is *the* way (cf. *Tao*):

> But faith and hope abide only as and because love abides. It is in love that faith and hope are active, and that there takes place that which is specifically Christian in the life-act of the Christian. Thus love is the "greatest of these." It is the future eternal light shining in the present. It therefore needs no change of form. It is that which continues. For whatever else may be revealed in and with the coming of that which is perfect, in whatever new form Christian activity and the life of the community may attain its goal with everything that now is and happens, one thing is certain and that is that love will never cease, that even then

the love which is self-giving to God and the brother, the same love for which the Christian is free already, will be the source of the future eternal life, its form unaltered. Already, then, love is the eternal activity of the Christian. This is the reason why love abides. This is the reason why to say this is to say the final and supreme thing about it. This is the reason why we had to say previously that it is love alone that counts and love alone that conquers. This is the reason why it is *the* way. (IV/2: 840).

Summary Remarks

Sanctification, as a central doctrine of theology, speaks of how to be radically human in the Christian paradigm. It proposes a radical humanization, in correspondence to God's gracious election and good creation. It involves one's recognition of the ontological connection between Jesus and the human race and one's continuous renovation, collectively and individually, in a concrete-universal way.

Shifting the sequence of two modes of the Word of God from Luther's law and Gospel to Gospel and law, Barth emphasized the nondualistically ultimate reality of the foundation of Christian faith according to God's Grace. The law is the unambiguous, necessary form of the Gospel whose content is grace. With this paradigm shift Barth affirmed the unity of theology and ethics.

Humanitas Christi, metaphorically described as the homecoming of the Son of Man, is the foundation of sanctification. The humanity of Christ manifests the concrete-universal act of God: God's gracious election, the concrete action of His incarnation, and the universal event of His resurrection and ascension. The life-act of the royal man Jesus reveals the root-paradigm of radical humanization in the unity of speech and act, of being and doing, of theology and ethics, and of knowing and acting. Through the event of crucifixion and resurrection, the royal man shows the most concrete signpost of the Christian faith and opens the most universal basis for our sanctification.

Analogously to inter-trinitarian co-existence and reciprocity, humanity in the image of God means a joyful co-humanity, being-in-togetherness, being-in-encounter, life in fellowship, or history in partnership. In the light of the radical and new humanity of Christ, sin is defined as sloth to participating in the work of sanctification. Hence, sin as sloth is contradictory to real human nature, violating its basic structures of relationship. Furthermore, the humanity of Christ reveals the miserable human condition in the boundless state of self-alienation and self-contradiction under the bondage of the will.

Nevertheless, the Holy Spirit authenticates and sanctifies human beings as really and radically human, by giving direction (*die Weisung*). A Christian is defined as a disturbed sinner by the *Weisung*. According to the critical but totally free direction of the Spirit, sanctification entails discipleship (simple obedience), collective and individual conversion (continuous renovation), works (as co-workers of God), and the bearing of the cross in dignity.

Agape is a human total self-giving in correspondence with the total self-giving of God. And it is the Christian Way, the metaphor of Christian life. Christian love is not merely a prolongation of the divine love, but a fully human act in a concrete-universal way. It begins as a differentiated love in a concretely shared praxis, but the circle of mutual love must be widened to universal extension.

PART III

AN ATTEMPT AT CONFUCIAN-CHRISTIAN DIALOGUE

Chapter 9

•

Methodology of the Dialogue

Presuppositions

In the preceding two parts, I have engaged in an exposition of Wang Yang-ming's confuciology of self-cultivation and Karl Barth's theology of sanctification. These expositions were to provide a basis for a comparative dialogue between Confucianism and Christianity, illustrated by these two paradigmatic thinkers. To begin the dialogue, I suggest the following three presuppositions:

(1) Confucianism and Christianity are both expressions of faith.

(2) A constructive enterprise of confuciology is a necessary heuristic and protective device for a more genuine Confucian-Christian dialogue. Analogously as theology refers to a coherent reflection of the Christian faith in a given context, confuciology does that for the Confucian faith. Confuciology as well as theology have been developed through continuous paradigm-shifts. The encounter of the two cultural-linguistic matrices can be appropriately examined in the correlation between confuciology and theology, as their thick-descriptive explications.

(3) The concrete subject of humanity is a more proper area for a genuine Confucian-Christian dialogue than other theological questions such as God, a subject not salient in the Confucian discourse. Particularly, the question of how to be fully human or the orthopraxis (*Tao*) of radical humanization is an appropriate locus to begin the dialogue. Self-cultivation, a prime project of Confucianism, and sanctification, a central project of Christianity, point to this same

problematic, namely, radical humanization. Thus, self-cultivation and sanctification is a point of contact from which we can begin a Confucian-Christian dialogue.

First of all, whether Confucianism is an articulation of "faith" is a controversial issue. The term faith in this context means neither merely a belief or a credo, but has a much broader definition than the Christian one, i.e., the informed trust in the salvific person. It is "genetically human" (W. C. Smith)[1] and "a constitutive human dimension" which necessitates orthopraxis rather than orthodoxy and orthopoesis (R. Panikkar).[2]   If faith is defined tentatively as an integrated human attitude toward salvific transcendence (or *"existential openness toward transcendence"* (Panikkar), then Confucianism is a faith. Confucianism has a capacity for religious transcendence (see Chap. 1). Tu Wei-ming has defined Confucianism as "a faith in the living person's authentic possibility for self-transcendence."[3] Although it is no institutional and dogmatic religion, it has a dimension of "being religious."[4]   Being religious in Confucianism means to be engaged in "ultimate self-transformation as a communal act and as a faithful response to the transcendent."[5]   In the Confucian sense, salvation means "the full realization of the anthropocosmic reality inherent in our human nature."[6]   As I elaborated in Chapter 1, there is a Neo-Confucian version of the soteriological leap in the confuciology of Wang.

Furthermore, this position is enhanced by Wang's emphatic endorsement of the establishment of the will (*li-chih*), which is analogous to the Kierkegaardian notion of qualitative change (faith), as the point of departure for confuciology. The establishment of the will is not totally different from the Christian notion of faith (see Chaps. 2, 10). For the mature Barth, faith is not merely an either-or leap related to the passive justification, but, rather, a spontaneous human self-determination for subjectivity that entails the process of sanctification. The point of departure for both Confucianism and Christianity is not so much a logically construed metaphysics or a philosophy of religion, as a full ethicoreligious commitment for the integrated human subjectivity. For both of them, the starting point is rather an establishment of one's will on the orthopraxis of the communally informed *Tao* (the Way).

However, using the traditional theological distinction between faith as a subjective act (*fides qua creditur*) and as objective knowledge (*fides quae creditur*), we can glimpse a comparison of Confucian faith and Christian faith. On the one hand, both Wang and Barth agree that the subjective act of faith entails a concrete-universal mode of radical humanization with an engagement of rigorous hermeneutical process. On the other hand, Wang and Barth appear different on the dimension of objective knowledge. Whereas Barth believes in the ontological connection between God and human beings through Jesus Christ, Confucians presuppose a person's primordially authentic capacity for self-transcendence (see Chap. 11).

Secondly, theology articulates a coherent refection on faith in a theistic paradigm (*fides quaerens intellectum*). Analogously, confucio-logy is a type of discourse that articulates coherently a faith in the Confucian paradigm. Confuciology as a heuristic device designates an interpretative explication of Confucian faith in a specific context.[7] According to George Lindbeck, the nature of doctrine is "to give a normative explication of the meaning a religion has for its adherents."[8] If theology is a thick description of the intratextuality of the Christian faith, confuciology is that of the Confucian faith.[9] Confuciology is a heuristic device to describe intelligibly the stories of Confucian ethicoreligious persuasions within its own context. Analogous to theology (at least similar to Barthian-Reformed or liberation theology), being secondary to the faith itself, confuciology explicates rules of the game for understanding the Confucian cultural-linguistic matrix. It prevents an eclectic and fragmentary approach to the texts (or intratextuality) of other faiths whose dangerous decontextualization can jeopardize and violate the integrity and the inner coherence of the other traditions such as Confucianism. To be a genuine dialogue, each story must be told freely in its own structure. Hence, confuciology is also a protective device to enable Confucian stories to be told authentically and thickly in their own structures. This also implies the significance of a structural or formal comparison between the dialogue partners. A structural comparison is as important as a substantial one. A conceptual comparison without considering the structural thrusts of related religio-cultural matrices is as arbitrary as the eclectic and fragmentary approach. After this formulation of confuciology, the Confucian-Christian encounter can be examined appropriately in the relation of and in the dynamic interplay between confuciology and theology.

Both confuciology, as an articulation of Confucian faith, and Christian theology, as that of Christian faith, have evolved through continuous paradigm shifts[10] based on the changes of their contexts. Many contemporary theologians have adopted Thomas Kuhn's notion of paradigm shift, and invite a search for new paradigms to interpret historical Christian faith in new contexts of "the emancipatory, ecological, and dialogical quest"[11] (e.g., feminist, black, Latin American liberation, and Asian theology of religion models). For example, Hans Küng noted the paradigm changes in the history of theology (see his *Theology For The Third Millennium*). In the history of Confucianism, paradigm shifts did not appear as saliently as in the history of Christian theology. Yet, Wang Yang-ming's confuciology illustrates a clear Confucian paradigm change (see Chap. 1). Both Wang and Barth made crucial paradigm changes within their respective traditions. Wang made a key Neo-Confucian paradigm shift by identifying mind-and-heart with principle, while Barth made a decisive theological paradigm change from law and Gospel (Martin Luther) to Gospel and law (see Chap. 10).[12]

Thirdly, the common subject of humanity is a more proper area for a genuine Confucian-Christian dialogue than other theological questions such as God, a subject not salient in the Confucian discourse. Furthermore, the primary problematique of Confucianism and Christianity lies in the question of how to be fully or radically human or the *Tao* of humanization. Since it is a concrete point of contact, this orthopraxis of radical humanization is a proper locus to begin a Confucian-Christian dialogue. Julia Ching argued for a similar point:

> For the dialogue between Christianity and Confucianism, as understanding of faith in man as openness to the transcendent remains the most promising point. It is this faith which has given Confucianism its dynamism, which has also counteracted the abuses of Legalism--and so many crimes attributed to Confucianism have emerged from the infiltration of Legalists concepts into the Confucian system. It is this faith which provides a starting point for contemporary theology itself, and which also, for the Christian, takes priority over law and precepts, being itself the only *rationale* for any authentic legal order. And lastly, it is this faith, in each case, which makes possible that creative exercise of freedom which brings man nearer to his transcendent goal, the achievement of a *radical* human-ity.[13]

In confuciology and theology, this common issue is treated as the doctrines of self-cultivation and sanctification. Self-cultivation, i.e., learning how to be fully human is the primary Confucian project. The locus of Confucian discourse is the concrete human situation of the living person here and now (orthopraxis). Since Confucianism focuses on the practice of self-realization, rather than the theoretical problem of God or transcendence, the Confucian paradigm appears to be anthropocentric. But it presupposes a vigorous process of self-cultivation, a serious engagement with the transcendent and creative communal and cosmic transformation, i.e., harmonizing the human and cosmic relationships (see Chap. 2).

Sanctification, which also involves how to be real or radically human, is a central doctrine of Christian theology. However, in the Christian theistic paradigm, the themes of salvation and the transcendence of God are highlighted. Since Martin Luther, many Protestant theologies hold justification as the central theological problem. However, Barth emphasized sanctification also as a central doctrine of Christian theology, following Calvin in shifting Gospel over law. Sanctification is understood as parallel and equal in value to justification. Sanctification, the perspective from below, and justification, the perspective from above, are different, but unified moments of one divine action. Being not interchangeable, they are inseparable in such a way that sanctification is the consequence of justification (see Chap. 6). This points to the thesis of this book, *in the light of two paradigmatic teachings of Wang Yang-ming and Karl Barth, self-cultivation and sanctification are thickly resemblant views of a common issue, i.e., how to be fully human, or radical humanization.*

My point at this juncture is twofold. First, radical humanization is a common issue of confuciology and theology (self-cultivation and sanctification), and this point of contact constitutes an appropriate locus to facilitate a Confucian-Christian dialogue. This point has been explained. Secondly, the nature of this point of contact is primarily not a static concept or a psychological consciousness but a living person's dynamic engagement with a shared practice. The basic locus of the dialogue should be not a metaphysics, a psychology, or a philosophy of religion, though they are constitutive, but a faith (more related to the orthopraxis or spirituality) in radical humanization. For their point of contact as well as their common ground first and foremost refers to the spiritual orthopraxis, an ethicoreligious embodiment of each faith in a historical context.

Methodology

Both theology and confuciology articulate descriptively and normatively the fabrics and intratextualities of their cultural-linguistic matrices. A Confucian-Christian dialogue can be formulated as an interplay of confuciology and theology (or their "homologous correlation").[14] Descriptively, the interplay is more related to a secondary level, a reflective level to examine the practical encounter, than to a primary level. Normatively, the discourse elicits an a posteriori thematization of the ethicoreligious and theological meaning for a community in the historic Confucian-Christian encounter. This enterprise, thus, consists of two stages: (1) a descriptive-comparative stage and (2) a normative-constructive stage.

Confuciology constitutes the main device for the first stage. Pointing out the methodological dangers of a simple juxtaposition of Confucian categories with those of other religions, Henry Rosemont, Jr., proposed a method of "a concept cluster," the formulation of a conceptual framework for a more appropriate process of decontextualization and recontexualization.[15] Partially agreeing with this method, the significance of the contextual consideration, the method of confuciology involves the much wider scope of the historical horizon, a systematic explication of Confucian intratextuality. Although it uses modern categories for the sake of communication, its purpose is to tell its story in its own categories, properly resisting impositions of other categorical schemes. Hence, this stage takes equivocity more seriously than univocity.[16] In this regard, its purpose is congruent with the aim of the "intrareligious dialogue." Raimundo Panikkar said:

> The aim of the intrareligious dialogue is understanding. It is not to win over the other or to come to a total agreement or a universal religion. The ideal is communication in order to bridge the gulfs of mutual ignorance and misunderstandings between the different cultures of the world, letting them speak and speak out their insights in their own languages.[17]

In the second, normative-constructive stage, the locus is shifted to the concrete context; namely, East Asian churches, Christian communities in the historic collision of the two spiritual traditions. Those communities need a holistic articulation of the Christian faith in their given cultural-linguistic matrix, namely, Confucianism. Hence, this stage inevitably focuses on their univocities. However, the goal of finding those univocative dimensions is primarily toward an a posteriori articulation of the Christian faith in the context of the fusion of the two horizons, more concretely, the two powerful stories of radical humanization. This enterprise does not refer to an arbitrary deliberation of speculative comparison, but an imperative thematization of a Christian community for the wholistic understanding of their faith. However, the result will enhance the theology of the Christian community as a whole.

The Structure of the Confucian-Christian Dialogue

The last two parts are a preparation to apply the method. This part is its case study. The following three chapters will be used for the stage of descriptive-comparative study, and the conclusion for the normative-constructive stage. In accordance with the categories described in the introduction, I will use the three main categories: prolegomena (Chap. 10), humanity (11), and humanization (including root-metaphor; 12). These will be further classified in nine sub-categories: (1) source, (2) paradigm-shift, (3) the point of departure, (4) the relation of theory and praxis, (5) root-paradigm, (6) the paradigm of humanity, (7) the problem of evil, (8) the humanization method, and (9) root-metaphor. In a nutshell, these may be set forth in the following diagram. For each category, I will briefly summarize the arguments of Wang and Barth, attempt to compare their concepts and themes, and draw the result of the comparison in a table.

Starting Question: "How to Be Fully Human?"

	<u>Confucian Paradigm</u>	<u>Christian Paradigm</u>
	Wang Yang-ming	**Karl Barth**
Project	*Self-cultivation*	*Sanctification*

A. Prolegomena (Chap. 10)

Source:	mind-and-heart	the Word of God
Paradigm-shift:		
to	the identity of mind and principle	Gospel and law
from	the investigation of things	law and Gospel
Point of Departure:		
	the establishment of the will	faith
Theory and Practice:		
	the unity of knowing and acting	
		the unity of theology and ethics

B. The Humanity Paradigm (Chap. 11)

Root-paradigm:	*liang-chih*	*humanitas Christi*
Paradigm of Humanity	*jen*	*Imago Dei*
Problem of Evil:	selfish desires	sloth

C. The Humanization Method: How to be Fully Human? (Chap. 12)

Method:	*chih liang-chih*	
		the direction of the Holy Spirit
Root-Metaphor:	*ch'eng* (sincerity)	*agape*

Chapter 10

•

Prolegomena

Source: Mind-and-Heart vs. the Word of God

Although both Confucianism and Christianity are expressions of faith, they have radically different orientations. Generally speaking, Confucianism is "human-centered," whereas Christianity is "God-centered."[1] Although it is not so transparent in the deeper level, the distinction is helpful at this beginning of dialogue. Confucianism is conducive to a subjective religion, while Christianity is conducive to an objective religion. As noted in the previous chapter, though both traditions are similar in the subjective dimension of faith (*fides qua creditur*), they are different in the objective dimension of faith (*fides quae creditur*). The objective source of Christian faith is clearly the revelation of God, most importantly the Bible, which Barth designated as the Word of God. That of Confucian faith is elusive. Certainly, the Classics hold a canonical status, however, the more important source is the human mind-and-heart, at least in the Wangian sense.[2]

Mind-and-heart (*hsin*) is a principle concept in East Asian thought since Mencius and has both cognitive and affective dimensions. In the Mencian sense, mind-and-heart has an intrinsic possibility for self-transcendence, which entails an ontological basis for self-realization. Wang underscores the Mencian tradition that mind-and-heart is the source and foundation of the Confucian project of self-cultivation (Chap. 1).

The foundation of the Christian faith is the Word of God. Barth formulated the doctrine of the Word as event in a threefold form: the written (the Holy Scriptures), the revealed (Jesus Christ), and the proclaimed (preaching and sacraments). He defined dogmatic theology as nothing but a radical self-examination of the language and experience of a community of faith according to the Word in a specific context.

Whereas confuciology takes the mind-and-heart as the source and the locus of realizing the transcendent principle *(li)*, theology takes the Word of God as its most authentic source and foundation. The primary Confucian source is in the inner forum, while the Christian source is in the outer forum. Metaphorically, they suggest two types of person: a sincere digger and an obedient hearer. If a Confucian profound person is a *sincere digger* of anthropocosmic realization latent in human mind-and-heart, then a Christian saint is an *obedient hearer* of the Word of God.

	Confucianism human-centered **Wang Yang-ming**	**Christianity** God-centered **Karl Barth**
Source	mind-and-heart inner forum sincere digger	the Word of God outer forum obedient hearer

Paradigm Shift: *Hsin chi li* vs. Gospel and Law

Both Wang Yang-ming and Karl Barth take seriously the status of these foundational loci within the whole structure of their hermeneutical paradigms. For Wang, it is the relationship between mind-and-heart and principle *(li)*, whereas, for Barth, the relationship between the two modes of the Word of God, Gospel and law. Both Wang and Barth challenged the established paradigms and contributed crucial paradigm changes, revolutionizing their traditions.

<u>Wang's doctrine of *hsin chi li*</u> (Chap. 1): Since *li* was adopted as a key concept of Neo-Confucianism, the relationship between *li* and *hsin* has become a crucial Neo-Confucian issue. In his emphasis on the transcendent dimension of *li*, Chu Hsi diminished the innate capability of mind-and-heart. Establishing *ko-wu* (the investigation of things) as the fundamental stage for the eightfold process of self-cultivation in *the Great Learning*, Chu Hsi focused on the gradual, intellectual pursuit of self-realization through external investigation. This move fostered an unfortunate dualism in Chu Hsi's confuciology, between mind-and-

heart and principle, the inner or outer, or the self-knowledge and external learning.

Until his own enlightenment, Wang had followed faithfully the teachings of Chu Hsi in searching for the Confucian *Tao*. However, Wang experienced severe spiritual crises and discovered anomalies in Chu Hsi's paradigm. Through his sudden enlightenment during his exile, Wang discovered that *li* is not external but fully immanent (literally, sufficient) in one's mind-and-heart. Hence, Wang proclaimed the precept of *hsin chi li*, meaning that mind-and-heart is none other than the principle. This constituted his radical departure from the orthodox tradition of Chu Hsi and resulted in a key paradigm change (following Lu Hsiang-shan). Through this shift, Wang reaffirmed the ontological identification of mind-and-heart with the Heavenly Principle. Although *li* is transcendent, it is not statically external, but also dynamically immanent in mind-and-heart (which means immanent-transcendence).

In this context of immanent-transcendence, the meaning of the investigation of things lies not so much in epistemological and intellectual study, as in serious moral practice. Philologically, Wang argues that the first word of *ko-wu* does not imply an intellectual inquiry as in Chu Hsi's thought, but a process of rectification in concrete existence, which involves a serious inner decision (*li-chih*) and an ethicoreligious action.

Barth's doctrine of Gospel and law (Chap. 5): In the history of theology, the two modes of the Word of God have been distinguished in sequence, first law and then Gospel. The distinction between law and Gospel was Luther's way of correcting two opposite doctrinal confusions: Roman Catholicism's reduction of the Gospel to law and the Radical Reformers' perversion of law into the Gospel. This hermeneutical criterion emerged from Luther's experience of existential struggle with the power of his conscience (internalized law). He endeavored to liberate the redemptive power of the Gospel over conscience's hindrance through the proper distinction of law and Gospel. However, this correction confined the law to a negative or restraining influence—the political and theological uses of the law, and diminished the positive (or a third use) of the law. Furthermore, Luther's dualistic distinction resulted in theological and anthropological problems. The distinction divided the foundation of Christian faith (the Word of God) into a dialectical dualism. Theologically, this constitutes a 'dualist peril' in which the God of the Gospel confronts the God of

the law. Anthropologically, it generates an 'anthropological narrowness' in which a person was understood merely as a passive receiver.

Barth's reversal of law and Gospel to Gospel and law (following
John Calvin) comprised a paradigm shift, correcting these problems.
The Word of God, as the foundation of Christian faith, cannot be
dualistically formulated from the outset, and the apparent duality
between law and Gospel must be theologically overcome. Barth
rejected Luther's formula of law and Gospel, with its theological
dualism and anthropological narrowness. Reversing the sequence,
Barth subordinated law to the Gospel. The Gospel reveals nondualistically the ultimate reality of God's grace. Law is the necessary
form of the Gospel whose content is grace. The law must be
understood in the context of the Gospel. This is shown in how Barth's
doctrine of sin was primarily related to Christology, not law. The
nature and specificities of sin (in contrast to the law) is fully revealed in
the context of Christology (the Gospel).

Hsin chi li vs. Gospel and law: This is not to show a parallelism
between *li* and the Word of God. (Instead, I have shown a parallelism
between *hsin* and the Word of God as the prime sources of faith, though
a comparison of the latter with *li* is intriguing because both of them are
related to the notion of *logos*). Rather, the point is, through observing
their paradigm shifts, to discern similarities in their modes of thinking.
Even though Confucianism and Christianity are radically different
religious paradigms, the paradigm changes made by Wang and Barth
share two converging goals; (1) maintaining a unified foundation of
faith, guarding against dualism, and (2) dynamically opening up the
possibility of human involvement in the process of realization. On the
one hand, through the precept of *hsin chi li*, Wang pled for a return to
the Mencian tradition of mind-and-heart as the authentic foundation of
Confucian persuasion, which had been diminished by Chu Hsi's
emphasis of *li* (*ko-wu*). On the other hand, Barth's reversal to Gospel
and law establishes the unity of the two modes of the Word of God, and
overcomes the dualism of Luther's doctrine of God and the narrowness
of his theological anthropology.

Chu Hsi's and Luther's concern for the proper distinction (a duality)
for the prime sources--*hsin* and *li* and law and Gospel--presuppose that
hsin and law are ambiguous, while *li* and the Gospel are transparent.
This constitutes the anthropological narrowness which diminishes the
possibility of dynamic human involvement in ethicoreligious practice.
Both Wang's doctrine of *hsin chi li* and Barth's doctrine of Gospel and

law overcome this anthropological narrowness. Both endorsed the positive capacities of *hsin* and the law for a person's authentic life, emphatically advocating that *hsin* and the law are also unambiguous.

Paradigm Shift

Wang's Paradigm Shift	**Barth's Paradigm Shift**
Chu Hsi:.	Luther:
the distinction of *hsin* and *li*	the distinction of law and Gospel
Li alone is unambiguous.	The Gospel alone is unambiguous
Wang: the unity of *hsin* and *li*.	Barth: the unity of Gospel and law.
Hsin is also unambiguous.	The law is also unambiguous.

Point of Convergence between the Two Paradigm Shifts:
    1) the unified source of faith in avoidance of dualism
    2) the emphasis of one's subjective involvement

The Point of Departure: *Li-chih* vs. Faith.

As noted already, both Wang and Barth advocated a converging point of departure, a qualitative change in a person's full determination and commitment. *Li-chih* (the establishment of the will) involves an ethicoreligious commitment to a fully integrated humanity and refers to a fundamental determination that effects the totality of one's being and needs constant reassurance. Hence, *li-chih* is analogous to the Kierkegaardian notion of qualitative change, and similar to the ethicoreligious meaning of *metanoia* (repentance), a radical turn of the will.[3] However, *li-chih* does not mean an "either-or" leap in response to the revelation of the divine ("the 'wholly other'"), but signifies a "both-and" return to human subjectivity in immanent- transcendence.[4] This conception is not totally different from the Christian notion of faith. For the mature Barth also, faith is not merely an either-or leap related to the passive justification, but, rather, a spontaneous human self-determination for subjectivity that entails the process of sanctification (continuous repentance, conversion, and regeneration), corresponding to the divine election. Barth defined being human as free self-determination in action. A dimension of Barth's dynamic understanding of faith converges with Wang's notion of *li-chih*. Thus, *li-chih* enhances the interpretation of Confucianism as a faith. For neither confuciology or theology is metaphysics or philosophy of religion a point of departure, but rather an ethicoreligious commitment of qualitative change, *li-chih* and faith (with the sense of *metanoia*).

For both, paradigm shifts—the identification of mind-and-heart with principle and the reversal of law and Gospel—enhance the dynamic inclusivity to the notions of *li-chih* and faith. Wang's return to the original Mencian understanding authenticates *li-chih* as the spark for the transcendence immanent in the mind-and-heart. Barth's doctrine of supralapsarian election in the reversal to Gospel and law opens up an ontology of universal humanity in which election, the sum of the Gospel, authenticates sanctification, the goal of the law. In short, whereas the goal of self-cultivation is to realize the true self latent in original human nature, the goal of sanctification is to realize true (elected) nature. Both self-cultivation and sanctification point to the authentication of full humanity—radical humanization. Furthermore, both *li-chih* and faith, as self-determination and fundamental change (*metanoia*), demand costly discipleship and even a doctrine of "martyrdom."[5]

Theory and Praxis: The Unity of Knowing and Acting vs. the Unity of Theology and Ethics.

Their congruent point of departure--the ultimate commitment--and similar mode of paradigm shifts involve an additional point of convergence, the unity of theory and praxis. Wang and Barth converge at the radical assertion in the inseparability of knowing and acting, being and acting, or ontological knowledge and ethical practice. This assertion in the unity of theory and practice enabled both Wang's confuciology and Barth's theology to make very powerful ethico-political influences on their traditions and societies.

Wang's doctrine of the unity of knowing and acting (Chap. 2): The goal of self-cultivation is attaining sagehood (ultimate humanity). The main Confucian concern does not lie so much in metaphysical questions as in the concrete and immediate problem of how to become a sage. Wang argued that the true Confucian point of departure is not an external method, such as Chu Hsi's formulation of *ko-wu*, but an inner, existential decision, i.e., the establishment of the will (*li-chih*). The establishment of the will, as a fundamental decision for ultimate commitment, is the true foundation for Confucianism, as expressed in Confucius' paradigmatic statement, "At fifteen, I set my heart on learning." The establishment of the will involves a qualitative change from a partial humanity (*hsiao-t'i*) to a fully integrated humanity (*ta-t'i*); in other words, it is an ethicoreligious authentication of humanity. It is an ultimate commitment to self-transformation for full humanization. Since the locus of self-cultivation is the everyday real situation, it takes socio-political conditions seriously. Wang, a radical political critic in the history of China, had lived a life of 'a hundred deaths and a thousand hardships,' a Confucian paradigm of costly discipleship.

Since the will is the directionality of the mind-and-heart in the Mencian sense, the establishment of the will also involves both cognitive and affective dimensions. The establishment of the will involves both knowing, a transforming self-reflection, and acting, a serious ethicoreligious embodiment. In the structure of the establishment of the will, knowing and acting form a unity. Therefore, Wang advocated the doctrine of the unity of knowing and acting (*chih-hsing ho-i*). This doctrine affirms the original nature of humanity in the inseparability of knowing and acting. True knowing is itself transformative, and real acting presupposes a transcendent self-knowledge, as manifested in the process of love. However, selfish desires are the source of evil that breaks this ontological inseparability and fosters a false dualism between knowing and acting.

Through the doctrine of *chih hsing ho-i*, Wang distinguished the salient features of his paradigm shift from Chu Hsi's doctrine of *ko-wu*. *Ko-wu*, an epistemological approach, falls into a subject and object dualism. *Chih hsing ho-i* denies this dualism and affirms that the true point of departure lies not in intellectual inquiry but in a real experience and commitment (*li-chih*). While *ko-wu* stresses external deeds in response to quantified codes, leading to a static and objectified self-cultivation. *Chih hsing ho-i* dynamically bridges the gap between the inner and outer, focusing on a qualitative change, or inner transformation. *Ko-wu* understands moral principle under the rubric of empirical knowledge, and presupposes the gradual attainment of enlightenment. *Chih-hsing ho-i* focuses on immediate, spontaneous ethicoreligious practices, and presupposes sudden self-realization.

Barth's doctrine of the unity of theology and ethics (Chap. 5): The reversal of Gospel and law is directly linked to Barth's affirmation of the unity of theology and ethics. The fundamental understanding of Gospel on the relationship between God and humanity is covenantal. The sum of the Gospel is God's gracious election of the human race as

God's covenant partner(s). This loving attitude of God claims a corresponding human response toward God. God's election as the Lord of covenant enables a person to be and become fully human, as God's covenant partners. Sanctification is our corresponding action, realizing our true (elected) nature, which is radical humanization. In Barth's supralapsarianism, sanctification is human participation corresponding to divine election. It involves ethics, the way of human action in correspondence to that divine action (theology), as the law ensconced and guided by grace.

To explain this process, Barth used the analogy of a human being whose essence is free self-determination in action. As there is unity in a human person between one's inward determinations and outward acts, there is unity between the Gospel and the law. Thus, the true meaning of being and becoming a Christian is in the unified action of hearing (dogmatics) and doing (ethics). Barth employed this internal human relationship and the ontological analogy between God and humanity. The ontological characteristics of humanity allow us a spontaneous response to the direction of the Holy Spirit.

Barth included ethics (law) as a part of dogmatics (Gospel). For Barth, content always precedes form; hence, Gospel precedes law, and dogmatics precedes ethics. A human being, as a self-determined being, is a doer of the Word, in correspondence to the divine being (being-in-action). To be and become an authentic Christian entails the unity of hearing and doing, the unity of being and doing; thus, the unity of theology and ethics. Barth underscored the spontaneity of human action in response to the work of the Holy Spirit. Not only is there a corresponding relationship between God and human being, but also an ontological connection through Jesus Christ. While Luther claimed the law is ambiguous, Barth said that the law is also unambiguous since it is the concrete form of the Gospel. While Luther focused on the existential problem of the distinction of the law and Gospel, Barth was concerned with the ontological unity of Gospel and law. Since law is the responsive corresponding human action to the divine action revealed in the Gospel, ethics (as law) cannot be separated from dogmatics (theology). Barth included ethics as a part of dogmatics in each of the three major volumes of the *Church Dogmatics*. From Volume II to Volume IV, from election to sanctification, his emphasis shifts from the commanding position of God to the commanded position of humanity. This concern with ethics is one reason that Barth's theology was able to have a strong political impact.

The unity of knowing and acting vs. the unity of theology and ethics: Whereas Wang thematized his doctrine of the unity of knowing and acting from the primordial non-dualism in the structure of mind-and-heart (*li-chih*), Barth developed his doctrine of the unity of theology and ethics from the doctrine of election as the sum of the Gospel (faith). Both of them held a positive vision of an ultimately transcendent reality (immanent-transcendence in Confucianism, Grace in the Christian term). Generally, while theology thematizes explicitly, placing this vision to the forefront (focusing on justification), confuciology brackets it off, placing it in the background (focusing on self-cultivation). However, both Wang and Barth lessened these differences. Wang constructed a dynamic confuciology of self-cultivation, further developing the *Chung-yung*-ian vision of Heavenly embodiment into human nature (*liang-chih*). Barth brought the doctrine of sanctification to the forefront, thematizing the Christian vision of God's gracious election of the human race.

Both Wang and Barth affirmed the ontological unity of the human. Both emphasized the unity of the inner and the outer of the whole person, the self-determined being. Both agreed that true humanity embraces the unity of knowing and acting (in the Confucian sense) or hearing and doing (in the Christian sense), between ontological knowledge and ethical practice, or simply between theory and praxis. The unity so conceived constitutes both Wang's confuciology and Barth's theology to produce the most dynamic, radical social hermeneutics in their traditions, called "dynamic idealism" (Wang) and "theo-ethical realism" (Barth).[6] The dynamism and radical realism are possible by overcoming the epistemological fallacies (dualism) of the established paradigms (Chu Hsi's interpretation of *ko-wu* and Luther's doctrine of law and Gospel), and securing a solid ontological (hermeneutical) foundation, an important converging point. Furthermore, radical humanization, in both, does not mean merely individual piety. Rather, it employs a collective process such as the team work of a community (communal acts), and serious socio-political involvement.

Theory and Praxis

	Wang	**Barth**
Paradigm shift		
from	*ko-wu* (Chu Hsi)	law and Gospel (Luther)
to	*chih-hsing ho-i*	Gospel and law
Foundation	immanent-transcendence	God's gracious election
Point of departure	*li-chih*	faith
Theory and praxis		
	unity of knowing and acting	unity of theology and ethics
Social implication	dynamic idealism	theo-ethical realism

Chapter 11

•

The Humanity Paradigm

Root Paradigm:
Liang-chih vs. *Humanitas Christi*

The root-paradigms of radical humanization (self-cultivation and sanctification) for Wang and Barth are *liang-chih* (the innate knowledge of the good) and *humanitas Christi* (the humanity of Christ). Each presents the Confucian and Christian visions of ultimate humanity or radical humanity, human being's transcendent goal. Whereas *humanitas Christi* is the incarnation of the Word (logos) in history, *liang-chih* is the primordial awareness of immanent-transcendence in the human mind-and-heart. Both *liang-chih* and *humanitas Christ* are somewhat related to the notion of incarnation, though it is hidden in the Confucian case. However, their emphases are different. Wang thematizes incarnate wisdom as the innate knowledge of good (or inner sage), whereas Barth understands the *assumptio carnis* of Jesus Christ as the Son of God. One the one hand, Wang focuses on immanent potentiality; on the other hand, Barth emphasizes historical revelation.

Wang's doctrine of *liang-chih* (Chap. 3): The genius of Wang is in his thematization of *liang-chih* as the transcendent subjectivity of humanity. *Liang-chih* is the great principle of Wang's mature Neo-Confucian thinking. He reasserted that mind-and-heart is identical and coextensive with original human nature (*hsin chi li*). Mind-and-heart, as a heavenly endowment, has an innate, or original, ability to discern the Heavenly principle and know the good. Wang defined this primordial faculty of mind-and-heart as *liang-chih*. Involving both cognitive and affective dimensions, *liang-chih* entails a prereflective knowledge and spontaneous natural feeling. As the innate knowledge of the Heavenly principle in human original consciousness, it is also called the 'primordial awareness'—'an innermost state of human perception' which generates values of human understanding as it encounters the world.

Wang's mature confuciology is *liang-chih*-centered. *Liang-chih* is taken as the hermeneutical principle for all the Confucian *Classics.* Exemplary deeds of Confucian sages are regarded as the 'histories of *liang-chih* in action.' Furthermore, Wang advocates a radically egalitarian perspective—*liang-chih*, the inner sage, is naturally endowed in all people. The distinction between sage and ordinary people is not in quality, but in quantity, the degree of extension. Every person has some innate power to exert the self to be authentically human.

In Neo-Confucian metaphysics, *liang-chih* is in a state of equilibrium before feelings are aroused. Wang identified it with mind-and-heart-in-itself, which is a Confucian notion of being-in-itself analogous to Heidegger's *Dasein*. *Liang-chih*, dynamic being-in-itself, transcends all dualistic distinctions and penetrates everything. Wang identified *liang-chih*-in-itself with the Great Vacuity, the Neo-Confucian expression for the Ultimate Primordiality. Like the Great Vacuity, *liang-chih*-in-itself is self-transcendent. And this self-transcendent *liang-chih* is also the creative Spirit which capacitates cosmic differentiations and warrants them into the anthropocosmic identification through the work of its material force (*ch'i*).

Furthermore, *liang-chih* is the life-giving True Self, the "subjectivity" of genuine humanity. *Liang-chih*, as the 'inner-most and indissoluble reality' of humanity, is radical humanity which has both internality and universality. Internality means both "a self-generative 'intellectual intuition'" and "a self-sufficient 'anthropocosmic feeling.'"[1] But these internal dimensions are to be extended beyond anthropocentric subjectivism in universal extension (*chih liang-chih*), where all things are in unity. Radical humanity in the Confucian anthropocosmic vision envisages "cosmic togetherness" in the triadic unity of Heaven, Earth, and the myriad things which entails 'a spiritual sensibility and loving care' with the cosmos as a whole.

Barth's doctrine of *humanitas Christi* (Chap. 6): Barth's Christ-centered theology establishes the foundation of sanctification on *humanitas Christi*, the being and becoming of Jesus Christ in human existence. Metaphorically, he describes the homecoming of the Son of

Man as the basis of the exaltation of humanity. Hence, sanctification does not mean a destruction or an alteration of humanity. The doctrine of *humanitas Christi* is related to election, incarnation, and resurrection and ascension, a theology of glory grounded in a theology of the cross.

The humanity of Christ, both the electing God and the elected humanity, is the root-paradigm of God's gracious election. The incarnation (*assumptio carnis*) of Jesus' becoming and being of human existence, in totality, signifies ultimately the exaltation of human essence to divine essence. The resurrection and ascension are an inseparable, revelatory and historical event in which the risen Christ manifests Himself as the ultimate foundation of sanctification.

Hence, *humanitas Christi* involves the threefold concrete-universal act of God. First, *humanitas Christi* was the concrete-universal manifestation of God's election of the human race. Second, the *assumptio carnis* of the Triune God in the particular person Jesus (incarnation) was the historical, and thus the concrete, fulfillment of God's salvific love for the human race. Third, the event of resurrection and ascension of the particular humanity of Jesus has opened once and for all the ontological basis for the redemption of humankind, and thus has established the universal foundation for the exaltation of the human race. Through the humanity of Christ in these events of election, incarnation, and resurrection and ascension, God has accomplished His gracious will to humanity as His covenant partner. Hence, the humanity of Christ is the revelation of God's most concrete-universal way of including humanity in His intratrinitarian history that establishes the ontological space of human sanctification. At the same time, *humanitas Christi* is God's presentation of the most concrete-universal paradigm of humanity.

Royal Man Christology: *Humanitas Christi* as the most concrete-universal humanity was manifested in the life-act of the royal man Jesus (traditionally, the kingly office). The royal man Jesus (as both the paradigm of full humanity and a mode of God's being) exhibits a revolutionary attitude "in a preferential option for the poor" against the exploitative established order. His life-act is the history of the Word in unity with deed (the unity of speech and act). Also it manifests the unity of knowing and acting, being and doing, hence theology and ethics. In other words, the life-act of the royal man Jesus reveals the paradigm of the unity of knowing and acting and theology and ethics par excellence. Paradoxically, the cross of Jesus, the final negativity, constitutes all-embracing positivities (the resurrection). The cross, the

most concrete point of the Christian faith, opens the new aeon of
universal actualities. This dangerous memory of the Crucified, the most
concrete point of the Christian faith, points to the inseparable dangerous
memory of the resurrection of the Crucified, the most universal point of
the Christian faith.

Liang-chih vs. *humanitas Christi*:   *Liang-chih* and *humanitas
Christi* are the centers and hermeneutical principles of Wang's
confuciology and Barth's theology. *Liang-chih* and *humanitas Christi*
are the foundations for self-cultivation and sanctification. Both of them
articulate radical humanity—full, real, authentic, and true human
subjectivity—the root paradigm for radical humanization. These two
central notions of Wang and Barth provide their salient material points
of convergence and divergence, constituting the bases for further
discussions.

Some points of convergence: First, both Wang and Barth took these
as the hermeneutical principle for understanding their texts and
traditions.   Whereas Wang's confuciology is *liang-chih*-centered,
Barth's theology is Christ-centered.   Second, Christ also can be
understood as an innate knowledge of the good (*liang-chih*) for
Christians in relation to sin and evil. The knowledge of Christ reveals
the specificities of sin, just as *liang-chih* (the primordial awareness)
illuminates those of evil.   Third, they congruently affirm the
inseparability of ontological knowledge and ethical practice. While
liang-chih manifests the proto-paradigm of the unity of knowing and
acting, the life-act of Christ reveals the historical paradigm *par
excellence* of the unity of logos and ethos, theory and praxis, and
theology and ethics. Fourth, both manifest the most concrete-universal.
Jesus Christ, the true humanity and the true God, is the most concrete-
universal of the Christian faith. *Liang-chih*, the immanent transcendent
of the Heavenly *Tao* in humanity is the most concrete-universal in the
Wangian sense. Fifth, both *liang-chih* and *humanitas Christi* as the
most concrete-universal are self-transcendent, life-giving human
subjectivity (true self).

Some points of divergence: First, these two concrete-universals
have divergent conceptual contexts. Whereas *liang-chih* is based on the
anthropocosmic vision of immanent-transcendence, *humanitas Christi*
is founded on faith in the gracious election of God (salvation history).[2]
Second, hence, their points of departure are divergent. While Wang
thematized *liang-chih* as the immanent potentiality of the Heavenly
principle in the human mind-and-heart, Barth articulated the humanity

of Christ as the historical and personal incarnation of the divine *logos*. Third, there is a nuance in their characterizations of ultimate humanity. Whereas *liang-chih* is viewed as the inner sage or incarnate Wisdom endowed in every person's mind-and-heart, Jesus of Nazareth, a historical person, is believed as the *assumptio carnis* of the Triune God and Christ, the messiah. In short, confuciology articulates the root-paradigm as the *Wisdom,* an immanent transcendence, while theology declares it as the *Christ,* a historico-transcendence. Fourth, they have accordingly different foci. Whereas confuciology focuses on ontological identification (e.g., the unity of all things), theology concentrates relatively on existential differentiation (e.g., the problem of evil). Also, Julia Ching is right to say, "Confucian teachings have focused more upon human perfectibility where Christianity has tended to stress human fallibility."[3] Fifth, this nuance constitutes their strengths and weakness. On the one hand, confuciology is strong in its all-embracing, anthropocosmic-sapiential articulation, and relatively weak in dealing with the historical-existential problems of the human predicament, suffering, and death. On the other hand, theology is strong in dealing with existential-historical problems, while falling easily into an exclusivism or historical anthropocentricism.

The Root-Paradigm of Humanization

	Wang	Barth
Root-paradigm	*liang-chih*	*humanitas Christi*
Most concrete-universal		
	of immanent transcendence	of election/incarnation
Subjectivity	radical humanity	royal humanity
Ethical paradigm	unity of knowing and acting	unity of theology and ethics
Good knowing	Good and evil	Christ and sin
Characterization	*Wisdom*	*Christ*
	inner sage	historical incarnation
	immanent-transcendence	*historico-transcendence*
Focus	immanent potentiality	historicality
	ontological identification	existential differentiation
	human perfectability	human fallibility

The Paradigm of Humanity: *Jen* vs. *Imago Dei*

The root-paradigms of ultimate humanity, *liang-chih* and *humanitas Christi*, can be divided into two dimensions: vertical (transcendental) and horizontal (human-to-human). Vertically, they are divergent (roughly, immanent-transcendence versus historico-transcendence). Horizontally, however, they are congruent. The Confucian notion of *jen* and Barth's understanding of the image of God show a remarkably substantial point of convergence Whereas the cardinal Confucian virtue, *jen*, is grasped as benevolent co-humanity, Barth understands *imago Dei* as joyful *Mitmenschlichkeit*. Hence, both Confucianism and Barth arrive at the same conclusion that the ontological paradigm of humanity is benevolent or joyful co-humanity (*Mitmenschlichkeit*), being-for-others, being-in-togetherness, or being-in-encounter.

The Confucian notion of *Jen* (Chap. 3): Etymologically, *jen* , the cardinal Confucian virtue, means togetherness of human beings, "co-humanity," or "co-humanization."[4] Confucians expand *jen*'s notion of togetherness to the cosmic dimension; namely, the cosmic togetherness represented in the organismic unity of Heaven, Earth, and the myriad things (Wang's doctrine of the unity of all things). *Jen* as cosmic togetherness entails a spiritual sensibility and loving care with the cosmos as a whole. *Jen*, a manifested structure of radical humanity, is a life-giving, creative spirituality through which reconciliatory communion is made possible. Hence, it is also designated as "cosmic life-force."[5]

In terms of *The Great Learning*, *jen*, as the substance, is "the clear character" (the ontological structure of radical humanity), while *jen*, as function, is "loving the people" (the ethicoreligious realization of radical humanity). This functional dimension of loving the people has a dynamic socio-political implication. However, such a concept as "universal love" is not tenable, from this vantage point, because it is abstract and vulnerable to misuse (cf. Barth's concept of *agape* in Sec. 9). Rather, it must be manifested in a concrete-universal way.

Humanity (*jen*) in Chinese is etymologically the related word and has the same pronunciation as human being (*jen*). Human beings, as bearers of radical humanity, are the mind-and-heart of the universe. Human beings possess innate spiritual powers for self-realization and dynamic capacities for self-transformation. Human beings as sole servants of the sovereign *liang-chih* participate in the cosmic hermeneutical process of reconciliation, transformation, and nourishment.

Barth's understanding of *Imago Dei* (Chap. 6): In the doctrine of creation (CD III/2), Barth formulated the paradigm of the human as (1) real human being in relation to God (vertical), (2) humanity in relation to others (horizontal), and (3) the whole person in relation to self (selfhood). (1) Analogously to Jesus Christ who is from, to, and with God, real human being is defined as a person with Jesus in the hearing of the Word of God, as a historical being in gratitude, and as subjectivity in pure spontaneity to the grace of God. (2) Since Jesus is a human being with and for other human beings, a person is the cosmic being that exists absolutely with and for its fellow beings. In the paradigm of Jesus, humanity (*Menschlichkeit*) means a joyful *Mitmenschlichkeit* (co-humanity). This image of God, fulfilled in the *humanitas Christi*, signifies humanity as co-humanity, being-in-encounter, life-in-fellowship, or history-in-partnership. Analogous to inter-trinitarian co-existence, co-inherence, and reciprocity, humanity, as image of God, means a plurality as being-in-togetherness or a being-with-others. (3) Jesus Christ is also the paradigm of the whole person in the unity of soul and body. The human nature of the whole person is constituted by an interconnected unity of creaturely life (soul) and creaturely being (body).

Jen vs. *Imago Dei*: Barth's understanding of *imago dei*—the paradigm of humanity as joyful *Mitmenschlichkeit*—is remarkably convergent with the Confucian perception of *jen* (humanity) as creative co-humanity. This entails an important, material point of convergence beyond their formal resemblances: Humanity (*jen* or *Menschlichkeit*) is co-humanity (*jen* or *Mitmenschlichkeit*).

Furthermore, Barth's third notion of the whole person, as integrated soul and body resonates strikingly with Wang's characterization of self-cultivation as "the learning of the body and mind" (*shen-hsin chih hsüeh*).[6] Self-cultivation emphasizes the integration of body and mind-and-heart (cf. *ch'eng-i*). The Chinese *shen*, the last character of the Chinese word for self-cultivation, originally denotes body but means a person in totality. Bracketing off the Christian vertical dimension (though we could also find a similar Confucian notion), both Wang and Barth hold the same understanding of being human: being human in both Confucian and Christian senses means being radically human, that is, a radical realization of being-in-togetherness in the unity of body and soul. Confuciology and theology represented by Wang and Barth strongly hold a common mode of "thinking in relationships and communities."[7]

However, their divergent emphases, i.e., immanence and historicality, also appear in this case. Whereas Wang extended the notion of togetherness to the cosmic dimension (the unity of all things), Barth focused on the meaning of co-humanity within the historical dimension. The Neo-Confucian understanding of humanity as cosmic togetherness would be a helpful insight to evoke theology to move beyond its captivity of anthropocentric understanding of historical process which, some say, is responsible for the present ecological crisis.

The Paradigm of Humanity

	Wang	Barth
Root-paradigm	*liang-chih*	*humanitas Christi*
Paradigm of Humanity	*jen*	*imago Dei*
Co-humanity	*jen*	*Mitmenschlichkeit*
	being-in-togetherness	life-in-fellowship
Implication	cosmic togetherness	history-in-partnership

The Problem of Evil: Selfish Desires vs. Sloth

Both Wang and Barth converge in understanding the ontology of humanity as transcendent being-in-togetherness and cosmic life-in-fellowship. Then, how can evil come about? In answering this question, both also agree that evil arises when radical humanity is violated. Wang viewed the root of evil as selfish desires which constitute a deviation from the original state of humanity. Barth understood sin as rejection of the reality of the sanctified, reconciled state (sloth) in the ontological connection with Jesus Christ. Both of them believe that the root-paradigm of radical humanity—*liang-chih* or *humanitas Christi*—has the power to fully reveal the insidious structure and specificities of evil.

Wang's notion of evil (Chap. 3): Confucianism holds that mind-and-heart in the original state is full of the Heavenly principle. This highest and transcendent state is beyond the distinction of good and evil. However, when mind-and-heart deviates from this state, evil ensues, and its equilibrium and harmony are broken. However, evil is not a separate entity in opposition to good. Confucianism does not see human mind-and-heart in a battle between two opposite supernatural forces. Evil takes place when a person's will is motivated by selfish attachment to personal interests, preferences, or perspectives. Selfish desires unbalance and perturb the *liang-chih* of mind-and-heart. Then evil emerges as a consequence of the dysfunction of mind-and-heart.

Even good intentions, thoughts, and efforts are vulnerable, like "gold or jade dust in the eye." Taoism and Buddhism, though valuable like gold or jade, are like dust in the eye of *liang-chih*. Their quest for personal immortality and emancipation from *samsara* are actually other forms of attachment, something extra added to the natural state of *liang-chih*. However, Wang's suspicion of religion was self-critical, first and foremost, toward his own tradition. He said that the real source of evil in his time was degenerated Confucians who forgot the real content of learning, self-cultivation, and only imitated its external forms, while pursuing their own fame and profit.

Confuciology divides mind-and-heart into two realms: the mind of the Way (*tao-hsin*) and the human mind (*jen-hsin*). The mind of the Way is the primordial state of mind-and-heart beyond good and evil, where human desires do not come into being. The human mind signifies the existential situation of mind-and-heart in which human desires arise and contradict the Heavenly Principle. Human desires obscure the radical humanity of cosmic togetherness and diminish its original inclusiveness, impartiality, and creativity. While the material force (*ch'i*) and feelings are not evil *per se*, human desires agitate them which, in turn, disturb the highest good, so that the distinction between good and evil appears. Nevertheless, *liang-chih*, as primordial awareness, naturally reveals these erroneous movements and empowers us to discern good and evil. *Liang-chih*, as transcendent subjectivity, has an innate power to remove this obscuring and restore original goodness. Hence, the real task of self-cultivation lies in the disciplined practice of attentive self-exertion of *liang-chih* (*chih liang-chih*).

Barth's notions of sin[8] (Chap. 6): In the Christian view, the human situation is determined by sin. For Barth, a person cannot grasp fully this situation without the preknowledge of Jesus Christ, because he or she is corrupt in his or her self-knowledge. In the light of the humanity of Christ, a person perceives sin as an aberration of peace with God. The knowledge of sin discloses our shaming which is inescapable and indefensible. As the unmerited free grace that liberates humanity from sin for God, *humanitas Christi* (the royal, real, and most concrete-universal humanity) becomes and is the most radical humanity, i.e., the most affirmative, critical self-judgment of humanity.

In the light of this radical and new humanity, sin is defined as sloth in the context of sanctification. Sloth as a refusal of the direction of God is a sin of disobedience and unbelief. Sloth makes a person self-contradictory in his or her basic structures of relationship. In relation to God, sloth drives a person to folly or stupidity. In relation to fellow human beings, sloth involves inhumanity to violate the meaning of being human as life in fellowship. In relation to self, sloth involves dissipation (disunity of soul and body) that is unnatural to human nature and against its proper order and discipline (cf. the life of Jesus Christ as the normalization of human nature). In relation to time, sloth involves futile human care and anxiety. Hence, sin as sloth in being radically human can be defined as insincerity (to one's nature).

Furthermore, the radical humanity in Jesus Christ reveals the corruption of human nature into a miserable human condition. Misery, the boundless state of self-alienation and self-contradiction, forms a vicious circle of actual sins under the bondage of the will. In this context, Christian freedom does not signify a choice at the crossroads, but the real freedom to be genuinely human with no possibility of sinning (*non potest peccare*). *Humanitas Christi* sets the limitation of the bondage for the sake of the sanctification of humanity.

Selfish Desires vs. sloth. Wang and Barth converge in understanding evil basically as deviation or aberration from primordial human nature. However, whereas Wang engaged primarily in restating the faith in the ontological structure of human nature, Barth focused on analyzing the historical and existential problems of sin in contrast to the Grace of God. Barth presented a more comprehensive analysis for the human condition, the misery under the bondage of will. Understanding evil basically as a dualistic break in a person's being and primal relationships, Confucianism has been not so much engaged in the analysis of this problem in contrast to Christianity. Evil is significantly more of a problem for Christians (or a problem in a theistic paradigm with respect to the righteousness of God). For Christianity, evil is basically a sin, the violation of a person's proper relation with God. The notion of God's Grace further radicalizes the Christian concept of evil, illuminating the human predicament and suffering, while evoking the problem of theodicy.[9]

Slightly similar to Mencius, Barth also understood shaming as the
spark to regain the original vision beyond the dysfunctional state of
human condition. Whereas Mencius viewed shaming as the gate to
recover the ontological state of mind-and-heart, Barth saw shaming as
the clue to realizing sin and the human situation.

Barth's understanding of sin as sloth—inhumanity, dissipation, and
anxiety—resonates with the Confucian insight of evil as the violation of
the ontological unity and totality (in relation to others, self, and the
mandate of Heaven). While Confucianism appeals to inherent, "normal"
human nature, Barth argued for Jesus Christ as the normalization of
humanity. Wang and Barth are congruent in their understanding of self-
cultivation and sanctification as the normalization of human nature
beyond the existential state of evil. In short, both Wang and Barth
agree that evil is an "insincerity" to one's own nature.

They share a dialectical understanding of the ontological reality of
human nature and the existential human condition.[10] Existentially, we
live (*de facto*) in the state of *jen-hsin* (Wang) or in the miserable human
condition (Barth). Ontologically, nevertheless, we are (*de jure*) in the
state of *tao-hsin* (Wang) or in the freedom of reconciliation (Barth).
Wang and Barth are congruent in focusing on the *de jure* (original) state
for radical humanization. For Wang, humanization (self-cultivation) is
an activation of good knowing fully latent in mind-and-heart. For
Barth, it (sanctification) is a participation in the Christian freedom (of
being not able to sin), once and for all, endowed by Jesus Christ.

The Problem of Evil

	Wang	**Barth**
Root-paradigm	*liang-chih*	*humanitas Christi*
Paradigm of Humanity	*jen*	*imago Dei*
The Problem of Evil	selfish desires	sloth
Ontological reality	*tao-hsin*	*non potest peccare* (freedom)
Human situation	*jen-hsin*	misery (bondage of the will)

Chapter 12

•

How to be Fully Human?

The *Tao* of Humanization:
Chih Liang-chih vs. Walking under
the Direction of the Holy Spirit

Wang and Barth believed that self-transcendent, ultimate humanity, *liang-chih* and *humanitas Christi,* empowers people to realize their radical humanity (self-cultivation and sanctification). In the final analysis, Wang articulated self-cultivation as the extension of *liang-chih,* whereas Barth formulated sanctification as walking under the direction (*Weisung*) of the Holy Spirit in the participation into Christ (*participatio Christi*).

Wang's doctrine of *chih liang-chih* (Chap. 4): The doctrine of the unity of knowing and acting does not abdicate the practice of *ko-wu* (the investigation of things). Wang's point is that "the sincerity of the will" (*ch'eng-i*) is the real issue of *ko-wu.* It is central among the four inner dimensions of self-cultivation: the rectification of the mind-and-heart, the sincerity of the will, the extension of the knowledge, and the investigation of things (*the Great Learning*). The sincerity of the will signifies a process through which a person's intention becomes truthful to the directionality of his or her mind-and-heart. From this vantage point, *ko-wu* is not so much a detached, objective, and static enterprise as a dynamic process through which a person's ontological being is manifested in existential becoming.

This task consists of two inseparable procedures: *ts'un T'ien-li* (the preservation of the Heavenly Principle) and *ch'ü jen-yü* (the extirpation

of human desires). The Heavenly Principle refers to the ultimate basis
on which we can become what we ought to be. However, human
desires tend to obstruct and distort this process of becoming.
Therefore, we need a twofold effort. (1) We have to preserve the
Heavenly Principle so as to protect and realize our ontological reality.
(2) At the same time, we need to extirpate human desires in order to
avoid their limitation of the full realization of authentic selfhood and
falsification of our original intention.

Wang's teaching of self-cultivation culminated in the doctrine of
chih liang-chih (the extension of *liang-chih*). *Chih liang-chih* needs
attentive efforts of self-exertion. The purpose of the twofold precept of
the preservation of the Heavenly Principle and the extirpation of human
desire is to free *liang-chih* from being obscured and to fully extend it.
This demands "single-minded," guarding against pride (egoism), "the
chief of all vices," but keeping humility (selflessness), "the foundation
of all virtue." Mencius' saying, "Always be doing something," is a
positive statement of the negative imperative, "Do away with your
selfish desires." Wang further identified *chih liang-chih* with the
Mencian notion of "the accumulation of righteous deeds." The four
inner dimensions of self-cultivation in the *Great Learning* can be
summarized in the one effort, *chih liang-chih*. We must focus on inward
transformation rather than outward imitation. We can attain the way of
sage only through personal experience of *liang-chih*.

By the doctrine of the extension of *liang-chih*, Wang overcame the
mistakes of two most powerful modes of thinking of his time, the Chu
Hsi school and Buddhism. On the one hand, in contrast to Chu Hsi's
external, empirical, and gradual method of self-cultivation, Wang
contended that *liang-chih* is innate, inborn, and spontaneous. Self-
cultivation, as the extension of *liang-chih*, involves not merely self-
effort but also self-realization. On the other hand, Wang also criticized
the Buddhists' attempt to realize "the Way" by separation from primal
ties as a form of subjectivism, which seeks "self-satisfaction of the great
ego." *Liang-chih* not only transcends human beings, but also is
immanent in social life. The locus of *chih liang-chih* is everyday social
life. *Liang-chih* is the true foundation of social solidarity, political
justice, and cosmic communion, and *chih liang-chih* entails serious,
ethicoreligious and sociopolitical involvement.

The uniqueness of being human lies not merely in the possession of
liang-chih, but also in the ability to extend *liang-chih* so as to embody
the universe as a whole. *Chih liang-chih*, as an actualization of the

inner sage, is to manifest radical humanity in cosmic togetherness and anthropocosmic communion. The Confucian way of radical humanization is summarized in expanding one's genuine humanity to its full potential. However, in the process, a person must be freed from subjectivism, and from any attachment or fixation to any thing, however small it is.

The doctrine of *chih liang-chih* implies the identification of radical subjectivity (*liang-chih*) and ontological reality (*t'ien-li*), a defining characteristic of Wang's mode of thinking. *Liang-chih*, as inner sagehood, true selfhood, or radical humanity, denotes a radical subjectivity which is fundamentally different from subjectivism. The process of *chih liang-chih* operates in a circular (more precisely, a spiral) movement of identification. Ontologically, *liang-chih* as radical subjectivity is identical with the Heavenly Principle. While, existentially, subjectivity is *de facto* obstructed and distorted, radical subjectivity is an irreducible reality which generates dynamism, creativity, and the power to entail a process of self-realization. The process of self-realization ultimately consists in the total manifestation of the Heavenly Principle. Finally, the Heavenly principle as the ontological reality, is also the original substance of mind-and-heart. The original substance of mind-and-heart, as radical subjectivity (*liang-chih*), must be fully self-exerted to manifest the Heavenly Principle completely, which is, *chih liang-chih* or radical subjectification.

Barth's doctrine of the direction of the Holy Spirit (Chap. 7): Barth conceived the direction of the Son as the basis of sanctification. The exaltation of Jesus as the royal man is its objective basis. Since the history of Jesus includes the history of all humanity, there is an ontological connection between the being of Jesus and all other beings (expressed in the Johannine writings in terms of abiding). Since this ontological reality which is the basis of the power of our conversion and our freedom is concealed, we need to recognize this ontological dignity to be and become radically and really human. Being and becoming a Christian is based on the operative power of transition from Jesus to us. This transitional power of being and becoming has characteristics of light, liberation, knowledge, peace, and life.

The New Testament testifies that this power is the work of the Holy Spirit. The Holy Spirit authenticates and sanctifies human beings as really human, and to be really Christian means to be radically human. Three decisive historical factors are: the royal man is the controlling center, the community is the goal, and the power of transition links the royal man and the community. The Holy Spirit effects the transition from Jesus to human beings in the distinctive history of the Trinity that is history as partnership (God is never solitary, but always has a partner). The history between the Father and the Son culminates in the concrete history of the Holy Spirit. The Holy Spirit is the basis of the riddle of the servant and royal man Jesus in the dialectic between humiliation and exaltation. The dialectic is not a paradox, but the *doxa* of God in the trinitarian life, entailing the powerful Yes of resurrection over the No of the cross. The Holy Spirit calls forth our response of thankfulness and brings us real joy, underscoring the theologies of resurrection and glory. The Holy Spirit also gives direction (*Weisung*) with its twofold meaning, wisdom and way. *Weisung*, similar to the Confucian notion of *Tao*, directs, corrects, and instructs us to a concrete and sapiential way (on the march, not static) to becoming radically human.

Further, sanctification is realized in the relationship between the Holy One and the saints. Often, *de facto* we have not grasped our transformation (sanctification and conversion) which *de jure* has been realized in the Holy One. Sanctification *de jure* has come to humanity as an a priori, as the ontological connection with the Holy One. However, it is achieved *de facto* by our participation in the Body of Christ. A Christian is defined as a disturbed sinner by this *Weisung* of the Holy One. By a critical, but totally free direction, sanctification entails discipleship, conversion, works, and the cross.

The commanding summons of Jesus "follow me" binds persons to the One in practice, which demands simple obedience in response to the irruption of God's coming Kingdom. Christian discipleship in the reign of God requires our resolute renunciation of possessions, honor or fame, fixed ideas, family, and the absoluteness of religion. Conversion means an awakening of human involvement in totality, and a movement in faith in the opposite direction, to new humanity (renovation). However, new humanity is still present with old humanity (*simul justus et peccator*). Thus, like a falling out or a quarrel, conversion still finds the human existence in a twofold movement. It also entails social relationship with others. Conversion is a public matter, as a public person acts in the totality of his or her being. Sanctification also entails works in mutuality (God's praise of our works and our praise of God's works). We do good works in correspondence to God's good works, and participate in God's works as His co-workers. Finally, the cross, as the limit and goal of our sanctification, reveals the most concrete form of fellowship between Christ and Christians. It involves persecution, sharing in tension, and temptations. However, it implies neither self-sought sufferings, nor the end of our life, but our sanctification. The cross is penultimate and provisional, for its real goal is to bring human beings joy in the eschatological hope of the coming Kingdom of eternal life.

  Chih Liang-chih vs. the Direction of the Holy Spirit. Wang and Barth articulate a similar structure of radical humanization. Both self-cultivation and sanctification point to radical humanization according to their root-paradigms, *liang-chih* and the life-act of Jesus Christ. Both Wang and Barth view these root-paradigms as radical subjectivity generating the spiritual power of our being and becoming radically, really, and fully human. Furthermore, they present the similar characteristics of this spiritual powers (from *liang-chih* and the Holy Spirit): light, liberation, knowledge, peace, and life.

  Both agree that self-cultivation and sanctification depend on the enactment of radical subjectivity beyond the existentially dysfunctional state. However, their foci diverge. Whereas confuciology focuses on human mind-and-heart (perfectibility), theology focuses on the sinful structure of human condition (fallibility). While Wang emphasizes the capacity of human effort through the sincerity of the will (immanent, internal power), Barth focuses on the transforming power of the Holy Spirit (transcendent, external power). Hence, while Wang consummated the insights of self-cultivation in the precept of the "extension" of *liang-chih*, Barth articulated sanctification as a participation in Christ (walking) under the direction of the Holy Spirit.

  Nevertheless, Barth's insight of the direction (*Weisung*) of the Holy Spirit resonates with the Confucian notion of *Tao* (the Way). In the same manner as the *Tao*, the *Weisung* does not offer us "a chance" like the ghosts "standing in decision," but "the reality of man [human being] concerning whom a decision has already been made" (IV/2: 363).[1] The *Weisung* does not put us "at a point or in a position," but sets us "on the way, on the march" (IV/2: 376).

  This metaphorical language for a dynamic action in progress or process rather than a static status echoes the radical of the Chinese character *Tao* which symbolizes a movement, process, or action. The Chinese word *Tao* is an outstanding linguistic rendition of what Barth had in mind when he plays with the German word *Weisung* (at least, *Tao* is a term far better than the English word *direction*). *Tao* designates precisely a sapiential way (*Weisung*) of life to be and become really, radically, fully human. Furthermore, the Way--Tao or Weisung--in both traditions primarily refers to the orthopraxis, salient in the notions of Confucian propriety and Christian discipleship. We see here a good case of a Confucian notion illuminating theological material.

Chih liang-chih sums up the four inner dimensions of self-cultivation, the rectification of mind-and-heart, the sincerity of the will, the extension of knowledge, and the investigation of things. Walking under the direction of the Holy Spirit entails the call to discipleship, awakening to conversion, praise of works, and the dignity of the cross. Both self-cultivation and sanctification require single-mindedness, recommending humility while rejecting pride. Both underscore the significance of deeds or works. While advocating a sudden enlightenment, Wang accommodated to the Mencian notion of the accumulation of righteous deeds as the result of *chih liang-chih*. Barth embraced the value of works often neglected by Protestant theologies.

In the final analysis, Wang's teaching of self-cultivation and Barth's doctrine of sanctification suggest a realization of radical subjectivity involving a similar circular or spiral movement (radical subjectification), a crucial point of convergence. On the one hand, Wang accommodated (though reluctantly) to an existential polarity in human mind-and-heart between *liang-chih* and *T'ien-li* which ought to be in unity. As Tu concluded, Wang's thesis concerning *chih liang-chih* is to see self-cultivation as the identification of subjectivity (*liang-chih*) and ontological reality (*T'ien-li*) at the locus of mind-and-heart. On the other hand, Barth presupposed an existential polarity between (*de facto*) human consciousness and (*de jure*) ontological reality of reconciliation through Jesus Christ. Barth understood sanctification as a realization of our real subjectivity in response to the ontological connection with Jesus Christ, under the direction of the Holy Spirit. Both advocate that subjectivity does not mean subjectivism, but has the real value in the context of community. Rather, it constitutes a radical criticism of subjectivism.

However, the direction of their moves differ. While Wang began from the inward (immanent transcendence) to the outward (extension), Barth looked from the outside (inclusive salvation history) to the inside (self-realization). Wang and Barth converge in saying that being either a Confucian, or a Christian means being radically human. However, their descriptions of being a person in the process are different: whereas confuciology names the human being a profound person, theology calls the person a disturbed sinner.

The Method of Humanization

	Wang's Self-cultivation	Barth's Sanctification
Foundation	*liang-chih*	the Holy Spirit (the Son)
Direction	*Tao*	*Weisung*

Way	*chih liang-chih*	
	(Identification of subjectivity and ontological reality)	
	under the direction of the Spirit	
	(*de facto* realization of de jure ontological connection)	

Human Image	profound person	disturbed sinner
Movement	inward/outward (exertion)	outward/inward (thematization)

Root-Metaphor:
Ch'eng (sincerity) vs. *Agape* (love)

The cardinal virtues of Confucianism and Christianity are *jen* and *agape*. However, as we have seen in the previous analysis, *jen* is a more ontological notion when regarded as the paradigm of humanity in contrast to the *imago Dei*. *Agape* relates to the existential fulfillment of the *imago Dei* in Christian theology. *Ch'eng* (sincerity), the "moral metaphysics" of *The Doctrine of Means*,[2] is the metaphor of Wang's confuciology. While the Christian disturbed sinner is a loving "hearer and doer" of the message of Grace, the Confucian profound person can be depicted as a sincere "digger" in the anthropocosmic vision. Hence, Barth's concept of *agape* (love) will be compared with the Confucian notion of *ch'eng* (sincerity). This comparison of these two root-metaphors may summarize the points of convergence and divergence between Wang's confuciology of self-cultivation and Barth's theology of sanctification.

<u>The Confucian notion of *Ch'eng* (sincerity)</u> (Chap. 2): Wang's doctrine of the unity of knowing and acting does not imply so much a closed inner transformation, as a dynamic adaptation to the real life situation. Self-cultivation as radical humanization must be manifested in the network of human-relatedness. This realization of true self as *jen* (creative co-humanity) commences with concrete existence and ends in universal extension. This points to the external dimension of the Confucian concrete-universal approach.[3] The internal dimension of the

Confucian concrete-universal approach is related to one of the fundamental Neo-Confucian notions, *ch'eng*. Since Confucianism presupposes human nature as a heavenly endowment, the locus of self-realization is the very structure of humanity. However, self-realization is not a process of individuation, but primarily a course of universal communion. The deeper one descends into the ground of one's being, the more one transcends one's anthropological structure, and "the closer one gets to the spring of common humanity and the source of cosmic creativity."[4] This paradox is based on "the Confucian belief that the true nature of man and the real creativity of the cosmos are both 'grounded' in *sincerity*."[5] Being sincere is not only the way to transcend one's anthropocentric structure, but also the way of ultimate humanization. The most sincere person is a sage, who manifests ultimate humanity. Ultimate humanity not only transcends egoism, but also realizes an anthropocosmic unity. In this process, self-realization (being) and self-transformation (becoming) are inseparable. The absolutely sincere person is the most authentic human being who participates in the reconciliating, transforming, and nourishing process of the cosmos as a whole. "To do so is to fulfill one's human nature," that is the meaning of humanization.

Barth's concept of *agape* (Love) (Chap. 8): Barth conceived Christian love as a total human self-giving, in correspondence with faith as the reception of the total self-giving of God. *Agape*, self-giving love, is the way and the act, distinguished from self-love (*eros*). Although both *agape* and *eros* are related to human nature, *agape*-love is in correspondence with real human nature, while *eros*-love is in contradiction. Vertically, *agape* fulfills and transcends real human being in proper relationship with God, but *eros* falls short of it. Horizontally, *agape* affirms and realizes radical humanity, but *eros* betrays or denies humanity (as co-humanity). Only through self-giving love (*agape*) can we liberate ourselves from the vicious circle of destructive self-love (*eros*).

The foundation of Christian love (*agape*) is faith in the self-giving love of God. Our love is a free action, but as a secondary love, responding to a primary love. God, who is love, forms the ultimate basis of love in His triune mode of being. Divine love, as the *opus Dei ad extra* as well as the basis of human love, is an electing, purifying, and creative love.

Although it is exclusively grounded in the love of God in the trinitarian mode of being, our own action of love is equally significant.

The act of love is new, free, sacrificial, and joyful. It is not merely a prolongation of the divine love, but a fully human act in return. This act of love has a twofold content: the love for God and Jesus (the first commandment) and the love for neighbors (the second commandment). First, Christians are those who love God and Jesus in the freedom of obedience to the command of Jesus "You shall love the Lord your God with all your heart, with all your soul, and with all your mind, and with all your strength." This vertical love for God is not a theomonistic conception, but involves a real human act in continual subjection to the command. Second, Christian love is the love for others, according to the other command of Jesus "You shall love your neighbor as yourself." This second commandment is as indispensable as the first. This commandment does not imply an abstract universal love of humanity, but a differentiated love in shared praxis. Thus, proximity is an important factor for its concrete realization. It always begins with specific fellow-people in the context of salvation history. Neighbor, in the biblical sense, means a reciprocal witness on the horizontal plane.

There is no revelation of love without a gracious inter-relating among people. While, in the final analysis, the emphasis on particularity is practical and provisional, the circle of mutual love must be widened to universal extension. Therefore, Barth's conception of horizontal Christian love is congruent with the Confucian notion of the concrete-universal approach. Finally, Christian love is the culminating manner of Christian life. Love is not merely an effluence of God's own life, but a real and concrete human act. Love, as the greatest among the manners of Christian life (faith, love, and hope), alone counts, alone conquers, and alone endures. In the last sentence of the *Church Dogmatics* IV/2, Barth said that "*agape* is the Way" (cf. *Tao*).

Agape vs. *Ch'eng*. We already have discussed the parallelism between the Confucian distinction of *tao-hsin* and *jen-hsin,* and the Christian distinction between *agape* and *eros*. *Tao-hsin* and *agape* refer to the ontological basis for human nature, whereas *jen-hsin* and *eros* describe the existential situation. Both *tao-hsin* and *agape* correspond to the radical human nature, whereas both *jen-hsin* and *eros* contradict human nature. Both *ch'eng* and *agape* refer to a realization of ontological reality onto existential totality, or in other words, a transformation of existential reality by ontological reality.[6]

Agape as the Christian *Tao* converges with *ch'eng* as the concrete-universal mode of the Confucian *Tao* in the unity of ontological knowledge and ethical action. *Ch'eng* and *agape* congruently point to the transcendent human subjectivity in the unity of being and becoming. Furthermore, similar to Confucianism, Barth advocated a concrete-universal approach in the horizontal execution of *agape*. According to Barth, Christian love also does not refer to the abstract notion of undifferentiated, universal love. On the contrary, both Confucian love (*ai*) and Christian love (*agape*) entail a concrete-universal realization of co-humanity through ever-expanding human relatedness; namely, through the channels of neighbors (in the sequence of Heavenly bonds or in the salvation history respectively).

However, *ch'eng* and *agape* are based on different perspectives. While *ch'eng* is based on the Confucian all-embracing anthropocosmic vision, *agape* is rooted in the divine-human convenantal relationship in the context of salvation history (a theohistorical vision). Their foci are also different. Whereas *ch'eng* focuses on the ontological dimension of humanity (as a self-realizing and self-transforming agent for cosmic equilibrium and harmony), *agape* primarily refers to an existential dimension of humanity (as a self-giving and reconciling agent, beyond the human predicament of alienation and separation).[7] This may be characterized: whereas *ch'eng* as the Confucian root-metaphor is more ontological (sincerity), *agape* as the Christian root-metaphor is more existential (love).

The Root-Metaphor of Humanization

	Wang's self-cultivation	Barth's sanctification
Root-Paradigm	*liang-chih*	*humanitas Christi*
	Wisdom	*Christ*
Paradigm	*jen*	*Imago Dei*
Ontological reality	*tao-hsin*	*agape*
Existential condition	*jen-hsin*	*eros*
Root-Metaphor	*ch'eng*-sincerity	*agape*-love
	sincere digger	*loving hearer*
Divergent Vision	*anthropocosmic vision*	salvation history
		(*theohistorical vision*)
Different Focus	ontological (cosmos)	existential (history)
Two Converging Ways:	*the concrete-universal way* of ever-expanding circle of human relatedness; ethicoreligious practice in the unity of knowledge and action	

Conclusion

•

A Confucian-Christian Dialogue
In Search for
the *Tao* of New Cosmic Humanity

Thick Resemblances Within Radical Differences

Now, let us turn to review the thesis I suggested in the introduction that, *in the light of Wang Yang-ming and Karl Barth, self-cultivation and sanctification are thickly resemblant views of a common issue: i.e., how to be fully human, or the* Tao *of radical humanization.* I have shown that self-cultivation and sanctification deal with a common issue, radical humanization. Whereas the goal of self-cultivation is to realize the true self (*liang-chih*) latent in original human nature, the goal of sanctification is to realize one's true (elected) nature. Both self-cultivation (how to be fully human) and sanctification (how to be really human) are concerned with the common problem of how to be radically human. Since Confucianism and Christianity converge at this point, I used this common issue (how to be fully human) as a point of departure for the Confucian-Christian dialogue I attempted in the last part.

Certainly, Confucianism and Christianity are two radically different religious paradigms that emerged from different historical-cultural-social-linguistic matrices; more human-centered versus more God-centered, more subjective versus more objective, soteriologically, more dependent on the inner power versus more on the external power, etc. These differences appear in the dialogue between Wang Yang-ming's confuciology of self-cultivation and Karl Barth's theology of sanctification.   The   two   paradigms   have   distinct   perspectives, emphases, and foci. Confuciology tends to emphasize immanence, and theology emphasizes historicality.   The Confucian source is the sapiential tradition transmitted through the human mind-and-heart. The Christian source is the prophetic tradition revealed through the Word of God.   Their   descriptions   of   the   root-paradigm   epitomize   their differences.   *Liang-chih* is immanent-transcendence, and *humanitas Christi* is characterized as historico-transcendence.   These different root-paradigms manifest the divergent visions of their wider contexts: the Confucian vision of anthropocosmic and inclusive humanism versus the Christian vision of salvation history (*theo-historical* vision)[1] which was consummated by the Christ event.

Characteristically, confuciology of self-cultivation is more ontolog-ical and cosmic, while theology of sanctification is more existential and historical. This distinction is revealed in the analysis of evil. Whereas confuciology   focuses   on   reaffirming   the   primordial   unity   and ontological goodness, theology analyzes the sinful structure of the existential human condition. This nuance is visible in the understanding of humanity. While confuciology construes *jen* as cosmic togetherness, theology articulates *imago Dei* rather as historical togetherness. These differences reflect divergent priorities in the movement of radical humanization: whereas self-cultivation first looks at the human inner self and makes an outward move (*chih liang-chih*), sanctification begins with the historical event and turns to subjectivity (the direction of the Holy Spirit).   While the Confucian model of a human being is the profound person, a sincere digger according to the *anthropocosmic vision* (*ch'eng*), the Christian model is the disturbed sinner, an obedient hearer and doer to the commandments of God according to the *theohistorical vision* (*agape*).

In the final analysis, these differences come from the fact that Confucianism and Christianity are based on two fundamentally different visions, *anthropocosmic versus theohistorical* respectively.   This visional difference explains the salient distinction in their emphases, immanence versus historicality. Hence, their differences can be summarized in two different modes of thinking; *the Confucian anthropocosmic mode of thinking* versus *the Christian theohistorical mode of thinking*.

Nevertheless, despite the fact that Confucianism and Christianity have fundamentally different visions and modes of thinking, the dialogue between Wang Yang-ming's confuciology of self-cultivation and Barth's theology of sanctification demonstrates remarkably thick resemblances. First of all, Wang and Barth begin their enterprises from crucial paradigm changes which present similar characteristics. (1) Their paradigm shifts (the identity of mind-and-heart and principle and the reversal of Gospel and law) share two converging goals: (a) Both maintain a unified foundation of faith (mind-and-heart and the Word of God), guarding against and overcoming dualism. And (b) both open up the dynamic possibility of human involvement in the process of realization (by claiming that mind-and-heart and the law are not ambiguous). (2) Both Wang and Barth take one's ultimate commitment (the establishment of the will and faith) as the point of departure for the explications of the meaning of their traditions (confuciology and theology), but not a metaphysics or a philosophy of religion. (3) Both radically assert the unity of theory and praxis--knowing and acting, being and acting, and ontological knowledge and ethical practice-- which entails profound socio-political implications.

Secondly, Wang and Barth articulate radical humanization in a similar way. (1) Both establish ultimate humanity, the root-paradigm or the most concrete-universal of true humanity, as the ultimate ontological reality in their own traditional categories—*liang-chih* and *humanitas Christi*. (2) Both define radical humanization as a transcendent process of realizing this ontological reality beyond the structure of the ambiguous human existential situation; namely, the identification of subjectivity and ontological reality in mind-and-heart (Wang) and the self-realization (or subjectification) of the ontological connection with Jesus Christ (Barth). (3) Both conceive that ultimate humanity endows the concrete spiritual direction (*Tao* and *Weisung*, respectively) through spiritual empowerment.

Thirdly, both Wang and Barth agree in understanding that evil arises existentially by a dysfunction and a denial of this ontological reality. Both believe that the root-paradigm not only illuminates but also has an intrinsic power to remove evil.

Fourthly, Wang and Barth present a similar material definition and paradigm of what the human is and ought to be. (1) Within their traditional categories of *jen* and *imago Dei*, Wang and Barth agree that being human means being-in-togetherness: a creative co-humanity (Wang) or a joyful *Mitmenschlichkeit* (Barth). (2) Both of them emphasize the understanding of selfhood (person) as a communal center of relationship, rejecting the modern understanding of self as an individual ego. For both Wang and Barth, radical humanization involves self-transformation as a communal act. (3) Both of them advocate the realization of what the human ought to be in the concrete-universal way of the ever-expanding circles or nexus of human relatedness and through the ethicoreligious realization rooted in the unity of ontological knowledge (being) and ethical action (becoming).

In this manner, Wang's confuciology of self-cultivation and Barth's theology of sanctification present similar concrete-universal ways of radical humanization. The resemblances manifested in the dialogue are remarkably thick, despite the fact that they are from two radically different religious paradigms. This may vindicate the thesis I have attempted to establish in this book: the Confucian teaching of self-cultivation and the Christian doctrine of sanctification are thickly resemblant views of a common issue, how to be fully human. Christianity meets Confucianism in the common quest for the *Tao* of humanization.

The Quest for the Tao of Common Humanity

There are some further implications of this study that need to be highlighted. First of all, this study endorses the hypothesis I argued in the Introduction that the thick resemblances between Neo-Confucianism and Reformed Protestantism (as illustrated in a comparison of Wang and Barth) explain why the miracle of the Presbyterian mission took place in Korea. These resemblances are such that there is a need for careful, conceptual scrutiny and critical, comparative studies of the two traditions. Without this, their commonalities may produce fragmentary and mischievous forms of religious synthesis (which already seems to have happened in the Korean Church such as the "individual churchism"). This false synthesis jeopardizes the integrity and true values of both traditions.

Secondly, this study supports the methodological presuppositions I suggested in Chapter 9. Even though defining Confucianism as a faith is problematic, interfaith dialogue provides a concrete and practical (and perhaps fruitful) way of thematizing a Confucian-Christian dialogue.[2] The locus where Confucianism and Christianity really meet each other lies in the transformative praxis *(Tao)* of radical humaniza-tion.[3] While not denying the value of comparative studies such as philosophy of religion and comparative theology, the task of East Asian constructive theology goes beyond this realm and takes a further step--

to see an a posteriori thematization for the communities of faith in a historic encounter between the two powerful stories of humanization. Theology and confuciology are thick-descriptive explications of these two stories in a more communicable cultural-linguistic matrix. In this enterprise, a confuciology was constructed to establish a proper symmetry so as to protect Confucianism from the categorical impositions by scientifically armed modern theologies. Through the correlation of confuciology and theology,[4] the collision and fusion of the two hermeneutical horizons can be appropriately scrutinized without the loss of their structural integrities and inner dynamics, or simply their intratextualities..

Thirdly, the starting question for the Confucian-Christian dialogue, *how to be fully human* or radical humanization, is a very significant one for the contemporary world. This issue has a global significance. The future of the human race and the planet earth appear gloomy and apocalyptic, with merciless technological warfare, massive ecological disasters, and the collapse of the balance of the cold-war ideologies, etc. And the process of dehumanization continues. The current context calls for radical humanization, once again, with its reassuring trust and confidence in the goodness of original humanity; a creative and joyful co-humanity which involves not only social but also cosmic togetherness. The Confucian "sincere diggers" and the Christian "obedient hearers" must share together the challenges of our time—the mandate of Heaven and the *kairos* of our time—in moral solidarity rather than in doctrinal contradiction.

Fourthly, the dialogue warrants the three modes of thinking that are originally Confucian and can be properly Christian and that need be emphasized with respect to the contemporary theological issues; i.e., *jen, ch'eng,* and *Tao.* First, the dialogue affirms that Confucianism and Christianity converge in *the jen mode of thinking*; in other words, "thinking in relationships and communities."[5] This mode of thinking is a proper corrective to contemporary individualism. Confucianism demands that the mode of thinking in relationship and community must be expanded to the widest horizon, in solidarity not only with the people of other races, sexes, classes, and cultures but also with nature, so as to actualize the goal of humanity as the cosmic being-in-togetherness. This *jen* mode of thinking has an affinity with feminist theology,[6] and thus can have a genuine dialogue with feminist theologies.

Further, the dialogue confirms that both Wang and Barth propose the concrete-universal mode of self-transformation as a communal act rooted in the unity of ontological knowledge and ethical practice. This *ch'eng mode of thinking* will be very important for our divided world. It may enable us to overcome difficult polarities such as religious or cultural particularity and universality, or diversity and unity, theory and practice, and orthodoxy and orthopraxis.

Furthermore, the dialogue establishes that Wang and Barth converge in *the Tao mode of thinking*, in the emphasis of orthopraxis in the communal interrelatedness (*propriety* and discipleship). They share a claim that radical humanization implies primarily *Tao* (the Way of life in transformation). *Tao* as the Way (propriety, orthopraxis) of Life in transformation refers to the Confucian expression of transformative praxis. Transformative praxis in the Confucian sense is *Tao*. The *Tao* mode of thinking, underscoring transformative praxis, also can make a productive dialogue with liberation theologies.

In the final analysis, all these modes of thinking reveal the real implication of the dialogue, i.e., an earnest participation in search of the *Tao* of common humanity. That is to say, Confucian-Christian dialogue is a genuine "dialogical participation" for the "common quest for a new humanism."[7]

Jesus Christ as the *Tao* of Humanity: Toward a Confucian Christology

For East Asian Christians, the quest for the *Tao* of common humanity--the common issue of how to be fully human--inevitably solicits Christology. For Christians, Jesus Christ is the truly humane human being and "the true and good human being *par excellence*."[8] Since *humanitas Christi* is the ultimate manifestation of full humanity and the root-paradigm of radical humanization, for Barth, Christology is the foundation for theological anthropology. Also, Karl Rahner said, "Christology may be studied as self-transcendent anthropology; anthropology as deficient Christology."[9]

At last, therefore, this study invites the most important theological theme for Christians in East Asia, where Christianity really has encountered Confucianism; namely, Christology, "Who do you say I am?"(Mark 8:29). Since Jesus himself asked it to his disciples, this question has been the most pervasive question for the Christian faith.

In the East Asian context, this question can be reformulated in this way: "Who do we, East Asian Christians from the Confucian tradition, say Christ is?"

Now, we are in a better position to pursue this most critical Christian question adequate to our own context. The dialogue between Wang Yang-ming and Karl Barth can furnish some bases for East Asian Christians to develop a more appropriate and authentic articulation for the faith in Christ. This refers to the second stage I mentioned in Chapter 9.

In the second, normative-constructive stage, we are turning to focus on individual Christians and Christian communities in the historic collision of the two spiritual traditions, including other East Asian communities outside of East Asia. These communities need a wholistic understanding of the Christian faith in their given cultural-linguistic matrix (Confucianism).

This is the moment for an East Asian constructive theology that impels us to move beyond an *a priori* level. As John Cobb said, it is a moment of the "beyond dialogue,"[10] beyond the hermeneutical moments of Wang Yang-ming and Karl Barth. The main task of this constructive moment is to construct an *a posteriori* articulation of the normative Christian faith for communities in the historic collision and fusion of two hermeneutical horizons, the two powerful stories of radical humanization. Primarily, this normative-constructive enterprise does not refer to an arbitrary deliberation of speculative comparison, but an imperative thematization of these Christian communities for the integrated understanding of their faith. However, this enterprise does not imply a naive, so-called religious syncretism.[11] On the contrary, it is more related to "a confessional method" of H. Richard Niebuhr[12] and to what R. Panikkar called "intrareligious dialogue."[13]

In this stage, the thick resemblances between Wang's confuciology of self-cultivation and Barth's theology of sanctification can furnish points of departure to develop an East Asian Christology with a Confucian horizon. Their understandings of humanity in traditional terms of *jen* and *imago Dei* respectively are not only homologous but also materially congruent; namely, co-humanity, being-in-togetherness, or being for others. East Asian Christians would have no difficulty in perceiving Jesus Christ as the paradigm of humanity who perfects both *jen* and *imago Dei*. Also, in Jesus Christ, they find a perfect unity for the two root-metaphors of radical humanization, *ch'eng* and *agape*. Hence, the thick resemblances and homologies between Confucianism and Christianity discovered by the dialogue of Wang and Barth become substantiated in the form of Christology. If East Asian Christians confess Jesus Christ as the ultimate paradigm of sincere humanity (Sage) who has authenticated once and for all the Confucian faith in humanity's intrinsic possibility of self-transcendence, the Confucian story of humanization would become a profound resource for deepening and enriching the reality and meaning of Jesus Christ. This East Asian understanding of Christ out of their Confucian-Christian experiences may introduce some profound insights and new dimensions to the history of Christology.

Although it is beyond the scope of this book, I suggest five models of Christology that can be developed from the dialogue which solicit further work: (1) Jesus as the *Tao*, (2) Jesus as the Sage, (3) Jesus as the *Ch'eng par excellence*, (4) Jesus as the Paradigm of Humanity in the unity of *jen* and *agape*, and (5) Jesus as the Ultimate Embodiment of *Liang-chih*.

1. Jesus Christ as the *Tao* of Radical Humanization

In fact, the *Tao* of Jesus Christ is a term more accurate than Christology. Christ is the *Tao* (the Way). Jesus called himself "the Way" (John 14:6). The Greek *hodos* (the Way, also meaning path, road, route, journey, march, etc.) was the original name for Christianity in the early Church (see Act 9:2; 19:9; 22:4; 24:14, 22). Jürgen Moltmann entitled his book on Christology *The Way of Jesus Christ*. He explained that the way-metaphor "embodies the aspect of process," "makes us aware that every human christology is historically conditioned and limited," and involves "an invitation" to follow "christopraxis."[14]

Furthermore, the Confucian insight of *Tao* may enrich the Christian understanding of Christ. Borrowing Fingarette's phrases, Jesus Christ as the *Tao* may mean that Jesus Christ is "the right Way of life, the Way of governing, the ideal Way of human existence, the Way of the Cosmos, the generative-normative Way (Pattern, path, course) of existence as such."[15] The life-act of Jesus signifies the culmination of propriety (*li*) according to a self-directing orthopraxis of *Tao* which Moltmann appropriately called "christopraxis."

The parallelism between *Tao* and Barth's notion of the *Weisung* of the Holy Spirit further illuminates the sapiential character of the self-directing *Tao*. The freedom of Christian discipleship by the following of christopraxis and the outpouring power of the Holy Spirit converges with the freedom of Confucian discipleship by the preservation of propriety (*li*) and the self-directing power of the *Tao*. Both of them do not mean a choice among alternatives but a capacity to freely take part in the orthopraxis (*Tao*) of radical humanization.

2. Jesus Christ as the Ultimate Sage.

Christ revealed full humanity in the complete freedom of *Tao*. The humanity of Christ, the ultimate human existence, accomplished once and for all the attention and purification of the mind-and-heart in its fullest capacity of awareness. Jesus Christ, as both the true God and true humanity, realized and manifested the ultimate human existence in complete unity with Heaven. Jesus is, in every respect, the perfecter of mindfulness and sincerity. His works were not intentional deliberations, but effortless, natural executions (*wu-wei*) of the *Tao* as they ought to be. Jesus is the absolutely sincere person, the true Sage, who manifested the very definition of humaneness as a self-transforming and self-realizing agent. Jesus, the foundation of sanctification, is also the royal humanity (King) who has completed the normalization of humanity, fully restored its original goodness, and perfected the goal of self-cultivation. Hence, he is the Sage-King who culminated the old Confucian axiom, "Sageliness Within, Kingliness Without."

3. Jesus Christ as the *Ch'eng Par excellence* (the Most Concrete-Universal).

In Jesus the Sage, the concrete-universal way of the *Tao* is extended to the fullest fusion of horizons. Here, the Confucian story of benevolent humanity meets, collides, and fuses with the Christian story of the gracious God. The Confucian *anthropocosmic* drama encounters the Christian *theohistorical* drama. Then, they are further substantiated and together retold in an "*theanthropocosmic*" theater.[16] Jesus Christ is both the concrete-universal authentication of full humanity in the theanthropocosmic vision and the concrete-universal embodiment of the Triune God in human history. The humanity of Christ is the concrete-universal action of God's gracious election for the human race. The incarnation of the Triune God in the particular person of Jesus is the historical, and thus the most concrete, manifestation of God's salvific love for the human race. The most concrete point of the Christian faith is the dangerous memory of the Crucified One, while its most universal point is the dangerous memory of the risen Christ.

The life-act of Jesus the Sage, as the single foundation of Christian theology and ethics, radically manifested the unity of ontological knowledge and ethical activities (the unity of knowing and acting). It is the history of a Word in unity with deeds, as the proto-paradigm of "human being as the doer of the Word." In His life-act, there is no distinction between *logos* and *ethos*, or speaking and action. Such a unity of word and deed is identical with the etymological connotation of the Chinese character, *ch'eng* (sincerization).[17] In the life-act of Jesus the Sage-King, a Christian sincere person perceives the historical manifestation of the *ch'eng*-sincerization *par excellence*.[18] The miracles of Christ constitute examples of the process of divine-human sincerization in cosmic history (theanthropocosmic *ch'eng*). The event of His crucifixion and resurrection consummates the concrete-universal drama of divine-human sincerization in the history of the Trinity with the world. The meaning of sincerity becomes transformed in a Confucian-Christian sense; namely, a faith in Jesus Christ.

4. Jesus Christ as the Paradigm of Humanity in the Unity of *Imago Dei* and *Jen*.

Jesus Christ is a human being with and for other human beings. His life-act was the full manifestation of *imago Dei* as co-humanity, being-in-togetherness, being-for-others, being-in-encounter, life and history-in-partnership. There is a remarkable parallelism between the notions of *imago Dei* and *jen*. *Jen* as the root-paradigm of humanity is discovered in the humanity of Christ as the image of God.

On the one hand, Jesus as the perfector of *agape*, a radically affirmative attitude of love through a self-giving, an action culminated on the cross challenged Confucians. On the other hand, the Christian attitude of self-giving *agape*-love is also challenged by the Confucian attitude of self-critical reciprocity. An excessive attitude of Christian love without a necessary self-reflection and humility invites an "epistemological immodesty" and an "moral hubris."[19]

5. Jesus Christ as the Ultimate Embodiment of *Liang-chih* (Wisdom)

Finally, Jesus Christ, the divine-human *ch'eng*-sincerization *par excellence*, is the historical and personal culmination of the immanent-transcendence in human mind-and-heart. Kant already viewed Jesus as "the Personified Idea of the Good principle."[20] Manifesting the unity of *jen* and *agape*, Jesus Christ is the ultimate embodiment of the innate knowledge of the good (*liang-chih*). Jesus Christ is the pure and good knowing which naturally discerns good and evil and radically uncovers specificities of sin and evil and reveals the misery of the human condition.

As the root-paradigm of radical humanization, Jesus Christ is the historical consummation of *chih liang-chih*, the omega point of the extension of *liang-chih*. In Jesus Christ, the true God and the true humanity, the theanthropocosmic connection of Heaven, humanity, and all things has been fully reestablished, and human subjectivity has been completely identified with ontological reality (*T'ien-li*).

In a Confucian Christology, more correctly, in the *Tao* of Jesus Christ, the two concrete-universal stories of radical humanization are fully encountered. Jesus Christ as the *Tao* of radical humanization elicits the two encountered stories to move beyond dialogue and to be transformed into a new wholistic story of inclusive humanity, profound human subjectivity, the novel paradigm of radical humanity in a new context, the eschatological, theanthropocosmic vision in the new aeon.

Postscript:
The *Tao* of New Cosmic Humanity

These christological models would have implications beyond the boundary of the Christian communities in traditionally Confucian contexts. Such a Christology of Confucianism can give a profound contribution to the understanding of Jesus Christ in this postmodern, global world. This paradigm would be more appropriate than traditional Western ones. Traditional Christologies such as the two-nature Christology in the Chalcedonian formula is not only inappropriate for people in traditionally non-Christian societies, but also "too narrow" for other people in the world today.[21] Some Western theologians also argued that traditional Christologies have too many problems ("impasses") for the contemporary world.[22]

Furthermore, this new paradigm of Christology has three important postmodern characteristics, corresponding to the three modes of thinking: namely, the *Tao* mode of Christology, the *jen* mode of Christology, and the *theanthropocosmic* mode of Christology. First, it is a *Tao* mode of Christology. The *Tao* (the Way) of Jesus Christ is a more preferable term than Christology, and it denotes explicitly a christology on the way. Moltmann argued, "I am no longer trying to think of Christ statistically as one person in two natures or as a historical personality. I am trying to grasp him dynamically, in the forward movement of God's history with the world." And he said, "Every confession of Christ leads to the way, and along the way, and is not yet in itself the goal." [23]

A Confucian Christology as the *Tao* of Jesus Christ also has a great potentiality to be a paradigm to move beyond the contradictions of scientific and technological civilization: the surplus masses of people and poverty in the Third World, nuclearism threatened by the nuclear inferno, and ecological disaster.[24] Primarily as a paradigm of equilibrium and harmony, it corrects contemporary paradigms of domination and expansion (see Jesus Christ as the Unity of *Jen* and *Agape*).

The *Tao* mode of Christology is emancipatory. It has a radical dimension, because it understands Jesus Christ as the *Tao* of radical humanization, that is to say, the root-paradigm, the orthopraxis, and the transformative praxis of human subjectivity in communal and cosmic relationships. Underscoring christopraxis and discipleship and receiving the messianic challenge affirmatively, the *Tao* Christology can develop a fruitful dialogue with political and liberation Christologies.

Further, the new paradigm is a *jen* mode of Christology that is dialogical by nature. It is a Christology in dialogue with Confucianism, and *jen* itself connotes a strong dialogical relationship. Dialogical nature is by no means alien to the history of Christology. In fact, Christology always has been developed by dialogue: "Christology is never final but always in dialogue."[25]

Since Confucianism is an inclusive humanism, this Christology has an affinity with modern, anthropological theology. Kant and Karl Rahner refer to Jesus as "the prototype of true humanity" and "the uniquely supreme case of the actualization of man's nature in general" (cf. Jesus Christ as the Ultimate Embodiment of *Liang-chih*).[26] However, this anthropological Christology from the context of the modern thrust of "the turn to anthropology" (Martin Buber), "modern man's revolt into subjectivity" (Martin Heidegger) also has some defects. This turn reduced the meaning and reality of Christ into a Jesusology, localized it in "the human heart" and in the existential experience of the individual self. And it forgot the external conditions of other societies, of the third world, and nature.[27]

However, the *jen* mode of Christology overcomes these defects. For it is not based on the modern anthropology of the isolated ego, but the Confucian anthropology that views a person as the center of a relationship. It is not a "logy," a metaphysical understanding, of the prototype of the ego, but a *Tao,* a transformative praxis, for a person to be fully human (*jen*), co-humanity, being-in-togetherness, being-in-encounter, being-for-others, and life in partnership (see Jesus Christ as the Paradigm of Humanity). It is based on the mode of thinking in relationship and community. Western theologies tend to remain under the captivity of an anthropocentric interpretation of history. The *jen* Christology can regain the epistemological humility and ethical modesty (see Jesus Christ as the Paradigm of Humanity). And this Christology may overcome "the crisis of history"[28] by introducing ecological and cosmic dimensions of Confucian-Christian theanthropo-cosmic vision. Envisioning Jesus, the root-paradigm of humanity (*jen*), as a cosmic, reconciled being-in-togetherness, it expands and empowers the Confucian principle of reciprocity and mutuality to the theanthropo-cosmic dimension. This would foster a liberation of humanity and nature from the principle of domination and exploitation.[29]

Furthermore, the new paradigm entails a *theanthropocosmic* mode of Christology. This theanthropocosmic Christology as an Asian theology of religion is ecological. In this Christology, the anthropo-cosmic vision of Confucianism fully encounters, collides, and fuses with the theohistorical vision of Christianity. These visions move beyond dialogue and are mutually transformed into a theanthropo-cosmic vision. It conceives Jesus Christ as the ultimate history of the theanthropocosmic sincerization (*ch'eng*). Hence, it is also the *ch'eng* mode of Christology that transcends every dualism; knowing and acting, theology and ethics, logos and ethos, orthodoxy and orthopraxis, etc. This *ch'eng* mode of Christology would further comprehend Jesus Christ as the Crucified and Risen Cosmic Sage who fully actualized the messianic *Tao* for the eschatological theanthropocosmic equilibrium and harmony. The Crucified and Risen Sage is also the Wisdom of Creation (*liang-chih*) who is the hermeneutical principle of new theanthropocosmic communion, traditionally expressed in terms of new Heaven, new Earth, and new Humanity. In other words, it confesses that Jesus Christ is the *Tao* of new cosmic humanity.

To articulate Jesus Christ as the *Tao* of new cosmic humanity in these *Tao, jen,* and theanthropocosmic modes implies a postmodern constructive paradigm of theology, yet on the way and in dialogue.[30] As Moltmann criticized succinctly, ancient cosmological, modern anthro-pological, and contemporary scientific-technological christologies which also have been developed in the process of dialogue are too narrow and problematic.[31] Conceiving Jesus Christ as the *Tao* of new cosmic humanity, Confucian Christology would be an appropriate, new paradigm for the coming third millennium.

Finally, the common and kairological issue of the Confucian-Christian dialogue, how to be fully human, arrives at the Christological question of who we say Jesus Christ is. Now, we may say: Jesus Christ is the *Tao* of radical humanization. He is the *Jen*, the paradigm of full humanity. He is the *Ch'eng*; a theanthropocosmic sincerization beyond both the Confucian anthropocosmic cultivation and the Christian theohistorical sanctification. He is the Crucified and Risen Sage. He is the Wisdom (*sophia*; cf. *liang-chih*) of Creation, the hermeneutical principle of theanthropocosmic communion (cf. Luke 7:35; 11:49).[32] In sum, Jesus Christ is the *Tao* of new cosmic humanity, a theanthropo-cosmic transformative praxis every human being needs to follow. [33]

Appendix:

•

The Life of Wang Yang-ming[1]

Wang's given name was Shou-jen (literally means "holding onto humanity"), and his courtesy name was Po-an. But he has been best known by the name Yang-ming. Wang Yang-ming is a seminal thinker in the history of Chinese Confucianism whose importance is surpassed only by Confucius (551-479 B.C.), Mencius (372-289? B.C.), and Chu Hsi (1130-1200). He is also the most important radical reformer in the history of Confucianism, analogous to Martin Luther (1483-1546) in the history of the Christian Church.[2] His spiritual journey reflects remarkable similarities with that of Luther. Wang had a personality of *k'uang*, "madness or eccentricity as the characteristic of a man fired with a single desire for true greatness," which might be also a good Chinese description of Luther's personality.[3]

Wang was born into a prominent *literati* family as a descendent of Wang Hsi-chih (321-379), the famous Chinese calligrapher. He had fervently searched for the *Tao* since childhood. His biography reveals that even on his wedding day he became so immersed in discussion with a Taoist priest about nourishing the vital force for longevity that he did not return home until the next day. Similar to young Luther, Wang spent a turbulent youth with spiritual crises and intellectual trials, passing through all the religious teachings available at his time. In Wang's epitaph, Chan Jo-shui, his best friend, wrote of the "five falls" Wang had gone through before he finally realized the Confucian *Tao*:

> His first fall was an absorbing interest in knightly ventures; his second was in the skills of horsemanship and archery. His third fall was an absorbing interest in letters; his fourth was in the art of pursuing

immortality [Taoism], and his fifth was Buddhism. Only in the year
1506, did he return to the correct teaching of the sages.[4]

Wang's relationship with Ch'an Buddhism is a controversial issue.
It has been often claimed that Wang's teaching which contributed
significantly to the development of Chinese Ch'an Buddhism
"represents an excellent case of synthesis between Confucianism and
Ch'an Buddhism."[5] Chan Wing-tsit took issue with this argument in his
article, "How Buddhistic is Wang Yang-ming?"[6] However, Tu Wei-
ming argued that, while there is "Ch'an-like wisdom" in Wang's
formulation of ideas, Wang had a closer relationship with Taoism.[7]
Wang's Taoist proclivity has been rather easily justified by the
authority of Tseng Tien whose Taoist carefreeness was accepted by
Confucius in the *Analects* as an authentic expression of self-cultivation.[8]
Wang disliked naive and indiscriminate attacks on Taoism and
Buddhism. For him, the real issue was not such arbitrary attacks on
other religions, but self-criticism of his own tradition, of "ideal
Confucians versus vulgarized Confucians." The targets of his vehement
criticism, were his colleagues in Confucian communities who used
"Confucian ethics as a pretext for avaricious and sycophantic practices
in the government." [9]

Wang's Neo-Confucian thought was vigorous, experiential, practical, dynamic, and contextual. Chan expressed the characteristics well:

> The philosophy of Wang Yang-ming is a vigorous philosophy born of
> serious searching and bitter experience. It is no idle speculation or
> abstract theory developed for the sake of intellectual curiosity. Rather,
> it is intended to provide a fundamental solution to basic moral and
> social problems. It calls for firm purpose and earnest effort, and for the
> actual practice and concrete demonstration of values. The intellectual
> and political situation of the time demanded just such a system.[10]

Politically, as de Bary said, the late Ming period in which Wang
lived, was "one of the most creative and stimulating periods in the
history of Chinese thought" which produced "the most searching
critique of political and social institutions China had ever known."
Among those radical intellectuals in sixteenth-century China, Wang was
"the most deeply committed and personally effective of Confucian
activists." The official Ming History called him a statesman who made
"the greatest achievement of any civil official in the Ming period,"
rather than a scholar.[11]

Intellectually, Wang radically attacked Ch'eng-Chu philosophy,[12] which had lost its original moral strength and had turned into a "pure scholasticism."[13] It was Chu Hsi's tradition, particularly, with which Wang painfully struggled. Eventually, the personal experience of enlightenment led to Wang's radical departure from Chu Hsi's orthodox interpretation. The controversy between Chu Hsi and Wang Yang-ming is an important issue. Traditionally, it has been understood under the rubric of two rival schools of Neo-Confucianism, the rationalistic wing of Ch'eng-Chu and the idealistic wing of Lu-Wang.[14] However, some argued that this bifurcation is "oversimplified" and "misleading" in the case of Wang Yang-ming.[15] For Wang developed the doctrine of identity of mind-and-heart and principle independently from the tradition of Lu Hsiang-shan, though he later aligned himself with Lu.

According to Tu Wei-ming, Wang's life can be divided into three periods.[16] The two pivotal points were his "sudden enlightenment" at Lung-ch'ang and his proclamation of *chih liang-chih* (the extension of the innate knowledge) because of which Wang was acclaimed as "one of the most original minds in the Confucian tradition."[17] The first period was from his birth in 1472, to 1509 when he was banished to Lung-ch'ang. There he affirmed his doctrine of the unity of knowing and acting. In 1510, he became the magistrate of Lu-ling. The second period was from 1510 to 1520, one year after his successful military campaign against the insurrection of Prince Ning. In 1521 he appeared to have reached the apex of his spiritual development. The third period was from this point to his death in 1529.

After his death, Wang was given a title of Marquis of Hsin-chien (1567) and honored with a posthumous title, Wen-ch'eng (Completion of Culture). In 1584, his tablet was included in the Confucian temple, which was the highest honor. Chan said, "Certainly he was, except for Chu Hsi, the most influential philosopher in China since the fifteenth century."[18] Wang's teachings profoundly influenced the history of East Asia as a whole, including late Ming China, seventeenth-century Korea, and late Tokugawa Japan.[19] Particularly in the period of modernization, Wang's legacy repeatedly supplied a dynamic basis for reforming and revolutionizing East Asian societies by revitalizing the old values and the ethos in response to the radical challenges from the Western civilization. It served a vital spiritual foundation for the radical reformation and modernization movement in nineteenth century Korea.[20] The influence of the Yang-ming school in modern Japan and China was even more striking.[21]

•

Notes

Introduction

1. Technically, Confucianism is distinguished from Neo-Confucianism (roughly, the Reformed Confucianism after the challenge of Buddhism and Taoism). In this book, the term Confucianism will be used loosely, covering both Classical Confucianism and Neo-Confucianism. For an introduction to Confucianism, see Tu Wei-ming, *Confucianism in a Historical Perspective* (Singapore: The Institute of East Asian Philosophies, 1989); its condensed version, Encyclopaedia Britannica, 15th ed. (1988), Vol. 16, s.v. "Confucius and Confucianism." Also, see Julia Ching, *Confucianism and Christianity: A Comparative Study* (Tokyo: Kodansha, 1977), 7-12.

2. Tu, *Confucianism*, 3.

3. Wm. Theodore de Bary divided the history of East Asian civilization into five stages: Classical, Buddhist, Neo-Confucian, Modern, and Post-Confucian periods. See *East Asian Civilizations: A Dialogue in Five Stages* (Cambridge, MA.: Harvard University Press, 1989), 107-122. Also see Tu Wei-ming, et. al., ed., *The Confucian World Observed: A Contemporary Discussion of Confucian Humanism in East Asia* (Honolulu: The East-West Center, 1992).

4. See Ezra F. Vogel, *The Four Little Dragons: The Spread of Industrialization in East Asia* (Cambridge: Harvard University Press, 1991); also Peter K. H. Lee, "Personal Observation on Religion and Culture in the four Little Dragons of Asia," *Ching Feng* 30:3 (1987), 154-169.

5. De Bary, *Neo-Confucian Orthodoxy and the Learning of the Mind-and-Heart* (New York: Columbia University Press, 1981), ix-x.

6. De Bary, *Civilizations*, 44.

7. Hans Küng and Julia Ching, *Christianity and Chinese Religions*, trans. Peter Beyer (New York: Doubleday, 1989).

8. Ibid., xii-xiii; xvii.

9. For an introduction to Christianity in Korea, see Donald N. Clark, *Christianity in Modern Korea* (Lanham: University Press of America, 1986).

Clark made an interesting conclusion that "Christianity is now a Korean religion" (51), though that might be still debatable.

10. Tu, *Confucianism*, 35.

11. James H. Grayson, "The Study of Korean Religions & Their Role in Inter-Religious Dialogue," *Inculturation* 3:4 (1988): 8.

12. J. H. Grayson, *Korea: the Religious History* (Oxford: Clarendon Press, 1989), 215-6.

13. See Kang-nam Oh, "Sagehood and Metanoia: The Confucian-Christian Encounter in Korea," *Journal of the Academy of Religion* 61:2 (1993): 303-20.

14. See Jean Sangbae Ri, *Confucius et Jesus Christ: La Premiere Theologie Chretienne en Coree D'apres L'oeuvre de Yl Piek lettre Confuceen 1754-1786* (Paris: Editions Beauchesne, 1979).

15. See Hector Diaz, *A Korean Theology* (Immense, Switzerland: Neue Zeitschrift für Missionswissenschaft, 1986).

16. See Chung Chai-sik, "Confucian-Protestant Encounter in Korea: Two Cases of Westernization and De-Westernization," *Ching Feng* 34:1 (1991): 51-8.

17. See the position paper of Korean Cardinal Stephen Kim, in Gerald H. Anderson and Thomas F. Stransky ed., *Mission Trends No. 2: Evangelization* (New York: Paulist and Grand Rapids: Wm. B. Eerdmans, 1975), 190-192.

18. H. Richard Niebuhr developed a typology of five relationships between Christ and culture; Christ against Culture, the Christ of Culture, Christ above the Culture, Christ and Culture in Paradox, and Christ the Transformer of the Culture. See his *Christ and Culture* (New York: Harper & Row, 1951).

19. Yoon, "The Contemporary Religious Situation in Korea," a paper presented in the Conference on Religion and Contemporary Society in Korea, Center of East Asian Studies, University of California at Berkeley, November 11-12, 1988. In this report, Yoon also made a helpful correction. The "self-identification" method is not appropriate to measure statistically the reality of East Asian religious phenomena. For East Asian religions, especially Confucianism, are not so much a "hard" religion (institutional) as a "soft" (institutionally diffuse, but rigorous in practice).

20. Here, I use Presbyterianism and the Reformed tradition interchangeably.

21. Kim Illsoo highlighted the fact that Korean Presbyterian Churches outnumbered the Korean Methodist Church by more than five times (as of 1982, 5 million versus some 800,000), whereas, in the U.S., Methodists outnumbered Presbyterians by almost three times. He suggested that the reason for this explosive growth of Korean Presbyterianism beyond all denominations in Korea lies in the "religious affinity" between Presbyterianism and Confucianism, particularly, the traditional propensity toward "personal community" (e.g., *Kye*) and social codes (i.e., five cardinal relationship). He also pointed out that the Nevius plan was also an effective strategy that enabled Korean Presbyterians to incorporate their new faith into their traditional organizational pattern of self-governance. See his article, "Organizational patterns of Korean-American Methodist Churches: denominationalism and

personal community," in Russell Richey and Kenneth Rowe, eds., *Rethinking Methodist History* (Nashville: Kingswood Books, 1985), 228-37 (229).

22. De Bary, *Neo-Confucian Orthodoxy*, 81f.; See Max Weber, *The Protestant Ethic and the Spirit of Capitalism* (Scribner's, 1958). This was already reported by an early American missionary:

"Many of the religious characteristics of the Korean people mark them for discipleship in the Christian faith. . . . Confucianism with its age-long insistence on the fact that man is a moral being and must obey moral laws, prepares them to sincerely exemplify Christian ethics in their life." (Gerge Herber Jones, *Korea: The Land, People and Customs* [Cincinnati: Jennings and Graham, 1907], 64)

23. "Individual churchism" (*gae gyohoe jueui*) is a salient example of this (see Kim Illsoo, "Organizational pattern"). The individual churchism which fosters a severe factionalism in Korean Churches is neither truly Confucian, nor true Christian. In fact, it is a pseudo religious syncretism, widely operative among Korean Churches, that must be systematically scrutinized.

24. Julia Ching also observed the reason for the different acceptance of Christianity in Korea and Japan: "the stronger Confucian influence in Korea has also been favorable to the development of Christianity, whereas the stronger Buddhist influence in Japan is more of a deterrent" (*Chinese Religions* [Maryknoll, N.Y.: Orbis Books, 1993], 199).

25. Aloysius Pieris, *Love Meets Wisdom: A Christian Experience of Buddhism* (Maryknoll, N.Y.: Orbis Books, 1988), 3.

26. This point seems to be very important for the contemporary Reformed theology that seems to be in the deadlock on the issue of wider ecumenism (perhaps, by the exclusive interpretation of John Calvin and Karl Barth [see "the theology of Karl Barth in the wider ecumenism" in Chap. 5]). Korean Reformed theology which has enabled Koreans to build the strongest Reformed Church in the non-Christian world has a global significance. A viable Reformed theology of religion may exist already in the Korean Church. The future of the global Reformed theology may depend on how effectively Reformed theologians make use of this development.

27. I have received two criticisms of this selection: (1) that the influence of Wang Yang-ming was relatively not important in the history of Korean Neo-Confucianism; and (2) that the theology of Karl Barth is too exclusive to be useful in dialogue with other religions. However, I argue:

First, though generally in the underground, the Wang Yang-ming school did exist in the history of Korean Neo-Confucianism. Wang's thought had played a significant role in motivating radical reform movements in the history of Korea. See Kim Gil-Hwan *The Study of the Korean Yang-ming School* (Seoul: Il Ji Sa, 1981); Yoon Nam-han, *The Study of the Yang-ming School in Chosun Period* (Seoul: Jib Mun Dang, 1982). Also see Chung Chai-sik, "Confucian-Christian Encounter. . ."

Second, Karl Barth is a very important figure who has greatly influenced the formation of Korean Reformed theology. If a genuine Confucian-Christian dialogue is to be historically grounded, then the study of Karl Barth and Neo-Confucianism is very important for Korean Reformed theology. It was not an accident that Yun Sung-bum formulated a Korean theology of Confucianism based on the theology of Karl Barth (see his *Han'gukjok Sinhak: Song ui Haesokhak* [The Korean Theology: The Hermeneutics of Sincerity] [Seoul: Son Myung Munhwasa, 1972]). Furthermore, a proper rereading of Barth in dialogue with Confucianism may open up a proper hermeneutics of Barth's theology in the non-Christian context and in a wider ecumenism (see Chap. 5).

28. For a summary of Wang's life and thought, see Tu Wei-ming, "Wang Yang-ming," in Mircea Eliade, ed. *Encyclopedia of Religions*, vol. 15 (1987), 335-337. Also see Chap. 1.

29. For a summary of the life and theology of Karl Barth, see Eberhard Jüngel, "Barth's Life and Work," in *Karl Barth: A Theological Legacy*, trans. Garrett E. Paul (Philadelphia: Westminster, 1986).

30. Chan Wing-tsit's translation of the title. For a complete translation, see Chan, *Instructions for Practical Living and other Neo-Confucian Writings by Wang Yang-ming* (New York: Columbia University Press, c. 1963); esp., "preface" and "translator's note" of Chan, *Instructions*, xi-xv. For English translation of *Ch'uan-hsi lu*, I will primarily use Chan's book. For the original texts in Chinese, I will refer to Chan's edition of *Wang Yang-ming Ch'uan Hsi Lu Hsing Chi P'ing* (Taipei, 1983) or *O Yomei Zenshu* in 10 vols. (1982ff.), Japanese collections of the Complete Works of Wang Yang-ming.

31. Chan, *Instructions*, xli.

32. See Mou, "Western Philosophy and Chinese Philosophy," in *Chung-kuo che-hsüeh te t'e-chih* [The Uniqueness of Chinese Philosophy] (Taipei: Student Book Co., 1974); trans. in Korean by H. Y. Song (Seoul: Donghwa Publishing Co., 1983), 9-20. Also, Cheng Chung-ying characterized their differences in philosophical orientation: namely, "natural naturalization" and "human immanentization" (Chinese Philosophy) vis-à-vis "rational rationalization" and "divine transcendentalization" (Western Philosophy); see Cheng, *New Dimensions of Confucianism and Neo-Confucian Philosophy* (Albany, N.Y.: State University of New York Press, 1991), 1-27.

33. See Mou, "Western Philosophy," 15, 20.

34. Tu Wei-ming, *Humanity and Self-Cultivation: Essays in Confucian Thought* (Berkeley: Asian Humanities Press, 1979), 139. Also see 138.

35. David S. Nivison, "The Problem of 'Knowledge' and 'Action' in Chinese Thought Since Wang Yang-ming," in Arthur F. Wright ed., *Studies in Chinese Thought* (Chicago: University of Chicago Press, 1953), 115.

36. For more discussions on this term, see Chap. 9.

37. For contemporary Confucian studies in the western world, see John Berthrong's article, "Trends in the Interpretation of Confucian Religiosity," in *All Under Heaven: Transforming Paradigms in Confucian-Christian Dialogue* (Albany, N.Y.: State University of New York Press, 1994), 189-207.

38. Generally, I will use G.W. Bromiley's translation, *Church Dogmatics, Vol IV, 2* (Edinburgh: T. & T. Clark, 1958). I recognize that both Barth's

German original text and English version do not use gender neutral terms to designate human beings. Although I have had to comply with author's own way of writings for citation, though I do not agree the exclusive use of male language.

39. Jüngel made an excellent analysis of Barth's doctrinal reversal of Gospel and law which is a central theme; see his *Barth*, 105-126. For Barth's doctrine of humanity, I will use Stuart McLean's analysis; see his *Humanity in the Thought of Karl Barth* (Edinburgh: T. & T. Clark Ltd., 1981), 1-71.

40. However, my primary goal is not a systematic treatise on Wang's teaching of self-cultivation, nor on Barth's doctrine of sanctification, but a comparative study of Confucianism and Christianity. Hence, my selection of topics and texts is governed by this purpose.

41. Cf., Ching, *Comparative Study*, 105.

42. Ibid., esp. Chap. 3, 68-105.

43. See Tu Wei-ming, *Confucian Thought: Selfhood as Creative Transformation* (New York: SUNY Press, 1985), 51-65.

44. M. Thomas, *Risking Christ for Christ's Sake: Towards an Ecumenical Theology of Pluralism* (Geneva: WCC Publications, 1987), 45, 113.

45. Ian G. Barbour, *Myths, Models and Paradigms: A Comparative Study in Science and Religion* (New York: Harper & Row, 1974), 124.

46. Hence, root-metaphor here does not exactly follow the definition of Sallie Mcfague: "the guiding fact in a paradigm" (*Metaphorical Theology: Models of God in Religious Language* [Philadelphia: Fortress, 1982], 109). Rather it simply means the essential metaphor that conveys the existential way to acquire the ontological reality of radical humanity (radical humanization).

Chapter 1: Prolegomena (Wang Yang-ming)

1. More accurately, Neo-Confucianism. See 1, no. 1.

2. See Gilbert Rozman, ed. *The East Asian Region: Confucian Heritage and Its Modern Adaptation* (Princeton, N.J.: Princeton University Press, 1991).

3. Wm. T. De Bary, *East Asian Civilizations: A Dialogue in Five Stages* (Cambridge: Harvard University Press, 1988), 109.

4. Max Weber's *The Religion of China: Confucianism and Taoism*, trans. Hans H. Gerth (Glencoe, Ill.: Free Press, 1951) is a famous example of these western reductionistic views. See Tu Wei-ming, *Confucian Thought: Selfhood as Creative Transformation* (Albany, New York: State University of New York Press, 1985), 55.

5. See de Bary, *Civilization*, and Rozman, *East Asian Region*.

6. For the formation of Confucian thought, see Fung Yu-lan, *A History of Chinese Philosophy*, vol. 1, 2nd ed., trans. Derk Bodde (Princeton: Princeton University Press, 1952); Benjamin I. Schwartz, *The World of Thought in Ancient China* (Cambridge, MA.: Harvard University Press, 1985); and A. C.

Graham, *Disputers of the Tao: Philosophical Argument in Ancient China* (La Salle, Ill.: Open Court Publishing Co., 1989).

7. For example, see Rodney L. Taylor's book exclusively on this issue, *The Religious Dimensions of Confucianism* (Albany: State University of New York Press, 1990).

8. Tu, *Confucian Thought*, 55.

9. See W. C. Smith, *The Meaning and End of Religion* (Minneapolis: Fortress Press, 1991), 19-74.

10. Tu, *Confucian Thought*, 132.

11. Tu Wei-ming, *Centrality and Commonality: An Essay on Confucian Religiousness*, rev. and enlarged (Albany: State University of New York Press, 1989), 94.

12. Ibid., 98.

13. Tu, *Confucian Thought*, 64.

14. Ibid., 52; 53.

15. A subtitle of Tu Wei-ming's books, see ibid., 7-16.

16. Ibid., 56.

17. CSL: 58.

18. Tu, *Confucian Thought*, 56; 57; 57.

19. Originally, *The Great Learning* was a chapter in *the Books of Rites*, which is one of *the Six Confucian Classics--Shih Ching (the Book of Poetry)*, *Shu Ching (the Book of History)*, *I Ching (the Book of Changes)*, *Ch'un Ch'iu (The Spring and Autumn Annals)*, *Li Chi (the Book of Rites)*, and *Yüeh Ching (the Book of Music)*. However, Chu Hsi separated out and regarded it as one of *the Four Books*: *The Great Learning (Ta Hsüeh)*, *the Doctrine of the Mean (Chung Yung)*, *the Analects (Lun Yü)*, and *the Book of Mencius (Mêng Tzû)*. Since then, *the Four Books* became even more significant than the *Six Classics* in Neo-Confucianism and the basis for the civil examination. For a complete translation of *The Great Learning*, see Chan Wing-tsit, trans. and compiled, *Source Book in Chinese Philosophy* (Princeton, N.J.: Princeton University Press, 1963), 85-94, or James Legge, trans., *The Chinese Classics*, Vol. 1 (New York: Paragon Book, 1966), 219-245.

20. Chan Wing-tsit, trans. and ed., *Source Book,* 84.

21. Ibid., 85-86.

22. Ibid., 86-87.

23. See Michael C. Kalton, *To Become a Sage: the Ten Diagrams on Sage Learning by Yi T'oegye* (New York: Columbia University Press, 1988), 81.

24. See Wing-tsit Chan, trans. and ed., *Neo-Confucian Terms Explained (The Pei-hsi tzu-i) by Ch'en Ch'un, 1159-1223* (New York: Columbia University Press, 1986), 112-113.

25. See Kalton, *Sage*, 216.

26. See Chan Wing-tsit, "The Evolution of the Neo-Confucian Concept *Li* as Principle," in *Neo-Confucianism, Etc.: Essays by Wing-tsit Chan* (Hanover,, N.H.: Oriental Society, 1969), 47 and 64-66; 73-74; 65, 74.

27. Kalton, *Sage*, 214.

28. Korean Neo-Confucianism, under the leadership of Yi T'oegye and with "its exclusive devotion" to the Ch'eng-Chu School, continued this line of thought and achieved remarkable Neo-Confucian results such as *the Four Seven Debate* between Yi T'oegye and Ki Taesong (1527-1572). See Kalton, *Sage*, 135-141.

29. See Chan, *Neo-Confucianism*, 77.

30. Chan Wing-tsit, *Source Book*, 86-87.

31. Cf. A. C. Graham, *Two Chinese Philosophers--Ch'eng Ming-tao and Ch'eng Yi-Ch'uan* (London: Lund Humphries, 1958), xix-xx.

32. Tu Wei-ming, *Neo-Confucian Thought in Action: Wang Yang-ming's Youth (1472-1509)* (Berkeley: University of California Press, 1976), 164.

33. *Nien-p'u*, chronological biography, written by Wang's favorite disciple Ch'ien Te-hung; cf. *Wang Wen-ch'eng kung ch'üan-shu*, 32-36.

34. See Tu, *Action*, 49-51.

35. This resonates with the anecdote of Martin Luther, the *Anfechtungen* in an Augustinian monastery. Luther also repeatedly failed to achieve a faith in salvation despite his rigorous practice of penitence.

36. Tu, *Action*, 50; 51; 51.

37. Ibid., 121.

38. Ibid., 120

39. Tu, *Confucian Thought*, 70.

40. I will use this translation, the mind-and-heart for *hsin*. However, Chan translated *hsin* as mind in CSL. When citing, I will follow the translation of the author of the work cited. In the case of a citation, generally, mind means mind-and-heart.

41. Tu, *Confucian Thought*, 70.

42. Note that, in CSL, Chan translates *T'ien-li* (the Heavenly Principle) as the Principle of Nature.

43. Julia Ching, *To Acquire Wisdom: The Way of Wang Yang-ming* (New York: Columbia University Press, 1976), 58.

44. See Tu, *Action*, 164.

45. Wang said in his "Inquiry on the *Great Learning*," Chan, *Instructions*, 279.

46. Cheng Chung-ying, *New Dimensions of Confucian and Neo-Confucian Philosophy* (Albany, N.Y.: State University of New York Press, 1991), 19-21.

47. The original Chinese word *jen* is a gender neutral term, and means human being[s] inclusively and collective. However, Chan generally translates *jen* as "man," and uses "he" as its pronoun. His use of exclusive language is not confuciologically correct. Sexist language is basically not a Chinese, East Asian, and confuciological problem, but more a Western and theological one. For citation, nevertheless, I will use Chan's authoritative translations. Hence, "man" or "he" in citations has an inclusive meaning beyond its English connotation.

48. Tu, *Confucian Thought*, 64.

49. See his book, *Theology of the Third Millennium*, trans. Peter Heinegg (New York: Doubleday, 1988), 131. I use the term "paradigm" based on the arguments of Thomas S. Kuhn in his book, *The Structure of Scientific Revolutions*, 2nd ed. (Chicago: University of Chicago, 1970). Kuhn defined paradigm as "recognized achievements [entire constellations of shared beliefs, values, techniques, etc.] that for a time provide model problems and solutions to a community of practitioners" (viii).

50. Cf. his "The Evolution of the Neo-Confucian Concept Jen" and "The Evolution of the Neo-Confucian Concept Li as Principle," in his book, *Neo-Confucianism*, 1-44 and 45-87. See the conclusion.

51. Philip Ivanhoe argued that Wang invented a fundamentally different way of self-cultivation, "unknown to Mencius," namely, the "discovery model," instead of Mencius' "development model." See his *Ethics in the Confucian Tradition: The Thought of Mencius and Wang Yang-ming* (Atlanta: Scholars Press, 1990), 3.

Chapter 2: Root-metaphor (*Ch'eng*)

1. Tu Wei-ming, *Neo-Confucian Thought in Action: Wang Yang-ming's Youth (1472-1509)* (Berkeley: University of California Press, 1976): 146; 146; 168.

2. See ibid., 142-6.

3. Cf. the Christian notion of repentance (*metanoia*). See ibid., 142.

4. Ibid., 143.

5. See Tu Wei-ming, *Humanity and Self-Cultivation: Essays in Confucian Thought* (Berkeley: Asian Humanities Press, 1979), 89.

6. Ibid. 89; 90.

7. Ibid., 89, quoting *Analects* 2:4.

8. Tu, *Humanity*, 89, quoting *Hsün Tzu*.

9. Tu, *Humanity*, 87.

10. Ibid., 90.

11. See Dietrich Bonhoeffer, *The Cost of Discipleship*, trans. R. H. Fuller (New York: Macmillan, 1959).

12. Mencius said, "When the mind directs, a 'bodily energy' follows," *Mencius*, 2A:2, Tu, *Humanity*, 91.

13. Ibid., 139-40; cf. *Nien-P'u*, ch. 34.

14. Literally, *chih* signifies "the faculty of knowing," *hsing* "the function of acting," and *ho-i* "unity or identity." See ibid., 91.

15. Tu, *Action*, 172.

16. Ibid.

17. Tu, *Humanity*, 146.

18. Tu, *Action*, 173.

19. David S. Nivison, "The Problem of 'Knowledge' and 'Action' in Chinese Thought," Arthur F. Wright, ed., *Studies in Chinese Thought* (Chicago: University of Chicago Press, 1953), 118; 119.

20. Julia Ching, *To Acquire Wisdom: The Way of Wang Yang-ming* (New York: Columbia University Press, 1976), 66.

21. Nivison, "The Problem of," 121.

22. Tu, *Humanity*, 145-6. However, Tu insisted that Wang's original intention was not so much to "reject the method of *ko-wu* nor to disparage its importance" as "to restore *ko-wu* its original position in the *Great Learning.*"

23. He wrote a fascinating contemporary interpretation of *the Analects* under this title, *Confucius--the Secular as Sacred* (New York: Harper & Row, 1972).

24. Tu, *Humanity*, 87; 87-8.

25. Mencius, 7A. See D.C. Lau, trans., *Mencius* (Harmondsworth: Penguin, 1970), 182.

26. From the *Inquiry on the Great Learning*, Chan, *Instructions for Practical Living and Other Writings by Wang Yang-ming* (New York: Columbia University Press, 1963), 272.

27. Tu, *Humanity*, 94.

28. Ibid., 95. Tu underscored that this term in Chinese has no negative meaning as English word sincerity does. See Tu's commentary on the notion of *ch'eng* in *Chung-yung, Centrality and Commonality: An Essay on Confucian Religiousness*, rev. ed. (Albany: State University of New York Press, 1989), 67-91.

29. This book was originally another chapter of the *Book of Rites* and became also one of the *Four Books* together with the *Great Learning*. The *Doctrine of the Mean* and the *Great Learning* are a pair in many ways. The latter focuses on the mind-and-heart, methodology, rationality, socio-political implications, whereas the former is more interested in human nature, existential reality, religiosity, psychological and metaphysical implications. See Chan Wing-tsit, *A Source Book in Chinese Philosophy* (Princeton: Princeton University Press, 1963), 95.

30. Chan, *Source Book*, 98.

31. Tu, *Humanity*, 95.

32. *The Doctrine of the Mean*, ch. 20; Chan, *Source Book*, 107.

33. Ibid., 96.

34. Ibid., 107-8.

35. Tu, *Humanity*, 96.

36. Ibid., 96-7.

37. *Doctrine of the Mean*, ch. 23, cited Tu's translation, *Humanity*, 97.

38. Tu, *Humanity*, 97.

39. *Doctrine of the Mean*, ch. 25, Chan, *Source Book*, 108

40. Tu, *Humanity*, 97.

41. *The Doctrine of the Mean*, ch. 32, Chan, *Source Book*, 112.

42. Tu, *Humanity*, 98.

43. Ibid., 98-9.

Chapter 3: The Humanity Paradigm

1. *Ching* is an important notion of the Ch'eng-Chu school; it is also translated as "seriousness" or "mindfulness." See Chan Wing-tsit, trans. and ed., *Neo-Confucian Terms Explained* (The Pei-hsi tzu-i) *by Ch'en Ch'un, 1159-1223)*, 100ff.; and Michael C. Kalton, trans. and ed., *To Become a Sage: the Ten Diagrams on Sage Learning by Yi T'oegye* (New York: Columbia University Press, 1988), 212ff.

2. Julia Ching, *To Acquire Wisdom: The Way of Wang Yang-ming* (New York: Columbia University Press, 1976), 107.

3. This term is difficult to translate, as is clear from the variety seen in the following translations: "good conscience" (*liang-hsin*), "innate knowledge" (Wing-tsit Chan), "conscious wisdom" (Thomé H. Fang), "intuitive knowledge of the good" (David S. Nivison), "conscientious consciousness" (T'ang Chün-i), "subjectivity" or "primordial awareness" (Tu Wei-ming), "knowledge of the good" (Julia Ching), or "pure knowing" (Philip Ivanhoe). The term in the Chinese romanization will be used unless translation is necessary.

4. Ching, *Wisdom*, 107.

5. Ibid., 108.

6. Mencius said: "If men [a person] suddenly see a child about to fall into a well, they will without exception experience a feeling of alarm and commiseration. *They will feel so*, not as a ground on which they may seek the praise of their neighbors and friends, nor from a dislike to the reputation of having been unmoved by such a thing." (*Mencius*, 2A:6; trans., James Legge, *The Chinese Classics*, v. 2 [New York: Paragon Books, 1966], 78)

Mencius stipulated four moral principles in primordial human nature: commiseration, modesty and deference, shame and dislike, and approving and disapproving; see ibid. These are also called the Four Beginnings; see Yi Hwang's "Diagram of the Saying 'the Mind Combines and Governs the Nature and the Feelings," Kalton, *Sage*, 123-4. For Yang-ming's comment on the feeling of commiseration, see CSL, 272.

7. Hitoyuki Iki characterized *liang-chih* as a revelation which is "neither knowledge nor ignorance." See his "Wang Yang-ming's Doctrine of Innate Knowledge of the Good," *Philosophy East and West* 11 (1961), 27-44, esp. 41-2.

8. Ching, *Wisdom*, 108. Ching distinguished *liang-chih* from the Kantian notion of the "categorical imperative" as the means of discovery. Whereas the categorical imperative was discovered by an analytical examination of common knowledge, *liang-chih* was acquired through an intuitive experience of inner enlightenment.

9. In Chan's translation, "innate knowledge" signifies *liang-chih*.

10. Tu Wei-ming, *Confucian Thought: Selfhood as Creative Transformation* (Albany: State University of New York Press, 1985), 32.

11. Philip Ivanhoe, *Ethics in the Confucian Tradition: The Thought of Mencius and Wang Yang-ming* (Atlanta, Ga.: Scholars Press, 1990), 104.

12. *Hsiang-shan ch'üan-chi*, cited from ibid., 104.

13. Ibid.

14. Martin Heidegger identified the threefold structure of interpretation as *Vorhabe* ("forehaving" or "a taken-for-granted background"), *Vorsicht* ("foresight"), and *Vorgriff* ("fore-conception"). This fore-structure of interpretation raises the problem of the hermeneutical circle, where all interpreting is necessarily circular. See Heidegger, *Being and Time*, trans. John Macquarie and Edward Robinson (Harper & Row, c. 1962), 191-5.

15. I use this Bultmannian term in a broader definition. Here demythologization means not only a scientific interpretation but also other interpretive attempts "to recover the deeper meaning behind the mythological [and traditionally mystified] conceptions." See Rudolf Bultmann, *Jesus Christ and Mythology* (New York: Charles Scribner's Son, 1958), 18.

16. From Wang's poem, *"Four Hymns to Liang Chih Shown to My Students, in Wang Wen-ch'eng-kung ch'üan-shu* 20:629a, citing Ivanhoe, *Ethics*, 109.

17. Wang said in *"Shu Wei Shih-meng chüan,"* "The knowledge of the good *(liang-chih)* which is [present] in the mind and heart may be called sagehood *(sheng);"* cited from Ching, *Wisdom*, 113.

18. James Legge, trans., *Chinese Classics*, Vol. 1(London: Truber, 1861), 248.

19. See *Chan, Source Book,* 566.

20. See ibid., 600-2.

21. *Dasein* literally means "there is." Heidegger defined the term: "[T]o work out the question of being adequately, we must make an entity [being]--the inquirer--transparent in his own being. . . . This entity [being] which each of us is himself and which includes inquiring as one of the possibilities of its Being, we shall denote by the term Dasein" *(Being and Time*, 27). Similar to Wang, Heidegger also rejected traditional (Cartesian and Husserlian) distinctions of Western philosophy such as mental content and independent object, subject and object, immanent and transcendent, representation and represented, conscious and unconscious, explicit and tacit, reflective and unreflective.

Julia Ching compared *hsin-chih-pen-t'i* to *Dasein*; see Ching, *Wisdom*, note, 112. Tu also tried to establish a Neo-Confucian ontology in a dialogue with this notion; see Tu's article, "Neo-Confucian Ontology: A Preliminary Questioning," *Confucian Thought*, 149-170.

22. See Chang Tsai, *Correcting Youthful Ignorance*; Chan, *Source Book*, 501.

23. See Ching, *Wisdom*, 145.

24. See Tu, "Subjectivity and Ontological Reality--An Interpretation of Wang Yang-ming's Mode of Thinking," in *Humanity and Self-Cultivation:*

Essays in Confucian Thought (Berkeley: Asian Humanities Press, 1979), 138-61. This section relies on Tu's interpretation.

25. See ibid., 156, 159; also *Confucian Thought*, 33.

26. Tu, *Humanity*, 156.

27. Webster's New Universal Unabridged Dictionary, 2nd. ed., 1486.

28. Tu, *Humanity*, 156.

29. Chan, *Instructions*, 272.

30. Tu, *Humanity*, 157.

31. Tu, *Confucian Thought*, 33.

32. Chan, *Source Book*, 497-8.

33. For a general discussion of this cardinal notion of Confucianism, see Chan Wing-tsit, "The Evolution of the Confucian Concept Jen," *Neo-Confucianism Etc.: Essays by Wing-tsit Chan* (Hanover, N.H.: Oriental Society, 1969), 1-44.

34. See Peter A. Boodberg, *"The Semasiology of Some Primary Confucian Concepts," Philosophy East and West* 2:4 (1953), 329-30.

35. Chan, *Instructions,* 272

36. Humanity *(jen)* also means "seed."

37. Chu Hsi revised the term to "renovating the people" *(hsin-min)*. But Wang argued for the original rendition, "loving the people." See Chan, *Instructions*, 276.

38. Ibid., 273-4. Italics are added.

39. CSL: 56f.. Cf. Ching, *Wisdom*, 129.

40. For the Neo-Confucian concept of human being, see Tu's article, "The Neo-Confucian Concept of Man," in Humanity, 71-82.

41. Ching, *Wisdom*, 145.

42. See *Boodberg,* "The Semasiology of," 327-9.

43. Iki designated the master-servant relationship between *liang-chih* and human beings; see "Wang Yang-ming's," 43.

44. CSL: 257, revised; cf. Ching, *Wisdom*, 145.

45. For a general discussion on Neo-Confucian solutions of the problem of evil, see Wing-tsit Chan's "The Neo-Confucian solution of the problem of Evil," in Chan, *Neo-Confucianism,* 88-116.

46. See Ching, *Wisdom*, 148.

47. Ivanhoe, *Ethics,* 61.

48. Wang said, CSL: 237: "As one's effort [*kung fu*] reaches the point of the greatest refinement, it will be increasingly difficult to express it in words or to discuss it. If one attaches any personal ideas to what is refined and subtle, the entire effort will be obstructed."

49. Wang said, CSL: 142:

"However, the Buddhists are different from us because they have the mind that is motivated by selfishness. Now to wish to think of neither good nor evil and to want the mind of innate knowledge to be clear, tranquil, and at ease, means to have a mind of selfishness, leaning forward or backward, arbitrariness of opinion, and dogmatism. This is why if one exerts effort to extend knowledge at the time of thinking of neither good nor evil, one will have the trouble of already being involved in thinking of good."

50. Wang Chia-hsiu, one of Wang's disciples, said:

"The Buddhists lure people into their way of life by the promise of escape from the cycle of life and death, and the Taoists who seek immortality do so with the promise of everlasting life. But in their hearts they do not wish people to do evil. In the final analysis, they also see the upper section of the Way of the Sage. But their paths to attainment are not correct. . . .

"On the other hand, Confucians of later generations have only the lower section of the Sage's doctrine. They mutilated it and lost the true nature and degenerated into the four schools of recitation and memorization, the writing of flowery composition, the pursuit of success and profit, and textual criticism, and thus at bottom are no different from the heterodox schools. People of these four schools work hard throughout their lives and benefit their bodies and minds not a bit. They seem to compare unfavorably with the Buddhists and Taoists, whose minds are pure, whose desires are few, and who are free from the worldly bondage of fame and profit. Nowadays students need not first of all attack Taoism and Buddhism. Rather, they should earnestly fix their determination on the doctrine of the Sage." (CSL: 40-41)

51. Wang said, CSL: 123:

"But in the final analysis there was nothing in these doctrines that could destroy the view of success and profit. For up to the present time it has been several thousand years since the poison of the doctrine of success and profit has infected the innermost recesses of man's mind and has become his second nature. People have mutually boasted of their knowledge, crushed one another with power, rivaled each other for profit, mutually striven for superiority through skill, and attempted success through fame."

52. Wang said, CSL: 229:

"Pleasure, anger, sorrow, fear, love, hate, and desires are the seven feelings. . . . When the seven feelings follow their natural courses of operation, they are all functions of innate knowledge, and cannot be distinguished as good or evil. However, we should not have any selfish attachment to them. When there is such an attachment, they become selfish desires and obscurations to innate knowledge. Nevertheless, as soon as there is any attachment, innate knowledge is naturally aware of it. As it is aware of it, the obscuration will be gone and its substance will be restored."

53. CSL: 243, revised

Chapter 4: Self-cultivation as *Chih Liang-chih*

1. See Tu Wei-ming, *Humanity and Self-Cultivation: Essays in Confucian Thought* (Berkeley: Asian Humanities Press, 1979), 151. Wang said:
   "The master of the body is the mind. What emanates from the mind is the will. The original substance of the will is knowledge, and wherever the will is directed is a thing. For example, when the will is directed toward serving one's parents, then serving one's parents is a "thing.'"
   (CSL: 14)
2. Tu, *Humanity*, 152.
3. Ibid.
4. Wang said, CSL: 30; cf. 8, 61, 70, 189: "The only way is to get rid of selfish desires and preserve the Principle of Nature."
5. Tu, *Humanity*, 152; 153.
6. Tu, *Humanity*, 153.
7. See Julia Ching, *To Acquire Wisdom: The Way of Wang Yang-ming* (New York: Columbia Univ. Press, 1976), 115.
8. Ibid.
9. Ibid., 117.
10. *Mencius* 2A:a; James Legge, trans., *The Chinese Classics* (New York: Paragon Book, 1966), Vol. 2, 190. See CSL: 143.
11. Ching, *Wisdom*, 118.
12. *Mencius*, 2A:2; Legge, *Classics*, vol. 2, 190. See CSL: 174.
13. Ching, *Wisdom*, 120.
14. Wang said, "One's innate knowledge is originally the same as that of the sage. If I personally realize my own innate knowledge with clarity, it means that the feelings and dispositions of the sage are not with the sage but with me." (CSL: 127-8)
15. See Hiroyuki Iki, "Wang Yang-ming's Doctrine of Innate Knowledge of the Good," *Philosophy East and West* 11 (1961), 35-8.
16. Ibid., 38; 37.
17. Masatsugu Kusumoto, "The Spirit of Wang Yang-ming's Doctrine," *Tetsugagku Zasshi*, 711 (1950), 63; quoting from Iki, 41, n. 72.
18. For this notion, see Shu-hsien Liu, "The Confucian Approach to the Problem of Transcendence and Immanence," *Philosophy East and West* 22:1 (1972), 45-52.
19. Tu, *Humanity*, 157; 157; 158.
20. Ibid., 159.

Chapter 5: Prolegomena (Karl Barth)

1. H. Kraemer, *The Christian Message in a Non-Christian World* (New York: Harper & Row, 1938).

2.   The wider ecumenism denotes. "the issue of unity among all world religions" (Peter C. Phan, ed., *Christianity and The Wider Ecumenism* [New York: Paragon House, 1990], ix). Cf. Eugene Hillmann, *The Wider Ecumenism* (New York: Herder and Herder, 1968); idem, *Many Paths: A Catholic Approach to Religious Pluralism* (Maryknoll, N.Y.: Orbis Books, 1989).

3.   See his *Christianity and Religious Pluralism* (London: SCM Press, 1983); cf. Gavin D'Costa, *Theology and Religious Pluralism: The Challenge of Other Religions* (Oxford: Basil Blackwell, 1986).

4.   Alan Race, *Religious Pluralism*, 11.

5.   See his *No Other Name?: A Critical Survey of Christian Attitudes toward the World Religions* (Maryknoll: Orbis, 1984)..

6.   For Knitter's criticism of Barth, see ibid., 70ff.

7.   See his *Beyond Dialogue* (Philadelphia: Fortress Press, 1983), 15-21.

8.   See David Lochhead, *The Dialogical Imperative: A Christian Reflection on Interfaith Encounter* (Maryknoll: Orbis, 1988), esp. 9f. and 31-9; and Donald W. Dayton, "Karl Barth and the Wider Ecumenism," in Phan, *The Wider Ecumenism*, 163-89, esp., 182.

9.   See *Natural Theology*, comprising "Nature and Grace" by Emil Brunner and the reply "No!" by Karl Barth, trans. Peter Fraenkel (London: The Centenary Press, 1946).

10.   See Eberhard Busch, *Karl Barth: His Life from letters and autobiographical texts*, trans. John Bowden (Philadelphia: Fortress Press, 1976), 235-55.

11.   Barth defined dogmatics in the beginning of *Church Dogmatics*: "As a theological discipline dogmatics is the scientific self-examination of the Christian Church with respect to the content of its distinctive talk about God" (I/1: 3).

12.   The title of a subsection in I/2: 297-325.

13.   It denotes a twofold freedom of a theologian in relation to culture, a theological freedom to criticize culture and the other freedom to use culture to praise God, in correspondence to the freedom of God. Cf. Robert J. Palma, *Karl Barth's Theology of Culture: The Freedom of Culture for the Praise of God* (Allison Park, PA: Pickwick Publications, 1983).

14.   "No Boring Theology! A Letter from Karl Barth," *The South East Asian Journal of Theology* (Autumn, 1969), 4-5. Italics are added.

15.   Lochhead, *Dialogical Imperative*, 39.

16.   For this paradoxical motif of Barth's theology, "No" for the sake of "Yes," see Eberhard Jüngel's tribute at Barth's death, in his *Karl Barth, a Theological Legacy*, trans. Garrett E. Paul (Philadelphia: Westminster, 1986), 16-21, esp. 18.

17.   Lochhead, *Dialogical Imperative*, 39.

18.   Jüngel, *Barth*, 19; 11.

19.   Hans Küng, *Theology for Third Millennium*, trans. Peter Heiengg (New York: Doubleday, 1988), 267.

20. For the Catholic reception of Barth's theology, see John Macken's dissertation, "The Autonomy Theme in Karl Barth's Church Dogmatics and in Current Barth Criticism" (Universität Tübingen, 1984), 1-20.

21. See his *The Theology of Karl Barth*, trans. John Drury (New York: Holt, Rinehart and Winston, 1971); also Macken, "The Automomy," 13-16; and Küng, *Third Millennium*, 266.

22. See his *Justification: The Doctrine of Karl Barth and a Catholic Reflection*, trans. Thomas Collins et. al. (New York: Thomas Nelson & Sons, 1964); also his summary in *Third Millennium*, 267.

23. Küng, *Third Millennium*, 267.

24. Jüngel, *Barth*, 11.

25. Küng, *Third Millennium*, 271 and 273; 275.

26. *The Christian Century*, 1963, no. 1, 7ff, quoted in Küng, *Third Millennium*, 283.

27. Küng, *Third Millennium*, 283.

28. See Palma, 10-14.

29. Ibid., 13.

30. Palma, 11 and 13; cf. Hans Frei, "Karl Barth--Theologian," in *Karl Barth and the Future of Theology*, ed. David L. Dickermann (New Haven: Yale Divinity School Association, 1969), 8f.

31. It simply denotes religions which are not theistically oriented, but it does not mean that such religions do not have theological or theistic dimensions.

32. See Lochhead, *Dialogical Imperative*, 40-5.

33. See ibid., 44; cf., Karl Rahner, "The Searching 'Memory' of All Faith is Directed Towards the Absolute Savior" and "The Question about the Concrete History of Religion," in *Foundations of Christian Faith: An Introduction to the Idea of Christianity*, trans. William V. Dych (New York: Crossroad, 1987), 318-21.

34. This book uses theology and dogmatics interchangeably.

35. For this topic, I rely on Eberhard Jüngel's article, "Gospel and Law: The Relationship of Dogmatics and Ethics," in his *Barth*, 105-26.

36. *D. Martin Luthers Werke, Kritische Gesamtaugabe* (Weimer: Hermann Böhlau, 1883-) [WA: The Weimer Edition of Luther's Work] 36, 9, quoted in Jüngel, 105.

37. WA 39/1, 361, quoted in Jüngel, *Barth*, 110.

38. Otto Weber, *Foundations of Dogmatics*, 2 vols., trans. by Darrel L. Guder (Grand Rapids: Wm. B. Eerdmans Publishing Co., 1981-3), 2: 366.

39. See Luther, WA, 19-21; also Jüngel, *Barth*, 109.

40. See *Lectures on Galatians* (1535), in the American Edition (LW) of *Luther's Works* (St. Louis: Concordia Publishing House, and Philadelphia: Fortress Press, 1955-1976), vol. 26, 336f. For a summary of the political and theological use of the law, see Weber, 381-98.

41. In his *Church Dogmatics*, Barth formulated the Word of God in three modes: revelation, Bible, and proclamation (see I/1, sec. 4, 88-124). Luther

formulated a dialectical relationship between law and Gospel in which the two modes of the Word of God oppose and contradict each other. Barth articulated an analogical relationship of the three modes of the Word of God in which they correspond to each other as different expressions (moments) of the same activity of God, i.e., the economy of salvation. Although these moments differentiate each other, they are in their unity, as the *only* analogy to the doctrine of the triune God, i.e., the only *vestigium trinitatis* (the vestige of the Trinity).

42. Barth continually made theological shifts throughout his career. Barth's mature theology is used loosely to denote Barth's dogmatic theology developed since 1927. Jüngel divided Barth's life into three periods; (1) theological beginning (to the first edition of *The Commentary on Romans*, 1919), (2) dialectic theology (to *The Christian Dogmatics in Outline*, 1927), and (3) dogmatic theology (*Church Dogmatics* and other writings); see his "Barth's Life and Work," in *Barth*, 22-52. For a more comprehensive treatment of Barth's life, see Eberhard Busch, *Barth*.

43. Karl Barth, "Gospel and Law," in *Community, State and Church*, (Garden City, New York: Doubleday, 1960), 71-100 (71).

44. See ibid., 72.

45. Jüngel, *Barth*, 113.

46. Barth, *Community*, 89; 94; 95; 95; 80. Jüngel summarized Barth's thesis:

"(1) The gospel alone determines what is to be taken as the law of God. (2) There is no gospel which does not also, as law, immediately lay claim to humankind. (3) The gospel is the Word of God addressed to humankind in the grace of God. (4) The law is the Word of God which lays claim to humankind for the grace of God. (5) The grace which is expressed as an indication in the 'content' of the gospel is expressed as a gracious imperative in the 'form' of the law.'" (*Barth*, 117)

47. Also see Barth, *Community*, 80.

48. For the pronouns (including possessive and reflexive) of God, I will follow the English translations of Barth's writings with capitalization. Although I believe in the inclusivity of God, the issue of gender for God is beyond the scope of this book.

49. Jüngel, *Barth*, 119.

50. Ibid. Generally, supralapsarianism denotes that God's election of individuals even before the Fall of Adam. However, rejecting the Calvinist doctrine of double predestination, Barth held this position to give a far more inclusive meaning of election.

51. Ibid.

52. Ibid., 121.

53. Ibid.

54. However, this does not imply that Barth has in fact a philosophical anthropology such as existentialism. This understanding comes directly from his doctrine of God.

55. Jüngel, *Barth*, 122.

56. Weber, *Dogmatics*, vol. 2, 377. A most salient aspect is that Luther's theology lacks of the third use of the law (roughly, the principle or positive use of the law); cf., ibid., 393-8.

57. I/2, 364, cited English translation from Latin in Jüngel, *Barth*, 123.

58. Jüngel, *Barth*, 123. Italics are added.

59. LW 26, 387, quoted in Jüngel, *Barth*, 123.

60. Jüngel, *Barth*, 124.

61. In each volume of the *Church Dogmatics*--i.e., the doctrines of creation (CD III), reconciliation (CD IV), and redemption (CD V), which was planned but never actually written--Barth included a corresponding theme of ethics as a part of dogmatics--i.e., "The Command of God the Creator," "The Command of God the Reconciler," and "The Command of God the Redeemer," which also was never written.

62. See Jüngel, *Barth*, 126.

63. Ibid.

64. Barth articulated the doctrine of Christ as a threefold expression according to its three different moments or movements: (1) the lord as servant, His divinity in His humiliation (the basis of justification); (2) the servant as lord, His humanity in exaltation (the basis of sanctification); and (3) the true witness, the unity of the God-man as the mediator (the basis of vocation). The three movements are expressed metaphorically in the Christological images of the prodigal son; (1) the way of the Son of God into the far country (the state of self-emptying), (2) the home-coming of the Son of Man, (the state of exaltation), (3) the light of life (the unity of both states).

Barth reformulated the traditional Protestant doctrine of the threefold office of Christ. (1) Justification is based on the obedience of the Son of God in which the judge was judged in our place (the priestly office). (2) sanctification is rooted on the exaltation of the Son of Man in His royal humanity (the royal office). And (3) vocation is related to the glory of this mediator in which Jesus is Victor (the prophetic office). See E. Jüngel, *Barth,* 47-51.

65. It was chosen as the topic for the seminar in celebration of his eightieth birthday (See Jüngel, *Barth*, 127-38). Barth's Christology of the royal man opens a legitimate basis for theological anthropology. Since the royal humanity of Jesus is the paradigm for every human being, Barth's Christology already includes humanity as its "implicit subject," which "marks the beginning of a new development in Protestant theology" (ibid., 128).

66. Barth criticized the older Protestant doctrine of *ordo saluis*. For its artificial schematization reduces theology into either a religious psychology or a "dualism between an objective achievement of salvation there and then and a subjective appropriation of it here and now" (IV/2: 503).

67. Barth said, "Even within the true human response to this one divine act the faith in which the sinful man may grasp the righteousness promised him in Jesus Christ is one thing, and quite another his obedience, or love, as his correspondence to the holiness imparted to him in Jesus Christ" (IV/2: 503).

68. See Calvin, *Institutes of the Christian Religions*, III, ii, 1. For English translation, 2 vols., ed. John T. McNeil, trans. Ford Lewis Battles (Philadelphia: The Westminster Press, 1960), 2:542-544. Also, cf. IV/2, 503-505.

69. This point implies Barth's criticism of the theology of R. Bultmann and of such a dimension in Roman Catholic and some Neo-Protestant theologies.

70. See Dietrich Bonhoeffer, *The Cost of Discipleship*, trans. R. H. Fuller (New York: Macmillan Publishing Co., 1959).

71. Barth praised Calvin as the theologian who expresses this point with a particular clarity (see IV/2: 505ff.).

72. See Barth's excursus of Calvin on this point, see IV/2: 510f.

Chapter 6: The Humanity Paradigm

1. As T. F. Torrance corrected in the Preface of IV/1, the German word *Versöhnung* for Barth includes both atonement and reconciliation in English. However, the translator, Bromiley translated it as atonement throughout the volumes. However, reconciliation is the more appropriate English term, because when Barth said *Versöhnung*, it has a more inclusive meaning than traditional atonement theories. See IV/1: vii.

2. For Barth's doctrine of the Trinity, see Claude Welch, *In This Name: The Doctrine of the Trinity in Contemporary World* (New York: Charles Scribner's Sons, 1952); also Eberhard Jüngel, *The Doctrine of the Trinity: God's Being is in Becoming* (Grand Rapids: Eerdmans, 1976); for its criticism, Jürgen Moltmann, *The Trinity and the Kingdom: the Doctrine of God*, trans. Magaret Kohl (San Francisco: Harper & Row, Publishers, 1981), esp. 139-44.

3. Barth said, "It does this *a posteriori*, with a reference to Him, to the Son of God actually existing in the flesh. It does not derive from a known *a priori*, a superior possibility, but only from the given actuality, from Him Himself." (IV/2: 62)

4. See Robert McAfee Brown, *Gustavo Gutiérrez: An Introduction to Liberation Theology* (Maryknoll, N.Y.: Orbis Books, 1990), 57-74.

5. Such an unity of word and deed is identical with the etymological connotation of the Chinese character, *ch'eng* (sincerity [see Chap. 2]). The Chinese character *ch'eng* consists of two graphs that mean word (or speech) and accomplishment (action); etymologically, it denotes a sincere actualization of one's word. The life-act of royal humanity manifests a paradigm of *ch'eng*, i.e., the sincere being and becoming in the unity of speaking and acting.

6. The primary theology of the cross refers to the cross of Jesus Christ, while the secondary theology of the cross refers to His disciples. See IV/2: 264.

7. See his commentary on Romans, *The Epistle To The Romans*, 6th ed., trans. Edwyn C. Hoskyns (London: Oxford *University* Press, 1933).

8. E. Jüngel, *Karl Barth, a Theological Legacy* (Philadelphia: Westminster, 1986), 132; see also Barth, IV/2, 10.

9. See his *The Humanity of God*, trans. John Newton Thomas and Thomas Wieser (Atlanta: John Knox Press, 1960), 45f. Underlines are added.

10. Barth established real human nature in the fourfold relationship: human-to-God, human-to-human, human-to-self, and human-to-time. However, this section focuses on the first three and is delimited to some basic issues (esp., the notions of humanity and *imago Dei*), those most relevant to the topic of sanctification. For an succinct analysis on this volume , see Stuart D. McLean, *Humanity in the Thought of Karl Barth* (Edinburgh: T.& T. Clark, 1981).

11. Ibid., 29.

12. Ibid., 31.

13. See, ibid., 33. This point may be viewed as a way of Barth's theological bracketing.

14. Barth said:

"If 'God for humanity' is the eternal covenant revealed and effective in time in the humanity of Jesus, in this decision of the Creator for the creature there arises a relationship which is not alien to the Creator, to God as God, but we might almost say appropriate and natural to Him. God repeats in this relationship *ad extra* a relationship proper to Himself in His inner divine essence. Entering into this relationship, He makes a copy of Himself. Even in His inner divine being there is relationship. To be sure, God is One in Himself. But He is not alone. There is in Him a co-existence, co-inherence and reciprocity. God in Himself is not just simple, but in the simplicity of His essence He is threefold--the Father, the Son and the Holy Ghost. He posits Himself, is posited by Himself, and confirms Himself in both respects, as His own origin and also as His own goal. . . . and in this triunity He is the original and source of every I and Thou, of the I which is eternally from and to the Thou and therefore supremely I. And it is this relationship in the inner divine being which is repeated and reflected in God's eternal covenant with human being as revealed and operative in time in the humanity of Jesus." (III/2: 218f.)

15. John D. Godsey, ed., *Karl Barth's Table Talks* (Richmond: John Knox, 1962), 57.

16. Barth said, "We gladly see and are seen; we gladly speak and listen; we gladly receive and offer assistance" (III/2: 265).

17. Barth differentiated the nature of humanity as the joyful being-in-togetherness from Christian love (*agape*). In doing so, he accomplished two things. On the one hand, he resisted theomonistic theologians' frequent custom to devalue the authenticity of humanity in contrast with Christian love. On the other hand, he put two important themes--the ontology of humanity (theological anthropology) and the Christian freedom to be fully human (sanctification)--in their proper places. This is precisely why he dealt with the

freedom of human being as joyful co-humanity in the context of the doctrine of Creation (III), and with Christian love in the context of the doctrine of Reconciliation (IV/2). However, when he treated Christian love, he did not make such a sharp distinction between natural humanity and Christian love (see Chap. 8).

18. Barth's definition of humanity as being-in-encounter, being-in-togetherness, or *Mitmenschlichkeit* renders a remarkable parallelism to the Confucian notion of *jen* which etymologically has the twofold meaning of both human and co-humanity. Barth seems to have known that Confucius (and Martin Buber) formulated humanity in a similar relational model (see III/2: 277). However, Barth differentiated his understanding as a purely theological viewpoint. Nevertheless, there is no actual difference at the point of seeing humanity as co-humanity between Barth's Christian understanding of humanity in the image of God--*Mitmenschlichkeit*--and the Confucian notion of humanity in the *jen*-paradigm.

19. Another example of Barth's theological bracketing. See McLean, *Humanity*, 45.

20. Barth's distinction between the old humanity and the new humanity does not imply that Barth conceives human nature in creation as bad. On the contrary, he said that human nature or natural humanity was originally good, though later perverted (see the previous section).

21. See IV/1, Sec. 60.

22. Barth said,

"True Christianity cannot be a private Christianity, i.e., a rapacious Christianity. Inhumanity at once makes it a counterfeit Christianity. It is not merely a superficial blemish. It cuts at the very root of the confidence and comfort and joy, of the whole *parresia*, in which we should live as Christians, and of the witness which Christianity owes to the world." (IV/2: 442)

Barth argued against the privatization of Christian faith. Cf. J. B. Metz's radical criticism on the privatization of the Christian faith as the middle class religion in *Faith In the History and Society: Toward A Practical Fundamental Theology*, trans. David Smith (New York: Seabury, 1980), esp. 32ff.

23. Barth said:

"His misery consists in the corruption of this best. The perverted use which he makes of it is followed at once by his corrupt state--the worst. Things which are bright in themselves are all dark for him. Things that he desires all slip out of his grasp. His true glory becomes his shame. The pure becomes impure. The joyful is enwrapped by the deepest sadness. That which uplifts becomes a temptation; every blessing a curse; salvation perdition. We do not see deeply enough if we think and say that there is here *only* darkness, want, shame, impurity, sadness, temptation, curse and perdition. In the strict sense, the misery of man is not a *status*, a *continuum*, but his being in a history in which there can be no abstract 'only.' Thus the light is still there, but quenched; the wealth as it slips away; the glory as it turns to shame; the purity to impurity; the joy to sadness." (IV/2: 489)

24. For this reason, Barth criticized the Tridentine doctrine of human co-operation in the accomplishment of justification. He agreed that its whole point is to maintain a delicate balance between divine grace and human sinfulness in a quantified measure (i.e., *augmentum gratiae* by good works). However, the conflicts between the Spirit and flesh, between the new humanity in Jesus and the old humanity in the flesh, between freedom and bondage "do not complement but mutually exclude one another" in totality (IV/2: 498). Barth argued that the Tridentine doctrine of justification does not take human misery as seriously as it deserves. However, Hans Küng argued that there is no real difference between Barth and the Tridentine teaching in the doctrine of justification; see his *Justification: the Doctrine of Karl Barth and a Catholic Reflection*, trans. Thomas Collins (Philadelphia: Thomas Nelson & Sons, 1964).

Chapter 7: Sanctification
under the Direction of the Holy Spirit

1. This chapter will examine these themes in four sections: (1) the direction of the Son (64.4a); (2) the direction of the Holy Spirit (64.4b); (3) the Holy One and the saints (66.2); and (4) four implications of sanctification, (a) the call to discipleship (66.3), (b) the awakening to conversion (66.4), (c) the praise of works (66.5), and (d) the dignity of the cross (66.6).

2. For the special meanings Barth gave to history, the characters of grace-thanksgiving within the covenant relationship of God and people, see III/2: 160-167.

3. Barth said, "[T]here is no Jesus existing exclusively for Himself, and there is no sinful man who is not affected and determined with and by His existence" (IV/2: 281).

4. Hans Küng, *On Being a Christian*, trans. Edward Quinn (Garden City, N.Y.: Doubleday & Co., 1984), 554.

5. This section can be regarded as a pneumatology.

6. See Moltmann, *The Crucified God: The Cross of Christ as the Foundation and Criticism of Christian Theology*, trans. R. A. Wilson and John Bowden (New York: Harper & Row, 1974).

7. The goal of Barth's attack on religion is not toward other world religions but self-criticism of his contemporary European Christianity. See Chap. 4.

8. Barth said, "The one who is under the determination and in the process of becoming a totally new man is in his totality the old man of yesterday" (IV/2: 571).

9. Barth said,

"in the direction unequivocally characterised by the radically different content of this twofold determination; not dualistically in a division or re-stabilised co-existence of an old man and a new, a sinner and saint; but monistically in the passing and death and definitive end and destruction of the one in favor of the development and life and exclusive, uncompromised and inviolable existence of the other" (IV/2: 574).

10. Barth said further,

"But it [God's work] binds it together. It directs it to a specific goal--His covenant with man, His own glory in this covenant and the salvation of man. It is His work in the history of this covenant, in which the history of the whole cosmos participates, and which constitutes the meaning and true content of the history of the whole cosmos." (IV/2: 588)

Chapter 8: Root-metaphor (*Agape*)

1. This chapter will examines Barth's analysis of *agape* in three sections: (1) the problem of Christian love (IV/2, 68.1), (2) the foundation of Christian love (68.2), and (3) the act and manner of Christian love (68.3,4).

2. Notice in the following treatment that *agape* and human nature are almost identifiable and that, as it is pointed out (Chap. 5), the distinction between Christian love and human nature which Barth had made in the *Church Dogmatics* III/2 is hardly detectable.

3. Barth said,:

"Even in Himself God is God only as One who loves. . . . God is *per se* '*der liebe Gott.*' . . . The statements 'God is' and 'God loves' are synonymous. . . . He is the origin and sum of all true being and therefore of all true good; the *summum esse* as the *summum bonum*. . . . As He loves, he fulfills His purpose, in accordance with which all His intentions regarding a being distinct from His own can be actualised only as purposes of His love. . . . Thus the love of God is free, majestic, eternal love." (IV/2: 755)

4. Barth said,:

"In this triunity of His essence God is eternal love. . . . In Himself He is both the One and the Other. And He is this, not in any reciprocal self-seeking, indifference, neutrality or even enmity, but in the self-giving of the Father to the Son and the Son to the Father which is accomplished in the fact that He is not merely the Father and the Son but also the Holy Spirit, and therefore as the Father is wholly for the Son, and as the Son wholly for the Father. In virtue of His trinitarian essence God is free and sovereign and competent and powerful to love us. He can and may and must and will love us. In so doing, He does not place us merely in an external and casual fellowship with Himself, but in an internal and essential fellowship in which our existence cannot continue to be alien to His but may become and be analogous. In virtue of His trinitarian essence the life and rule of love is the most inward and proper life and rule of God. It is on this ground that He loves us. And it is on this ground that, as He declares His love to us, it is decided that to His glory and our salvation the life and rule of love is also our determination--a determination which on this ground is truly eternal." (IV/2: 757)

5. For example, Arnold Come misunderstood Barth of this point. He said that Barth reduced "man as created by God to an empty and impotent vessel into which God later pours his grace, a purely animal substructure to which God later adds a totally new and unrelated spiritual superstructure" (*An Introduction to Barth's "Dogmatics" for Preachers* [Philadelphia: Westminster Press, 1963], 152).

6. Barth particularly argued against Anders Nygren's analysis of *agape* (see *Agape and Eros*, trans. Philip Watson [London: SPCK, 1953]); see IV/2: 737ff., 827, etc.

7. Barth said:

"In the last instance it is not we who have to decide whether or not this other man loves God. God may well have loved him as He has loved us, and his love for God (greater perhaps than our own) may have been a fact even though he has not so far been recognised by baptism as a member of the people and community of God." (IV/2: 807)

8. See his article, "Christianity and the Non-Christian Religions," in *Christianity and Other Religions*, ed. John Hick and Brian Hebblethwaite (Philadelphia: Fortress Press, 1980), 52-79, esp. 75ff.

9. Italics are added.

Chapter 9: Methodology of the Dialogue

1. See Wilfred Cantwell Smith, *Faith and Belief* (Princeton: Princeton University Press, 1979), 129-142.

2. See Raimundo Panikkar, "Faith as a Constitutive Human Dimension," *Myth, Faith and Hermeneutics: Cross-cultural Studies* (New York: Paulist Press, 1979), 188-229 (207).

3. Tu Wei-ming, *Confucian Thought: Selfhood As Creative Transformation* (Albany: State Univ. of New York Press, 1985), 55.

4. Smith, *The Meaning and End of Religion* (Minneapolis: Fortress Press, 1991), 19-74.

5. Tu Wei-ming, *Centrality and Commonality: An Essay on Confucian Religiousness*, rev. ed. (Albany: State Univ. of New York Press, 1989), 94.

6. Tu, *Confucian Thought*, 55.

7. The term confuciology needs two further clarifications. First, the term is not a Confucian counterpart to Christology. Although confuciology includes an interpretation of the teachings of Confucius, it does not mean a specific discourse on the person of Confucius in the way that Christology and Buddhology exclusively involve the interpretation of the person and work of Jesus Christ and Siddharta Gautama Buddha. Second, I am fully aware that not only Taoism but also Confucianism have an inherent suspicion and aversion against systematic discourse, because such a deliberation inevitably violates the natural flow of *Tao* (*wu-wei*). However, I argue that it is necessarily a heuristic device for a dialogue with Christian theology. Without such an attempt of post-modern construction, a necessity Tu wei-ming also proposed in terms of "the third epoch," Confucianism would be easy prey to be swallowed up by scientifically armed, modern, heavy-duty theological systems.

8. George Lindbeck, *The Nature of Doctrine: Religion and Theology in a Postliberal Age* (Philadelphia: The Westminster Press, 1984), 113.

9. See ibid., 113-6.

10. For this term, I adopt definitions of Thomas Kuhn and Ian Barbour: See Thomas Kuhn, *The Structure of Scientific Revolution*, 2nd ed. (Chicago: Univ. of Chicago Press, 1970), 123-169; Ian G. Barbour, *Myths, Models and Paradigms: A Comparative Study in Science and Religion* (New York: Harper & Row, Publishers, 1974). Also see Küng, *Theology for the Third Millennium*, trans. Peter Heinegg (New York: Doubleday, 1988).

11. Peter categorizes this new contact in these three quests. See his *Winds of the Spirit: A Constructive Christian Theology* (Louisville: Westminster/ John Knox Press, 1994), part II.

12. This statement is made in the context of the comparison between Confucianism and Christianity. It does not neglect that there were preceding figures in theses paradigm changes. In the history of Neo-Confucianism, Lu Hsiang-shan first claimed the identification of mind-and-heart and principles. In the history of theology, John Calvin originated the shift of Gospel and law.

13. Julia Ching, *Confucianism and Christianity: A Comparative Study* (Tokyo: Kodansha, 1977), 105

14. Raimundo Panikkar defined "homology" as "correlation between points of two different systems so that a point in one system corresponds to a point in the other." It discovers that "the notions play equivalent roles, that they occupy homologous places within their respective systems." See Panikkar, *The Intrareligious Dialogue* (New York : Paulist Press, 1978), 33.

15. See Henry Rosemont, Jr., "Why Take Rights Seriously," *Human Rights and the World's Religions*, ed. by Leroy S. Rouner, 168-9.

16. For this distinction, see Lee H. Yearly, *Mencius and Aquinas: Theories of Virtue and Conceptions of Courage* (Albany: State University of New York Press, 1990, 188-91.

17. Panikkar, *Dialogue*, xxvii.

Chapter 10: Prolegomena

1. Julia Ching, *Confucianism and Christianity: A Comparative Study* (Tokyo: Kodansha, 1977), 69.
2. This might be debatable, because, for Chu Hsi, the source is the *li* (principle) which seems to be objective. Although the notion means an objective principle, there is actually no objective way to ascertain the principle.
3. See Tu Wei-ming, *Neo-Confucianism in Action: Wang Yang-ming's Youth (1472-1509)* (Berkeley: Univ. of California Press, 1976), 142.
4. See Tu Wei-ming, *Centrality and Commonality: An Essay on Confucian Religiousness* (Albany, N.Y.: SUNY Press, 1989), 116-21.
5. Ching argued that Confucianism has a doctrine of martyrdom, if it means giving a testimony of truth. See her *Comparative Study*, 86.
6. Paul D. Mathany, *Dogmatics and Ethics: The Theological Realism and Ethics of Karl Barth* (Frankfurt am Main; New York: Verlag Peter Lang, 1990), see Chap. 5, Sec. A, "theological realism as Christian ethical performance."

Chapter 11: The Humanity Paradigm

1. Tu Wei-ming, *Humanity and Self-Cultivation: Essays in Confucian Thought* (Berkeley: Asian Humanities Press, 1979), 156.
2. The election of God through salvation history also has a dimension of immanent-transcendence. However, salvation history basically is grounded on the radical transcendence and focuses on its historical immanence. So I call this theo-historical (see the next chapter).
3. Ching, *Confucianism and Christianity: A Comparative Study* (Tokyo: Kodansha, 1977), 103.
4. Hence, Ching said, "The Confucian is a man for other, even in his pursuit of sagehood" (ibid., 88).
5. Ibid., 128.
6. See Tu, *Humanity*, 139.
7. J. Moltmann, *The Trinity and the Kingdom: Doctrine of God,* trans. Magaret Kohl, New York, 1981), 19.
8. In the doctrine of reconciliation, Barth formulated sin as pride (in the context of justification; IV/1) and as falsehood (vocation; IV/3). However, this book deals with his concept of sin as sloth in the context of the doctrine of sanctification.
9. Ching was right to say, "Confucian philosophy is to develop, not a theory of sin as offense against God, but a theory of moral evil and its relationship to human nature" (Ching, *Comparative Study*, 75). Concerning humanity, e.g., the human sense of self-alienation, she claimed that "the Confucian position is less 'dualistic' than the Christian one" (ibid., 88).

Although this comparison is generally true, it is not so clear in the theology of Barth. As we saw, Barth rejected all dualistic tendencies in the understanding of humanity.

10. Ching distinguished that Christian theology expresses three moments of human nature (integral, fallen, and redeemed) while Confucianism two moments (original and existential); see Ching, *Comparative Study*, 75. Again, this might be too simplistic. After the Christ-event, as Barth articulated, the real problem is rather as dialectical (ontological and existential) as confuciology generally conceives.

Chapter 12: The Humanization Method

1. Cf. Fingarette's explanation on the *Tao, Confucius--the Secular as Sacred* (New York: Harper & Row, Publishers, 1972), esp., 18-36. Compare the following two explanations of *Tao* (Fingarette) and *Weisung* (Barth):

"Thus there is no *genuine* option: either one follows the Way or one fails. To take any other 'route' than the Way is not a genuine road but a failure through weakness to follow *the* route. Neither the doctrine nor the imagery allows for choice, if we mean by choice a selection, by virtue of the agent's powers, of one out of several equally real options.

"Put in more general terms, the task is not conceived as a choice but as the attempt to characterize some object or action as objectively right or not. The moral task is to make a proper classification, to locate an act within the scheme of *li* [propriety].' (Fingarette, *Confucius*, 21, 22)

"He [the Holy Spirit] does not, therefore, make us an offer or give us a chance. . . [but] places us at once at a very definite point of departure, in a very definite freedom. . . . The Holy Spirit does not create the ghosts of a man standing in decision, but the reality of man concerning whom decision has already been made. . . . "(Barth, IV/2: 363)

2. Tu's transliteration of *ch'eng* in his commentary on *Chung-yung*; see his *Centrality and Commonality: An Essay on Confucian Religiousness*, Revised (Albany, N.Y.: State University of New York Press, 1985), 67-91.

3. See the explanation on the concept of *ai* in Sec. 6.

4. Tu, *Humanity and Self-Cultivation: Essays in Confucian Thought* (Berkeley: Asian Humanities Press, 1979), 87-8.

5. Ibid., 99.

6. Ching made a distinction that confuciology shows "more sense of self-reliance (*jiriki*)," while Protestant theology depends exclusively on the power from the outside (*tariki*). And she claimed that, therefore, Catholic theology is closer to confuciology. However, the distinction is not tenable in the case of Barth. See Ching, *Confucianism and Christianity: A Comparative Study* (Tokyo: Kodansha, 1977), 90f.

7. This does not mean that Barth's theology is existential. On the contrary, I said that Barth's theology is more ontological in comparison to Luther's

theology. But this statement implies the nuance that, while confuciology focuses on the goodness of mind-and-heart, theology generally inclines to underscore the existential human condition such as sin and misery.

Conclusion: A Confucian-Christian Dialogue in Search for the *Tao* of New Cosmic Humanity

1. I call the Christian vision of salvation history *theohistorical vision* in contrast to the *anthropocosmic vision* of Confucianism.

2. For interfaith dialogue, see David Lochhead, *The Dialogical Imperative: A Christian Reflection on Interfaith Encounter* (Maryknoll, N.Y.: Orbis Books, 1988), esp., 89-97. Also see R. Panikkar, *The Intrareligious Dialogue* (New York: Paulist Press, 1978). But interfaith here denotes a broader definition than that of Panikkar in his distinction between faith and belief; see ibid., 17-22.

3. Even Paul Knitter argued for "the *praxis of dialogue*;" see his *No Other Name? A Critical Survey of Christian Attitudes Toward the World Religions* (Maryknoll, N.Y.: Orbis Books, 1985), 206.

4. The correlation of confuciology and theology is not merely a comparison of concepts, but can be regarded as a homology, which Panikkar defined, "the notions play equivalent roles, that they occupy homologous places within their respective systems. . . . a kind of existential-functional analogy" (R. Panikkar, *The Intrareligious Dialogue* [New York: Paulist Press, 1978], 33).

5. Jürgen Moltmann, trans. by Margaret Kohl, *The Trinity and the Kingdom of God: Doctrine of God* (San Francisco: Harper & Row, 1981), 19.

6. Cf. Carter Heyward, *The Redemption of God: A Theology of Mutual Relation* (Washington, D.C.: University Press of America, 1980).

7. See M. M. Thomas, *Risking Christ For Christ's Sake: Towards an Ecumenical Theology of Pluralism* (Geneva: WCC Publications, 1987), esp, Chap. 3 "Common Quest for a New Humanism: Towards Dialogical Participation."

8. Jürgen Moltmann, trans. by Margaret Kohl, *The Way of Jesus Christ: Christology in Messianic Dimensions* (San Francisco: HarperSanFrancisco, 1990), 57.

9. Karl Rahner, *Theological Investigations* I, trans. C. Ernst (Baltimore: Helicon Press; London: Darton, Longman & Todd, 1961), 164 n. 1.

10. See John B. Cobb, Jr., *Beyond Dialogue: Towards a Mutual Transformation and Buddhism* (Philadelphia: Fortress Press, 1982).

11. See M. M. Thomas, "Christ-Centered Syncretism," *Religion and Society*, XXVI: 1 (1979), 26-35. Cf. Jerald Gort, et. al., ed., *Dialogue and Syncretism: An Interdisciplinary Approach* (Grand Rapids: Eerdmans, 1989).

12. H. Richard Niebuhr, *The Meaning of Revelation* (New York: Macmillan, 1962), 41.

13. This moment has an affinity with what Panikkar describes as "intrareligious dialogue." He defines it, "an inner dialogue within myself, and encounter in the depth of my personal religiousness, having met another religious experience on that very intimate level" (Panikkar, *Dialogue;* 40). However, there are differences: In the dialogue, I do not meet "another religious experience," but both Confucianism and Christianity are my personal religiousness. My concern is more related to the community of faith while his is more to the individual.

14. J. Moltmann, *Jesus Christ*, xiv.

15. Herbert Fingarettee, *Confucius--the Secular as Sacred* (New York: Harper & Row, 1972), 19.

16. This is a compound word (theos-anthropos-cosmos) coined by Raimundo Panikkar. For theanthropocosmic vision, see R. Panikkar, *The Cosmothenandric Experience: Emerging Religious Consciousness* (Maryknoll, N.Y.: Orbis Books, 1993). However, Panikkar prefers the other term cosmotheandrism. Panikkar defined the term, " the divine, the human and the earthly. . . are three irreducible dimensions which constitute the real" (ibid., 60).

17. The Chinese character *ch'eng* consists of two graphs that mean word (or speech) and accomplishment (action); etymologically, it denotes sincere actualization of one's word. In addition to sincerity, thus, I sometimes translate *ch'eng* into "sincerization" to emphasize its dynamically active dimension.

18. *Ch'eng* Christology is particularly important for the history of Korean theology. Yi Pyok who is often called the Father of the Korean Catholic Church basically understood Christ as the human being of *ch'eng* who completed Heavenly *Tao* and human *tao*; see Jean Sangbae Ri, *Confucius et Jesus Christ: La Premiere Theologie Chretienne en Coree D'apres L'oeuvre de Yi Piek lettre Confuceen 1754-1786* (Paris: Editions Beauchesne, 1979).

Yun Sung Bum, an initiator of the Korean Protestant debate for theological indigenization, also constructed a Korean Christology based on the functional equivalences, he thought, existed between Yi Yulgok's teaching of *ch'eng* and Barth's theology. With the notion of *ch'eng*, he attempted to overcome the dualism which appeared in the European debates between the historical Jesus and the kerygmatic Christ. He formatted the historical Jesus as the starting point of *ch'eng,* the kerygmatic Christ as the goal of *ch'eng*, and Jesus Christ as the completion of *ch'eng*; see his *Han'gukjok Sinhak: Song ui Haesokhak* [The Korean Theology: Hermeneutics of *Ch'eng*] (Seoul: Son Myung Munhwasa, 1972).

19. See Robert E. Allison, "The Ethics of Confucianism and Christianity: the Delicate Balance," *Ching Feng* 33:3 (1990), 168.

20. I. Kant, *Religion within the Limits of Reason Alone* (New York: Harper, 1960), Bk 2, Sec. I:A, 54-5..

21. Moltmann, *Jesus Christ*, 69.

22. For the impasses of two nature christology, see Moltmann, *Trinity*, 51-5. Moltmann called this type "ancient cosmological Christology."

23. Moltmann, *Jesus Christ.*, xv; 33.

24. Cf., ibid., 63-9.

25. Robert F. Berkeley and Sarah A. Edwards, *Christology in Dialogue* (Cleveland: Pilgrim Press, 1993), 24-5. . Berkeley said:

"Dialogue" is the key word, and it carries our conviction that Christology loses its vitality when it is not so engaged. Whether in their first-century or in their Chalcedonian or Enlightenment clothing, Christological formulations have always fallen short of finality. . . . Christology is never final but always in dialogue: with the early church, with the religious and mythological presuppositions and commitments of the Jewish and Hellenistic world, and perhaps most important, with the worldviews of our own age and time . . . Christologies, be they ancient or modern, are evoked first and always by dialogue"

26. Moltmann, *Jesus Christ*, 59 and 61.

27. For the assessment and criticism of modern, anthropological christology, see ibid., 55-63.

28. For its succinct analysis, see Panikkar, *Cosmotheandric*, esp., 108-19.

29. See Tu Wei-ming, *Centrality and Commonality: An Essay on Confucian Religiousness*, rev. ed. (Albany, N.Y.: State Univ. of New York Press, 1989), 102-7.

30. Peter Hodgson categorized three characteristics that postmodern constructive theology should have: (1) dialogical, (2) emancipatory, and (3) ecological (See Peter C. Hodgson, *Winds of the Spirit: A Constructive Christian Theology* [Louisville, Ky.: Westminster/John Knox Press, 1994], 53-118). Confucian Christology has all of these dimensions. Simply, the *jen* mode of Christology is dialogical by nature, the *Tao* mode has an emancipatory dimension, and the theanthropocomsic mode is more than ecological.

31. See Moltmann, *Jesus Christ*, 46-72.

32. Interestingly enough, the Gospel of Thomas emphatically depicts Jesus as the Wisdom teacher. See Marcus J. Borg, *Anchor Bible Dictionary*, Vol. 3, 803-12; also John Dominic Crossan*, Jesus: A Revolutionary Biography* (San Francisco: HarperSanFrancisco, 1989); Leo G. Perdue, "The Wisdom Saying of Jesus," *Forum* 2:3 (1986): 3-35.

33. Cf. John Berverley Butcher, ed., *The Tao of Jesus* (San Francisco: HarperSanFrancisco, 1994).

Appendix: The Life of Wang Yang-ming

1. This introduction is selectively made for those who are not familiar with Wang Yang-ming. For a summarized account of Wang Yang-ming's life and thought, Tu Wei-ming, "Wang Yang-ming," Mircea Eliade, ed., *Encyclopedia of Religions*, Vol. 15 (1987), 335-7.

2. Tu Wei-ming wrote a psychoanalytic biography on Wang Yang-ming's youth, in which Tu compared Wang Yang-ming to Martin Luther. See his *Neo-*

Confucian Thought in Action: Wang Yang-ming's Youth (1472-1509)
(Berkeley: University of California Press, 1976). Cf. Erik H. Erikson's *Young Man Luther* (New York: W. W. Norton & Co., 1958).

3. Julia Ching, *To Acquire Wisdom: The Way of Wang Yang-ming* (New York: Columbia Univ. Press, 1976), xxiii.

4. Tu Wei-ming, *Action*, 43.

5. Ibid., 64.

6. *Neo-Confucianism, Etc.: Essays by Wing-tsit Chan* (Hanover, N.H.: Oriental Society, 1969), 227-47.

7. See Tu's article, "An Inquiry into Wang Yang-ming's Four-Sentence Teaching," *Humanity and Self-Cultivation: Essays in Confucian Thought* (Berkeley: Asian Humanities Press, 1979), 162-78.

8. Tu, *Action*, 74.

9. Ibid., 84.

10. Chan, *Instructions*, xix.

11. Wm. T. De Bary, introduction to *Self and Society in Ming Thought* (New York: Columbia Univ. Press, 1970), 3; 6; 11.

12. The school inherited the teachings of Ch'eng I (1033-1107) and Chu Hsi (1130-1200). This school "dominated the Chinese intellectual world since the twelfth century" (Chan, *Instructions*, xix.). It influenced Korean Neo-Confucianism even more exclusively.

13. Chan, *Instructions*, xx.

14. The Lu-Wang school is named after Lu Hsiang-shan (1139-1193), the intellectual rival of Chu Hsi, and Wang Yang-ming. For this distinction, see Fung Yu-lan, *A History of Chinese Philosophy*, vol. 2. trans. Derk Bodde (Princeton: Princeton Univ. Press, 1953), 585-92.

15. Tu, *Action*, 157. He used the support from such contemporary Confucian scholars as Shimada Kenji, Araki Kengo, and Ch'ien Mu.

16. See Tu, *Action*, 10-1.

17. Ibid., 11.

18. Chan, *Instructions*, xxix.

19. See Ching, *Wisdom*, xxiii.

20. See Kim Gil-hwan, *The Study of the Korean Yang-ming School* (Seoul: Il Ji Sa, 1981), 277-83.

21. Tu said:

"The spirit of the samurai, which emphasizes firm purpose, self-mastery, and loyalty, and the dynamic leadership of the Meiji Restoration in 1868 were partly Wang Yang-ming's gifts to Japan. In China, reformers such as Liang Ch'i-ch'ao (1873-1929) and T'an Szu-t'ung (1865-1898), revolutionaries such as Sun Yat-sen (1866-1925), and philosophers such as Hsiung Shih-li (1885-1968) and Liang Sou-ming (b. 1893) have all been inspired by Wang's legacy, the *Ch'uan-hsi lu* (Instructions for Practical Living). ("Wang Yang-ming," 337)

Glossary of Chinese Terms

ai	love	愛
ai-min	loving the people	愛民
ch'eng	sincerity	誠
ch'eng-i	the sincerity of the will	誠意
cheng-hsin	the rectification of the mind-and-heart	正心
ch'i	material force	氣
ch'i-chia	the regulation of the family	齊家
chih	knowledge	知
chih chih	the extension of knowledge	致知
chih-hsing ho-i	the unity of knowing and acting	知行合一
chih-kuo	the order of the state	治國
chih liang-chih	the extension of liang-chih	致良知
ching	reverence	敬
chi-i	the accumulation of righteous deeds	集義
Chu Hsi		朱熹
Ch'uan-hsi lu	Instructions for Practical Living	傳習錄
chung	equlibrium	中
Chung-yung	The Doctrine of Means	中庸
ch'u yen-yu	the extirpation of human desires	去人欲
hsiao-t'i	a partial humanity	小體
hsin	mind-and-heart	心
hsin	faithfulness	信
hsin chih li	the identity of mind-and-heart and principle	心即理
hsin-chih-t'i	the substance of the mind-and-heart	心之體
hsing	human nature	性
hsing	action	行

hsing chi li	the identity of nature and principle	性即理
hsiu-shen	self-cultivation	修身
i	intention	意
i	righteousness	義
jen	humanity	仁
jen	human being	人
jen-hsin	the human mind	人心
ko-wu	the investigation of things	格物
kung-fu	effort/study	工夫
li	principle	理
li	propriety	禮
liang-chih	the innate knowledge of the good	良知
li-chih	the establishment of the will	立志
ming-te	the clear character	明德
nei	the inner	內
Nien-p'u	Chronological Biography	年譜
pen-t'i	the original substance	本體
p'ing t'ien-hsia	peace throughout the world	平天下
shen	body	身
T'ai-hsu	the Great Vacuity	太虛
Tao	the Way	道
tao-hsin	the mind of the Way	道心
ta-t'i	a fully integrated humanity	大體
t'i	substance	體
T'ien-li	the Heavenly Principle	天理
t'ou-nao	basis	頭腦
ts'un T'ien-li	the preservation of the Heavenly Principle	存天理
wai	the outer	外
Wang Yang-ming		王陽明
Wan-wu i-t'i	the Oneness of All Things	萬物一體
wu	thing	物
wu-shan wu-o	no distinction of good and evil	無善無惡
Yi T'oegye		李退溪
yung	function	用
yu-shan-yu-o	the presence of good and evil	有善有惡

•

Bibliography (Works Cited)

I. Works on Wang Yang-ming and Confucianism

A. Primary Sources

Chan, Wing-tsit. Trans. *Instructions for Practical Living and Other Neo-Confucian Writings*. New York: Columbia University Press, 1963.

_____. Trans. and comp. *A Source Book in Chinese Philosophy*. Princeton, N.J.: Princeton University Press, 1963.

_____. Trans. and ed. *Neo-Confucian Terms Explained* (The Pei-hsi tzu-i) *by Ch'en Ch'un, 1159-1223*. New York: Columbia University Press, 1986.

Kalton, Michael C. Trans. and ed. *To Become a Sage: the Ten Diagrams on Sage Learning by Yi T'oegye*. New York: Columbia University Press, 1988.

Lau, D. C. Trans. *Mencius*. Harmondsworth, Middlesex: Penguin Books, 1970.

Legge, James. Trans. *The Chinese Classics*. 5 Vols. Hong Kong: Legge; London: Trubner, 1861-1872).

O Yomei zenshu (Japanese translation of *Wang Wen-ch'eng kung ch'uanshu* [The Complete Works of Wang Yang-ming]). 10 vols. Tokyo, 1982ff.

Wang Yang-ming Ch'uan Hsi Lu Hsing Chu Chi P'ing. Ed. Chan Wing-tsit. Taipei, 1983.

B. Secondary Sources

Chan Wang-tsit. *Neo-Confucianism, Etc.: Essays by Wing-tsit Chan*. Hanover, N.H.: Oriental Society, 1969.

Cheng Chung-ying. *New Dimension of Confucian and Neo-Confucian Philosophy.* Albany, N.Y.: State University of New York Press, 1991.

Ching, Julia. *To Acquire Wisdom: The Way of Wang Yang-ming.* New York: Columbia University Press, 1976.

De Bary, Wm. Theodore. Ed. *Self and Society in Ming Thought.* New York: Columbia University Press, 1970.

_____. *Neo-Confucian Orthodoxy and the Learning of the Mind-and-Heart.* New York: Columbia University Press, 1981.

_____. *East Asian Civilizations: A Dialogue in Five Stages.* The Edwin O. Reischauer Lectures, 1986. Cambridge: Harvard University Press, 1988.

Fingarette, Herbert. *Confucius--the Secular as Sacred.* New York: Harper & Row, Publishers, 1972.

Fung Yu-lan. *A History of Chinese Philosophy.* Vol. 2. Trans. Derk Bodde. Princeton: Princeton University Press, 1952-1953.

Graham, A. C. *Two Chinese Philosophers--Ch'eng Ming-tao and Ch'eng Yi-Ch'uan.* London: Lund Humphries, 1958.

_____. *Disputers of the Tao: Philosophical Argument in Ancient China.* La Salle, IL.: Open Court Publishing Co., 1989.

Grayson, James H. *Korea: the Religious History.* Oxford: Clarendon Press, 1989.

Ivanhoe, Philip. *Ethics in the Confucian Tradition: The Thought of Mencius and Wang Yang-ming.* Atlanta, Ga.: Scholars Press, 1990.

Kim, Gil-Hwan. *The Study of the Korean Yang-ming School.* Seoul: Il Ji Sa, 1981.

Mou Tsung-san. *Chung-kuo che-hüseh te t'e-chih* [The Uniqueness of Chinese Philosophy]. Taipei: Student Book Co., 1974. Korean trans. Seoul: Donghwa Publishing Co., 1983.

Ro Young-chan. *The Korean Neo-Confucianism of Yi Yulgok.* Albany, New York: State University of New York Press, 1989.

Rozman, Gilbert. Ed. *The East Asian Region: Confucian Heritage and Its Modern Adaptation.* Princeton, N.J.: Princeton University Press, 1991.

Schwartz, Benjamin I. *The World of Thought in Ancient China.* Cambridge, MA.: Harvard University Press, 1985.

Taylor, Rodney L. *The Religious Dimensions of Confucianism.* Albany: State University of New York Press, 1990.

Tu, Wei-ming. *Neo-Confucian Thought in Action: Wang Yang-ming's Youth (1472-1509)*. Berkeley: University of California Press, 1976.

_____. *Humanity and Self-Cultivation: Essays in Confucian Thought.* Berkeley: Asian Humanities Press, 1979.

_____. *Confucian Thought: Selfhood As Creative Transformation.* Albany, N.Y.: State University of New York Press, 1985.

_____. *Centrality and Commonality: An Essay on Confucian Religiousness.* Revised and enlarged ed. Albany, N.Y.: State University of New York Press, 1989.

_____. *Confucianism in an Historical Perspective.* Singapore: The Institute of East Asian Philosophies, 1989.

_____ et al. *The Confucian World Observed: A Contemporary Discussion of Confucian Humanism in East Asia.* Honolulu: The East-West Center, 1992.

Yoon, Nam-han. *The Study of the Yang-ming School in Chosun Period.* Seoul: Jib Mun Dang, 1982.

II. Works on Karl Barth

A. Primary Sources (Works of Karl Barth)

The Church Dogmatics. 4 Vols. 2nd Ed. ET. Ed. G. W. Bromiley and T. F. Torrance. Edinburgh: T. T. & Clark, 1932-81.

The Epistle to the Romans. 6th ed. Trans. Edwyn C. Hoskyns. London: Oxford University Press, 1933.

"No! Answer to Emil Brunner." *Natural Theology.* Trans. Peter Fraenkel. London: The Centenary Press, 1946.

Community, State and Church. Garden City, New York: Doubleday, 1960.

The Humanity of God. Trans. John Newton Thomas and Thomas Wieser. Atlanta: John Knox, 1960.

Karl Barth's Table Talks. Ed. John D. Godsey. Richmond, VA.:John Knox Press, 1962.

"No Boring Theology! A Letter from Karl Barth." *The South East Asian Journal of Theology* (Autumn, 1969). 4-5.

B. Secondary Sources

Balthasar, Hans Urs von. *The Theology of Karl Barth*. Trans. John Drury. New York: Holt, Rinehart & Winston, 1971.

Busch, Eberhard. *Karl Barth: His Life from Letters and Autobiographical Texts*. Trans. John Bowden. Philadelphia: Fortress Press, 1976.

Come, Arnold B. *An Introduction to Barth's "Dogmatics" for Preachers*. Philadelphia: Westminster Press, 1963.

Jüngel, Eberhard. *The Doctrine of the Trinity: God's Being is In Becoming*. Grand Rapids: Wm. B. Eerdmans Publishing Co., 1976.

_____. *Karl Barth, a Theological Legacy*, Trans. Garrett E. Paul. *Karl Barth, a Theological Legacy*. Philadelphia: Westminster Press, 1986.

Küng, Hans. *Justification: the Doctrine of Karl Barth and a   Catholic Reflection*. Trans. Thomas Collins et. al. Philadelphia: Westminster Press or New York: Nelson & Sons, 1964.

Macken, John. "The Autonomy Theme in Karl Barth's Church Dogmatics and in Current Barth Criticism." Dissert. Universität Tübingen. 1984.

Matheny, Paul D. *Dogmatics and Ethics: The Theological Realism and Ethics of Karl Barth's Church Dogmatics*. Frankfurt am Main, New York: Peter Lang, 1990.

McLean, Stuart D. *Humanity in the Thought of Karl Barth*. Edinburgh: T.& T. Clark Ltd., 1981.

Palma, Robert J. *Karl Barth's Theology of Culture*. Allison Park, Pa.: Pickwick Publications, 1983.

Welch, Claude. *In This Name: The Doctrine of the Trinity in Contemporary Theology*. New York: Scribner's, 1952.

III. Other Works

Barbour, Ian G. *Myths, Models, and Paradigms: A Comparative Study in Science and Religion*. New York: Harper & Row, Publishers, 1974.

Berthrong, John. *All Under Heaven: Transforming Paradigms in Confucian-Christian Dialogue*. Albany, N.Y.: State University of New York Press, 1994.

Bonhoeffer, Dietrich. *The Cost of Discipleship*. Trans. R. H. Fuller. New York: Macmillan Publishing Co., 1949.

Brown, Robert McAfee. *Gustavo Gutiérrez: An Introduction   to Liberation Theology*. Maryknoll, N.Y.: Orbis Books, 1990.

Bultmann, Rudolf K.. *Jesus Christ and Mythology*. New York: Charles Scribner's Son, 1958.

Butcher, John Berverley. Ed. *The Tao of Jesus*. San Francisco: Harper San Francisco, 1994.

Calvin, John. *Institutes of the Christian Religions*. 2 Vols. Ed. John T. McNeil. Trans. Ford Lewis Battles. Philadelphia: The Westminster Press, 1960.

Ching, Julia. *Confucianism and Christianity: a Comparative Study*. Tokyo: Kodansha, 1977.

_____. *Chinese Religions*. Maryknoll, N.Y.: Orbis Books, 1988.

Clark, Donald N. *Christianity in Modern Korea*. Lanham: University Press of America, 1986.

Cobb, John B. Jr. *Beyond Dialogue: Toward a Mutual Transformation of Christianity and Buddhism*. Philadelphia: Fortress Press, 1982.

Crossan, John Dominic. *Jesus: A Revolutionary Biography*. San Francisco: HarperSanFrancisco, 1989.

D'Costa, Gavin. *Theology and Religious Pluralism: The Challenge of Other Religions*. Oxford, U.K.; New York, N.Y.: Basil Blackwell, 1986.

Diaz, Hector. *A Korean Theology: Chu-Gyo Yo-Ji, Essentials of the Lord's Teaching by Chong Yak-jong Augustine (1760-1801)*. Immense: Neue Zeitschrift für Missionswissenschaft, 1986.

Erikson, Erik H. *Young Man Luther: A Study in Psychoanalysis and History*. New York, London: W. W. Norton & Co., 1958.

Heidegger, Martin. *Being and Time*. Trans. John Maquarrie & Edward Robinson. New York: Harper & Row, Publishers, 1962.

Heyward, Carter. *The Redemption of God: A Theology of Mutual Relation*. Washington, D.C.: University Press of America, 1980.

Hick, John and Brian Hebblethwaite. Ed. *Christianity and Other Religions*. Philadelphia: Fortress Press, 1980.

Hillmann, Eugene. *The Wider Ecumenism*. New York: Herder and Herder, 1968.

_____. *Many Paths: A Catholic Approach to Religious Pluralism*. Maryknoll, N.Y.: Orbis Books, 1989.

Hodgson, Peter C. *Winds of the Spirit: A Constructive Christian Theology*. Louisville, Ky.: Westminster/John Knox Press, 1994.

Kant, I. *Religion Within the Limits of Reason Alone*. New York: Haper, 1960.

Knitter, Paul F. *No Other Name?: A Critical Survey of Christian Attitudes toward the World Religions*. Maryknoll, N.Y.: Orbis Books, 1984.

Kraemer, Hendrik. *The Christian Message in a Non-Christian World.* London: Edinburgh House Press, 1938.

Kuhn, Thomas S. *The Structure of Scientific Revolutions.* 2nd ed. Chicago: University of Chicago Press, 1970.

Küng, Hans. *On Being a Christian.* Trans. Edward Quinn. Garden City, N.Y.: Doubleday & Co., 1974.

_____. *Theology for the Third Millennium.* Trans. Peter Heinegg. New York: Doubleday, 1988.

_____ and Julia Ching. *Christianity and Chinese Religions.* Trans. Peter Beyer. New York: Doubleday, 1989.

Lindbeck, George A. *The Nature of Doctrine: Religion and Theology in a Postliberal Age.* Philadelphia: Westminster Press, 1984.

Lochhead, David. *The Dialogical Imperative: A Christian Reflection on Interfaith Encounter.* Maryknoll, N.Y.: Orbis Books, 1988.

Metz, Johann Baptist. *Faith in History and Society: Toward a Practical Fundamental Theology.* Trans. David Smith. New York: Seabury Press, 1980.

Moltmann, Jürgen. *The Crucified God: The Cross of Christ as the Foundation and Criticism of Christian Theology.* Trans. R. A. Wilson and John Bowden. New York: Harper & Row, 1974.

_____. *The Trinity and the Kingdom of God: the Doctrine of God.* Trans. Margaret Kohl. San Francisco: Harper & Row, 1991.

_____. *The Way of Jesus Christ: Christology in Messianic Dimensions.* San Francisco: HarperSanFrancisco, 1990.

Niebuhr, H. Richard. *Christ and Culture.* New York: Harper & Row, 1951.

_____. *The Meaning of Revelation.* New York: Macmillan, 1962.

Nygren, Anders. *Agape and Eros.* Trans. Philip S. Watson. London: SPCK, 1953.

Panikkar, Raimundo. *The Intrareligious Dialogue.* New York: Paulist Press, 1978.

_____. *Myth, Faith and Hermeneutics: Cross-cultural Studies.* New York: Paulist Press, 1979.

_____. *The Cosmotheandric Experience: Emerging Religious Consciousness.* Maryknoll, N.Y.: Orbis Books, 1993.

Phan, Peter C. Ed. *Christianity and The Wider Ecumenism.* New York: Paragon House, 1990.

Pieris, Aloysius. *Love Meets Wisdom: A Christian Experience of Buddhism.* Maryknoll, N.Y.: Orbis Books, 1988.

Race, Alan. *Christianity and Religious Pluralism.* London: SCM Press, 1983.

Rahner, Karl. *Theological Investigations I.* Trans. C. Ernst. Baltimore: Helicon Press; London: Darton, Longman & Todd, 1961.

_____. *Foundations of Christian Faith: An Introduction to the Idea of Christianity.* Trans. William V. Dych. New York: Crossroad, 1978.

Ri, Jean Sangbae. *Confucius et Jesus Christ: La Premiere Theologie Chretienne en Coree D'apres L'oeuvre de Yi Piek lettre Confuceen 1754-1786.* Paris: Editions Beauchesne, 1979.

Smith, Wilfred Cantwell. *The Meaning and End of Religion.* Renewed. Minneapolis: Fortress Press, 1991.

_____. *Faith and Belief.* Princeton, N.J.: Princeton University Press, 1979.

Thomas, M. M. *Risking Christ For Christ's Sake: Towards an Ecumenical Theology of Pluralism.* Geneva: WCC Publications, 1987.

Tillich, Paul. *Systematic Theology.* 3 Vols. Chicago: University of Chicago Press, 1951-63.

Vogel, Ezra F. *The Four Little Dragons: The Spread of Industrialization in East Asia.* Cambridge: Harvard University Press, 1991.

Weber, Max. *The Protestant Ethic and the Spirit of Capitalism.* Trans. Talcott Parsons. New York: Charles Scribner's Sons, 1930.

_____. *The Religion of China: Confucianism and Taoism.* Trans. Hans H. Gerth. Grencoe, Ill.: Free Press, 1951.

Weber, Otto. *Foundations of Dogmatics.* 2 Vols. Trans. Darrell L. Guder. Grand Rapids, Mich.: Wm. B. Eerdmans Publishing Co., 1981-3.

Yun, Sung-bum. *Han'gukjok Sinhak: Song ui Haesokhak* [The Korean Theology: The Hermeneutics of Sincerity]. Seoul: Son Myung Munwhasa, 1972.

Yearly, Lee H. *Mencius and Aquinas: Theories of Virtue and Conceptions of Courage.* Albany: State University of New York Press, 1990.

IV. Articles Cited

Allinson, Robert E. "The Ethics of Confucianism & Christianity: the Delicate Balance." Ching Feng 33:3 (1990): 158-175.

Boodberg, A. "The Semasiology of Some Primary Confucian Concepts." *Philosophy East and West* 2:4 (1953): 317-332.

Bibliography

Borg, Marcus. "The Teaching of Jesus." In *The Anchor Bible Dictionary*, Vol. 3: 804-12. Ed. D. N. Freedman. New York: Doubleday, 1992.

Chung Chai-sik. "Confucian-Christian Encounter in Korea: Two Cases of Westernization and De-westernization." *Ching-Feng* 34:1 (1991): 51-81.

Grayson, James. H. "The Study of Korean Religions & Their Role in Inter-Religious Dialogue." *Incluturation* 3:4 (1988): 2-10.

Iki, Hiroyuki. "Wang Yang-ming's Doctrine of Innate Knowledge of the Good." *Philosophy East and West 11* (1961): 27-44.

Kim Illsoo. "Organizational patterns of Korean-American Methodist Churches: denominationalism and personal community." In *Rethinking Methodist History*. Ed. Russell Richey and Kenneth Rowe. Nashville: Kingswood Books, 1985: 228-37.

Kim, Stephen, Cardinal. "Position Paper." In *Mission Trend No. 2: Evangelization*. Ed. Gerald H. Anderson and Thomas F. Stransky. New York: Paulist; Grand Rapids: Wm. B. Eerdmans, 1975: 190-2.

Lee, Peter K. H. "Personal Observation on Religion and Culture in the four Little Dragons of Asia." *Ching Feng* 30:3 (1987): 154-69.

Liu, Shu-hsien. "The Confucian approach to the problem of transcendence and immanence." *Philosophy East and West* 22:1 (1972): 45-52.

Nivison, David S. "The Problem of 'Knowledge' and 'Action' in Chinese Thought." In *Studies in Chinese Thought*. Ed. Arthur F. Wright. Chicago: University of Chicago Press, 1953: 112-145.

Oh, Kang-Nam. "The Encounter of Confucianism and Christianity in Korea: Past and Future." *Journal of the Academy of Religion* 61:2 (1993): 303-20.

Perdue, Leo G. "The Wisdom Saying of Jesus." *Forum* 2:3 (1986): 3-35.

Tu, Wei-ming. "Wang Yang-ming." Mircea Eliade. Ed. *Encyclopedia of Religions*. Vol. 15 (1987): 334-337.

Yun, Yee-heum. "The Contemporary Religious Situation in Korea." Presented in the Conference on Religion and Contemporary Society in Korea. Center of East Asian Studies. University of California at Berkeley. November 11-12, 1988.

About the Author

HEUP YOUNG KIM is Assistant Professor of Systematic Theology at Kang Nam University, Korea. He earned his M.Div. and Th.M at Princeton Theological Seminary and Ph.D. at the Graduate Theological Union, Berkeley. As a converted Christian who had been raised in a Korean family steeped in a thousand-year history in Confucianism, he is strongly committed in Confucian-Christian dialogue. He participated in and presented papers at the second and third International Confucian-Christian Dialogue Meetings held in Berkeley, July 1992, and in Boston, August 1994. He has also taught at the Graduate Theological Union, Seoul National University, and Ehwa Women's University, and was Visiting Professor of Theology at San Francisco Theological Seminary.